The Haunted History of Pelham, New York

The Haunted History of Pelham, New York

Including Ghostly Tales of The Bronx, Westchester County, and Long Island Sound

Blake A. Bell

excelsior editions

AN IMPRINT OF STATE UNIVERSITY OF NEW YORK PRESS

Published by State University of New York Press, Albany

© 2022 State University of New York

All rights reserved

Printed in the United States of America

No part of this book may be used or reproduced in any manner whatsoever without written permission. No part of this book may be stored in a retrieval system or transmitted in any form or by any means including electronic, electrostatic, magnetic tape, mechanical, photocopying, recording, or otherwise without the prior permission in writing of the publisher.

Excelsior Editions is an imprint of State University of New York Press

For information, contact State University of New York Press, Albany, NY
www.sunypress.edu

Library of Congress Cataloging-in-Publication Data

Name: Bell, Blake A., author.
Title: The haunted history of Pelham, New York : including ghostly tales of the Bronx, Westchester county, and Long Island Sound / Blake A. Bell.
Description: Albany : State University of New York Press, 2022. | Series: Excelsior editions | Includes bibliographical references and index.
Identifiers: LCCN 2021040585 (print) | LCCN 2021040586 (ebook) | ISBN 9781438486741 (pbk. : alk. paper) | ISBN 9781438486758 (ebook)
Subjects: LCSH: Ghosts—New York (State)—Pelham (Town) | Ghosts—New York (State) | Haunted places—New York (State)—Pelham (Town) | Haunted places—New York (State) | Pelham (N.Y. : Town)—History.
Classification: LCC BF1472.U6 B457 2022 (print) | LCC BF1472.U6 (ebook) | DDC 133.109747/277—dc23
LC record available at https://lccn.loc.gov/2021040585
LC ebook record available at https://lccn.loc.gov/2021040586

10 9 8 7 6 5 4 3 2 1

I dedicate this book to my beloved wife, Janice Faye Ingram, and our children, Brett Ingram Bell and Jennifer Anne Bell. Without my family's love, understanding, and nurturing for decades, I would not have been able to devote the time and effort it has taken to document Pelham history so thoroughly, collect the details of dozens of Pelham ghost stories, and assemble such work into this book. I further dedicate this book to my mother, Phyllis Anne Rose Bell of Columbia, Missouri, and my late father, Rondal Edward Bell, a career college professor and academic dean. Without their love, support, and care to educate and instill in me an appreciation for the importance of history and what it can reveal about us and our futures, the work it has taken to prepare this book would never have been completed.

Contents

List of Illustrations   xi

Preface   xiii

Part I. Indigenous American Hauntings | 1

Chapter 1   Headless Apparitions of the Haunted Cedar Knoll   5

Chapter 2   Spirit of the Siwanoy Brave   9

Chapter 3   Ghost of the Indian Maiden of Pelhamdale   13

Chapter 4   Dark Spirit of the Devil and His Stepping-Stones   19

Part II. Revolutionary War Specters | 23

Chapter 5   Shrieking Ghosts of Execution Rocks   32

Chapter 6   Ghostly Cow Rustlers of Pelham Road   36

Chapter 7   Specter of the British Spy   40

Chapter 8   Death March of a Vanishing Spirit   43

Chapter 9   Another Vanishing Soldier   48

Part III. Ghostly Treasure Guards | 51

| Chapter 10 | Ghost of Captain Kidd | 56 |
| Chapter 11 | Elegant Lady of the Old Stone House | 61 |

Part IV. Phantom Ships Off Pelham Shores | 67

Chapter 12	Fiery Phantom Ship of Long Island Sound	71
Chapter 13	Ghostly Gunship of Long Island Sound	75
Chapter 14	Ghost Ship *Palatine* and Its Mad Specter	79

Part V. Ghosts of the Murdered, Insane, and Suicidal | 83

Chapter 15	Ghost of Anne Hutchinson	91
Chapter 16	Ghost of the Murdered Traveler at Bartow-Pell Mansion	95
Chapter 17	Ghost of the Insane Pelham Lover	99
Chapter 18	Suicidal Specter of Manger Circle	104

Part VI. Wailing Ghosts of Pelham | 107

| Chapter 19 | Moaning Ghost of Hart Island | 109 |
| Chapter 20 | Shrieking Ghost of Wolfs Lane | 114 |

Part VII. Pelham Poltergeists | 117

| Chapter 21 | Melancholy Apparition of the Old Pelham Farmhouse | 119 |
| Chapter 22 | Phantom Bell Ringer of Christ Church | 123 |

Chapter 23	Whispering Bell of Saint Paul's Church	126
Chapter 24	Petulant Preacher Poltergeist	132
Chapter 25	Poltergeist of Pelhamdale	136

Part VIII. Haunted Houses and Ghosts of Pelham Mansions | 139

Chapter 26	Ghost of the Haunted Hardenbrook House	141
Chapter 27	Spirits of Bartow-Pell Mansion	148
Chapter 28	Ghostly Gardener of Bolton Priory	155
Chapter 29	Ghostly Matron of the Manor Club	159
Chapter 30	More Ghosts of the Old Stone House	164

Part IX. Quirky Apparitions and Shadow Ghosts of Pelham | 167

Chapter 31	Luminous Lantern-Bearer of Baychester and Pelham Bridge	168
Chapter 32	Wandering Ghost of the Mad Chemist	172
Chapter 33	Little Specter of the Field	177
Chapter 34	Floating White Phantom of City Island	181
Chapter 35	Faceless Shadow Ghost of City Island	184
Chapter 36	Faceless Shadow Ghost of James Street	187
Chapter 37	Fiery-Eyed Phantom of Pelham Heights	190

Notes	195
About the Author	207
Index	209

Illustrations

Figure 3.1	Glover's Rock	14
Figure 4.1	Pelham landmark known as Split Rock	21
Figure 5.1	Execution Rocks Light and keeper's house	32
Figure 6.1	Haunted Spy Oak	37
Figure 8.1	Horses and wagons crossing Pelham Bridge in 1865	44
Figure 10.1	Detail from 1867 map of Eastchester, Pelham, and New Rochelle	57
Figure 11.1	The old stone house at 463 First Avenue, Pelham, New York	65
Figure 15.1	*Massacre of Anne Hutchinson*	93
Figure 16.1	Pell Treaty Oak from an article published in *Scribner's Magazine* in 1892	96
Figure 16.2	Bartow-Pell Mansion in 1917	97
Figure 19.1	View of Hart Island in 1864	110
Figure 19.2	Military housing on Hart Island in 1864	111
Figure 22.1	Christ Church in 1848	124
Figure 23.1	Saint Paul's Church, Eastchester, in 1848	127
Figure 24.1	Saint Paul's Church from an engraving published in 1895	134

Figure 26.1	Newspaper depiction of Mrs. Gordon, Marvin R. Clark, and John A. Hardenbrook as they swapped ghost stories on the fateful night	143
Figure 26.2	One of the only known depictions of a Pelham ghost taken from eyewitness accounts	145
Figure 27.1	Bartow-Pell Mansion in Pelham Bay Park	149
Figure 27.2	Bartow-Pell Mansion and grounds in 1892	153
Figure 28.1	Bolton Priory in 1844, shortly after construction	156
Figure 28.2	Bolton Priory in 1855	158
Figure 33.1	Nineteenth-century map of City Island and the town of Pelham	178

Preface

Pelham, New York, is roughly triangular. A beautiful suburb of New York City, it is bounded by New York City's Pelham Bay Park in the borough of The Bronx, the city of New Rochelle, and the city of Mount Vernon. The town consists of two villages. Its northern half is the village of Pelham. Its southern half is the village of Pelham Manor.

Archaeological explorations, surveys, and excavations over the last century demonstrate that Pelham and its region were inhabited by Indigenous Americans for thousands of years prior to arrival of European settlers in the early seventeenth century. One such early European settler was Thomas Pell, an English immigrant who lived in Fairfield in the colony of Connecticut.

On June 27, 1654 (Julian Calendar), Pell purchased roughly fifty thousand acres of land from local Natives. Though Pell never lived on his lands, he immediately installed settlers on his purchase, later christened the "lordshipp and manner of Pelham."

The manor of Pelham initially included lands that comprise today's town of Pelham, much of the northeast Bronx, including Pelham Bay Park, City Island, and Throggs Neck; the city of Mount Vernon; the town of Eastchester (including its village of Bronxville); the city of New Rochelle; all the offshore islands in Long Island Sound; and more. Over the centuries, portions of the manor lands were sold to early settlers and, later, were annexed by New York City, until only about 1,400 acres remained. That remaining acreage comprises today's tiny town of Pelham, only 2.2 square miles of land adjacent to behemoth Gotham.

Pelham's ancient history provides a fascinating backdrop against which countless ghost stories have been handed down for generations. Indeed, some believe Pelham to be among the most haunted places in New York. In 2007, the magazine *Fate* (a US magazine about the paranormal) published an article designating the town of Pelham as the sixth most haunted town in New York out of the state's nearly one thousand towns and cities. Based on the number of Pelham ghost stories research reveals, it is unfathomable how Pelham did not finish first on the *Fate* list.

Admittedly, not many of today's Pelhamites have seen a ghost in the little town. There are some, however, who claim to have seen phantoms in the town. Such Pelhamites insist that if "one watches in the proper spirit on the right sort of night" (as one account puts it), such wonders still may be seen and heard in the region.

Among the most fascinating aspects of the several dozen ghost stories passed from generation to generation in Pelham is the fact that most accounts are tied to the history of the town or have arisen in connection with actual events. By telling and retelling these stories, Pelhamites preserve oral traditions that keep alive the region's rich history.

Academicians see ghost stories as useful tools that reveal insights about our lives and culture. As Jeannie Thomas, professor of English and chair of the English Department at Utah State University, has written:

> Ghost stories are a useful way to come to a better understanding of the worlds we inhabit. . . . [T]he narratives help us look more closely and analytically at culture, the environment, and the personal. [These] stories—whatever their level of believability—can point us outward and take us into realms of interest and significance.[1]

As Professor Thomas notes, when examining a culture's ghost stories, one should consider questions like:

- What cultures does the story reflect?
- What cultural values or "truths" (historical or contemporary) can be discerned in the narrative?
- Does it reveal or reinforce cultural values?
- Does the story present issues about which there is fear, stress, or conflict in the culture?
- How are these issues handled in the narrative?
- What views of trauma, death, and the body emerge from the story?[2]

Some Pelham ghost stories are frightening. Others are horrifying. A few are funny. All, however, provide fascinating glimpses of Pelham, its culture, and its storied history. Indeed, if thoughtful readers keep Professor Thomas's questions in mind while enjoying this book, the insights into Pelham's culture that these tales reveal will be as intriguing as the stories.

This text is organized to help readers understand the historical context underlying the stories. Thus, the book is organized in nine parts: (1) Indigenous American Hauntings; (2) Revolutionary War Specters; (3) Ghostly Treasure Guards; (4) Phantom Ships Off Pelham Shores; (5) Ghosts of the Murdered, Insane, and Suicidal; (6) Wailing Ghosts of Pelham; (7) Pelham Poltergeists; (8) Haunted Houses and Ghosts of Pelham Mansions; and (9) Quirky Apparitions and Shadow Ghosts of Pelham. Though some of the ghost stories fit more than one such category, each is included only once as a chapter within a relevant part.

At the beginning of each part there is a brief historical or informational sketch, documented with sources for students of history, to provide context for chapters that follow within that part. Each chapter is devoted to a single ghost story and ends with references where readers may "Read More."

Brace yourself and prepare to be entertained, enlightened, and frightened. You are about to read *The Haunted History of Pelham, New York*.

—Blake A. Bell
February 5, 2021

PART I
INDIGENOUS AMERICAN HAUNTINGS

In 1848, local historian Robert Bolton Jr. claimed that the Indigenous Americans who lived in and around the shores of today's Pelham and Pelham Bay Park comprised a band called "Siwanoys." He claimed such in his seminal two-volume history of Westchester County, presumably repeating local tradition.¹ Many scholars, professional archaeologists, anthropologists, and local historians have since assumed that a band of Native Americans known as "Siwanoys" populated the region.²

The notion seeped into popular culture. Pelham has a Siwanoy Elementary School. There is a Siwanoy Place. Nearby are the Siwanoy Country Club and the Siwanoy Trail. Tradition and local history books say that Siwanoys signed a 1654 deed with Thomas Pell selling him the lands that became Pelham and surrounding areas. Clearly, Indigenous Americans had a rich and lasting impact on Pelham and its lore. But were these early settlers "Siwanoys"?

Indigenous Americans, of course, populated the region long before European settlers arrived. Yet, contrary to Pelham lore there was no distinct group of Natives that might properly be labeled "Siwanoys." Recent scholarship supports, at best, a conclusion that the few early Siwanoy references were general in nature and not linked to identifiable groups of Natives or to specific individuals.

There may not have been a term in the Munsee dialect spoken by Lenape Natives in the Pelham region that sounded like "Siwanoy." Even if there were, any such term may not have had the meaning many ascribe. Noted anthropologist and Lenape scholar Dr. David Oestreicher has stated that his research suggests that the term "Siwanoy" did not apply to a specific band or group. Rather, a word sounding much like "Siwanoy" may have been used by Indigenous Americans to refer to others nearby. "It was a loose term used to reference people who lived in an area and surrounding lands extending as far south as Delaware and as far north as New York, Connecticut or even . . . northeastern Massachusetts." Today, of course, no one knows if the term "Siwanoy" had any meaning to the Indigenous Americans who lived in the area. Dr. Oestreicher, however, suggests that "it is guessed that the roots of the word 'Siwanoy' come from one of three other words meaning southerner, sea salt or wampum."[3]

Similarly, John Alexander Buckland has published an important book entitled *The First Traders on Wall Street: The Wiechquaeskeck Indians of Southwestern Connecticut in the Seventeenth Century*. According to Buckland, the term "Siwanoy" is a derivation of Munsee terms intended not as a "name" of a tribe or clan of local Natives, but rather as a descriptive term that denoted an activity pursued by Natives not only in the Pelham region but also in other locations, including Long Island, Pennsylvania, and Massachusetts. Buckland writes in his book:

> [Indigenous Americans in the Pelham region] have been called the "Siwanoy." Siwanoy referred to their occupation, however, and was not their tribal name. Many of their artisans made sewan, or wampum, along the shore, and they were the "Siwanoy" ("oy" means people), or "makers of wampum." Other Natives, who lived on Long Island, in Pennsylvania, and even in Massachusetts north of Boston, were also called "Siwanoy."[4]

Due at least in part to the mid-nineteenth-century work of Robert Bolton Jr., the term "Siwanoy" mistakenly emerged as a shorthand reference to local Indigenous Americans in the Pelham region who did not refer to themselves by any such appellation and may never have used the term.

Recent scholarship indicates that a group of Indigenous Americans with shared cultural traits, including a dialect of the Algonquian language known as "Munsee," lived in an area that encompassed a large portion of New Jersey, Manhattan and Staten Island, portions of the Hudson

Valley and all of the area of today's Pelham and Pelham Bay Park, and northward toward Connecticut and western Long Island. Dr. Paul Otto, professor of history at George Fox University, has studied this group of Indigenous Americans extensively. He writes that the Natives of the lower Hudson Valley and the surrounding region "can be grouped as the 'Munsees' because of their shared cultural traits and the use of the Munsee dialect."[5]

Dr. Otto has published a seminal work on the Indigenous Americans of the region who spoke Munsee: *The Dutch-Munsee Encounter in America*.[6] He writes that those to whom experts refer as Munsees did not group themselves as a nation, a tribe or even on the basis of small-scale villages. Rather, "their sociopolitical groups can be defined in a number of levels including villages, districts and maximal groups."[7]

The Munsees, according to Dr. Otto, commonly organized themselves in villages and related territories. He notes, however, that villages or even groups of villages also "claimed sovereignty over larger territories such as tracts and districts."[8] Such local associations could form into what Otto labels as "maximal groups" when the need for "broad cooperation or consultation" arose.[9]

Significantly, Munsees "used unique names to identify these various groupings (usually at the village level or close to it) by which the Dutch knew them and recorded in their observations." These included a host of collectives, among which was a grouping referenced repeatedly in seventeenth-century records as "Wiechquaeskecks."[10]

Early Dutch and English records indicate that the Munsee band or group known as Wiechquaeskecks ranged in an area on the mainland north of Manhattan from the Hudson River to the Long Island Sound, well north toward today's Connecticut border, and, perhaps, a little beyond.[11] The area included most, if not all, of the lands acquired by Thomas Pell from the local Indigenous Americans in 1654—lands that included today's Pelham, Pelham Bay Park, and much of the surrounding region.

Analysis of what is known about the Indigenous Americans who signed the Pell deed in 1654 by this author—analysis well beyond the scope of this book—indicates that several of the Natives who signed the deed can be identified as Wiechquaeskecks. These include an important sachem and signer of the deed referenced as Anhōōke.

Research suggests that Indigenous Americans who signed the Pell deed in 1654 were not "Siwanoys" as local lore maintains, but rather were part of a grouping known about that time as Wiechquaeskecks. That said, the romance and tradition passed from generation to generation of Pelhamites that Siwanoys once roamed the region prevails and has pervaded local ghost stories. Those stories, presented in the four chapters of part 1, are recounted as they have been told for generations with all references to Siwanoys retained.

Chapter 1

Headless Apparitions of the Haunted Cedar Knoll

She had heard the stories. Though a youngster, she had heard whispers of the haunted cedar knoll.

The ancient rocky knoll, strewn with hulking boulders, stood in Pelham Manor along Shore Road opposite Christ Church. Though it was the early nineteenth century, the youngster's grandmother had heard frightening stories during her own girlhood in the late eighteenth century. As her life ebbed, the grandmother warned her little granddaughter against visiting the knoll.

Such warnings only piqued the brash little girl's curiosity. She chose a windy night when a glowing full moon hung low in the sky to pick her way unsteadily up the boulders and rocks to climb the rocky knoll at its southern end.

Though the moon was bright, the furry branches of hundreds of ancient cedars on the rocky outcropping obscured much of the light. Because the moon hung low though, some light found its way beneath the branches. Shadows of the gnarled trunks and drooping branches striped the ground.

Each time the wind gusted, the furry branches shook and danced, casting confusing shadows that painted trunks, rocks, and ground. During one gust, the girl heard something eerie.

A howling shriek pierced the wailing gust. It curdled her blood. She knew howls of the wind. This was something sinister. As the shriek dissipated, she questioned her senses. Had she heard anything but wind?

Then shrieks rose again above the whining gusts. She knew then she should have taken her grandmother's warning to heart.

Instinctively the little girl crouched to lower her profile. Slipping from tree to tree and boulder to boulder, the courageously curious youngster crept toward shrieks and cries in the distance. As she made her way along the knoll toward its center, she could see an orange glow that flickered in the distance. The glow competed with the light of the moon and intensified the shadows of the furry branches that danced in the gusts.

The pungent smoke of burning green boughs brought tears to her eyes. She sneaked along and soon spied a fumy bonfire. Shadowy figures moved about the smoke and flames.

When she had made her way as close as courage allowed, she peered from behind a boulder. She spied a score of shrieking figures dancing around the fire. She first thought all had heads bowed, as though in prayer, as they danced about the flames. Soon she realized that she saw no heads, not because they were bowed and thus hidden from sight but because none of the furiously dancing figures had heads.

Wonder turned to horror. If the dancers had no heads, from where came the ear-piercing shrieks? Only then did she realize that the screaming dancers actually had heads. Each carried one.

Each dancer cradled within its arms a perfectly animated head that howled and shrieked. The eyes of each opened and closed, staring at the fire then looking toward the heavens as its wide-open mouth howled. Long dark hair cascaded from each head. The face of each was contorted and wrinkled.

Just as the little girl's grandmother had warned, the dancers once were Indians. Indeed, the spirits wore Indian garb and danced in a ring around the fire seemingly unaware that anyone spied nearby.

The hellish spirits bobbed diabolically. Though the eavesdropping little girl sensed evil, the spirits seemed to be hopping and whooping in a joyous celebration. Occasionally, each lifted a leg in unison with all others. The heads chanted in cadence. Other times the figures tightened the circle toward the fire, dancing in unison, then backed away in unison, expanding their circle.

Once, after the circle expanded, the shrieks ended abruptly. Howling winds halted. An eerie silence settled. The girl froze. She held her breath, fearing she might have been discovered.

The silence seemed eternal. The girl prepared to flee. Had she been seen? Had the terrible demons sensed her presence?

Each spirit then tossed its head toward the fire—not in the fire but near it. The heads rolled forward and stopped. Silence reigned momentarily. Each head then began to shriek in cadence again. With that, the winds gusted and the headless spirits linked arms and danced again both about the fire and the shrieking heads lying near the flames.

After dancing for what seemed an eternity to the girl, the headless dancers stopped. Again, the shrieks of the heads lying near the fire ended abruptly. The howling winds stopped. Another eerie silence washed over the knoll as each headless figure stood motionless and each head lay quietly by the fire.

The little girl feared what next might happen. She had a horrifying, uneasy feeling. She wished she had listened to her grandmother and never crept onto the cedar knoll.

As her regrets welled, every head lying on the ground came awake and shrieked a blood-curdling, piercing scream as though in monstrous pain. The unholy sounds reverberated throughout the knoll and across the little town of Pelham. Screams seemed to shake the headless Indian spirits back into motion. Each rushed forward and grabbed whatever head was nearest, whether its own or not, and cradled it, again, in careful arms. Once all held heads, the dancing and shrieking began anew.

"The stories are true," thought the little girl. But she had seen enough. How would she escape without being seen? What if she were discovered? Should she run or creep away?

As the shrieks continued, she glanced over a shoulder to choose an avenue of escape. As she did, the shrieks ended abruptly. All became dark and quiet. She glanced back toward the headless apparitions.

All were gone. The bonfire was gone. Neither smoke nor embers remained. The area was bare. The howling winds had ended. Tree branches no longer swayed. Moonlight once again cascaded through the treetops above, striping the ground below with the shadows of the cedar trees' trunks and branches.

Despite the serene moonlight, the little girl turned and ran to the edge of the haunted cedar knoll. She nearly tumbled down the rocky decline as she scrambled off the knoll and onto Shore Road. She ran for her life toward home.

As she ran, her mind raced. "The stories are true!" she gasped to herself. She thought of her grandmother's stories that rival tribes known as Siwanoys and Laaphawachkins[1] once lived in the region harmoniously until one of the Siwanoys murdered a member of the rival tribe. A blood feud followed and led to a deadly battle between the rival tribes on the great cedar knoll. The Siwanoys vanquished a score of their foes, decapitating each warrior and leaving their bodies on the top of the knoll. Each time the moon was full and the winds howled, the spirits of the dead Laaphawachkins danced in preparation for revenge against the Siwanoys.

The little girl ran frantically until she tumbled safely inside her home. Though brash, she never dared return to the haunted cedar knoll. Indeed, she was so frightened by what she saw that she never spoke of that frightening evening until her last years.

In 1901, however, a *New-York Daily Tribune* reporter convinced her, long after she had become an old woman, to tell her story. That story appeared in the December 15, 1901, issue of the newspaper. It is the only known eyewitness account of the headless apparitions of the haunted cedar knoll.[2]

Read More

Bell, Blake A. "Pelham's Ghosts, Goblins and Legends." *Pelham Weekly* (Pelham, NY). October 25, 2002, p. 1, col. 1.

Bolton, Robert. *The History of the Several Towns, Manors, and Patents of the County of Westchester, from Its First Settlement to the Present Time Carefully Revised by Its Author*, 2: 37. New York: Chas. F. Roper, 1881.

Comfort, Randall, ed. *History of Bronx Borough City of New York, Compiled for the North Side News*, 53. New York: North Side News Press, 1906.

Farnsworth, Cheri. *Haunted New York City: Ghosts and Strange Phenomena of the Big Apple*, 8. Mechanicsburg, PA: Stackpole Books, 2008.

New-York Daily Tribune. "Legends of Pelham." December 15, 1901, p. 2, cols. 1–4. See also *Hamilton Democrat* (Hamilton, OH), "Tragedy of Split Rock—Where Anne Hutchinson and Her Family Were Burned by Indians," p. 8, col. 2 (same text); *Hutchinson Democrat* (Hutchinson, KS), "Tragedy of Split Rock—Where Anne Hutchinson and Her Family Were Burned by Indians," p. 4, col. 3 (same text).

Twomey, Bill. *The Bronx in Bits and Pieces*, 227. Bloomington, IN: Rooftop, 2007.

Valenti, Ken. "Spooky Legends Are Part of Town's History." *Journal News* (White Plains, NY), October 31, 2004, p. 4B, cols. 1–5 (Local News—South Edition, Section B).

Chapter 2

Spirit of the Siwanoy Brave

Branches stung the face of the Siwanoy brave as he ran through the primeval forest. Underbrush clawed at his legs. Though blood streamed from scratches on his face, arms, and legs, he felt no pain, only fear.

The Siwanoy glanced over a shoulder as he ran, searching for pursuers. Though he could not yet see them, he could hear their shrieks. With each passing moment, the unearthly sounds seemed closer. He considered dropping the bow he carried in his left hand and the deerskin quiver with arrows slung across his back to make it easier to run, but he didn't. He ran.

Breathing heavily, he paused to rest against a tree, instinctively keeping its trunk between him and his pursuers. The shrieks were louder, almost drowning the sound of his heavy breathing. His temples pounded. His eyes darted as he searched for any refuge or avenue of escape. There was none.

Instantly, a strange sense of calm overwhelmed him. Momentarily, as he focused his thoughts on what next to do, the approaching shrieks melted away within his ears. Finally, he understood his heart. It was time to sprint to the Sacred Place ahead of his pursuers. He ran again, this time toward the Sacred Place.

The Sacred Place

Siwanoys knew the Sacred Place as the place of "Three Trees." Deep within the ancient Pelham forest was a monumental clearing in which stood three massive oaks. Each of the ancient, monumental trees spread its canopy nearly 150 feet from its trunk. The primeval oaks stood in nearly a perfect triangle. The sacred trees already were ancient, according to the Siwanoy brave's grandfather, when his grandfather's father was a young boy. One tree stood at the north point of an equilateral triangle. The second stood at the west point. The third stood at the east point.

In later historic times, those famous Pelham trees were aptly named the "North Tree," the "West Tree," and the "East Tree." Some in Pelham knew the area not as "Three Trees" but as the "North Oak Triangle." By the late nineteenth century, however, the West Tree had died and disappeared, though the North and East Trees still stood. Old photographs show that both of those ancient trees were, indeed, monumental.

The North Oak Triangle stood in part of Pelham that has been annexed by New York City. For many years there was a road that branched from today's Shore Road beginning about where the driveway entrance to the clubhouse for the Pelham Bay and Split Rock Golf Courses now begins. The road, known variously as Split Rock Road, Prospect Hill Road, and Prospect Lane, meandered from today's clubhouse driveway along the modern golf cart path that traverses beneath the New Haven Branch Line railroad tracks, then beyond where it passed the landmark Split Rock boulder and proceeded across what now is Interstate 95 and into a portion of today's town of Pelham, where a few blocks of the roadway still exist as "Split Rock Road" before ending at today's Boston Post Road.

The North Oak Triangle stood along Split Rock Road about a quarter mile from the roadway's beginning at Shore Road. The trees stood just past today's New Haven Branch Line railroad tracks on the side of the tracks opposite Shore Road. In the late nineteenth century, both the North Tree and the East Tree stood on that side of the branch line, although the West Tree was gone.

According to one author writing in the early twentieth century:

> These trees were regarded by the Indians with great reverence. Tradition tells us that, under their spreading branches the various tribes of Indians, some from Long Island and others from as far as Wappinger's Falls, met in the early part of every June and settled all their differences. This league of [Indigenous Americans] gathered together without any mental reservations and settled amicably their disputes.[1]

Cornered at the Sacred Place

Scratched and bleeding, the Siwanoy brave made it to the West Tree of the Sacred Place. He ducked beneath heavy drooping branches of the tree and leaned on it with his bloody bare back resting against the rough bark of the massive trunk. He could smell the stench of decay from the moist ground beneath the outspread branches of the tree. His chest heaved as he struggled to catch his breath. He shifted the deerskin quiver slung over a shoulder and the two arrows it held so the quiver and arrows dangled at his side. He dropped the bow to the ground.

Though young, the exceptionally handsome Siwanoy brave carried himself with nearly aristocratic bearing. He was a proud and successful warrior. He was strong. He held within his heart, however, a deep secret. The precise secret that he kept and refused to divulge to his tribe is now lost to history. However, it was this secret and his refusal to divulge it to the tribe that was responsible for the terrible and relentless pursuit by his fellow Siwanoys—members of his own clan.

According to legend, this proud Siwanoy brave "kept a secret from the rest of his tribe which he refused to divulge when ordered to do so." According to the story, members of the brave's tribe decided to conduct two trials to determine whether he should be called to account for his refusal to divulge his secret.

It was the supposed custom of local Siwanoys to treat members of their tribe accused of wrongdoing as innocent until proven guilty by *two* trials rather than one. This Siwanoy brave was dragged to the first such trial and was proven guilty of wrongdoing for refusing to divulge his secret to clan elders. Only days later, as he was dragged to the second trial, he overpowered a guard, took his bow and quiver, escaped, "and was pursued from the rocks near Travers Island to these sacred trees."

The brave's secret, however, was not in the forefront of his mind as he leaned against the great West Tree and awaited the arrival of his tormentors. The shrieks continued as the pursuers approached. He stood with his back to the great tree. Through the outspread branches of the tree, he finally could see them as they approached.

As the Siwanoys neared, the handsome brave reached into the deerskin quiver dangling by his side from a strap and removed a single arrow. He stood ramrod straight and pressed his back hard against the trunk of the tree. He closed his eyes and defied his pursuers by holding the tip of the arrow to his breast and shoving it violently so that it pierced his heart.

As the pursuers arrived, the proud Siwanoy brave fell at the foot of the great West Tree. He carried the secret with him to the grave.

In modern times those who visit the area of the Sacred Place on moonless nights have seen a spectral Siwanoy brave running frantically while carrying a bow with a deerskin quiver slung across his back. Usually when the spirit of the brave is seen, unearthly shrieks also can be heard in the distance, particularly when it is windy. It seems that the spirits of the Siwanoy band who chased the brave refuse to let the specter of the proud Siwanoy brave rest and, instead, will continue their chase for eternity until they learn the secret of the Siwanoy brave.

Read More

This tale is inspired by a tiny fragment of an unidentified, yellowed, and brittle newspaper clipping in the collection of the Office of the Historian of the Town of Pelham (copy in possession of this author). The clipping does not identify its date or source and has not yet been identified despite extensive research efforts.

Chapter 3

Ghost of the Indian Maiden of Pelhamdale

Dawn ignited. An orange glow from beneath the horizon lit the glimmering waters of Long Island Sound. Puffs of billowy clouds were backlit by a radiant glow. They shone from behind with violet, pink, and azure luminance.

Already hard at work gathering clams from the muddy edges of the sound at low tide, a young Native American woman stopped her work briefly to revel in the beauty of the moment. Her dark brown eyes sparkled with the fiery glow of the sunrise. A smile involuntarily crept across her small mouth as she watched a flock of geese spatter across the surface of the water in a cacophony of angry honks and splashes as they lifted heavily from the water into the morning sky.

This was the woman's ancestral land. She and her family were among the final few of their people to remain. Yet, a morning such as this reaffirmed the wisdom of her family's decision to remain.

As the sun edged above the horizon, the maiden returned to her work. She stooped to rake clams through the muck at her bare feet until something startled her. She straightened and looked toward the nearby peninsula some called Pell's Point. As she turned her head, she heard it again. She heard the unmistakable sounds of gunfire.

She heard a few distant pops. The retort, however, startled her. The few pops were met with staccato gunfire.

The maiden rushed from the muddy shoreline and hid her basket of clams near the path on the high ground above the water. That path ran parallel to Long Island Sound before it turned inland through the manor of Pelham and crossed the great horse path known by some as the Old Boston Post Road, then ran along the Hutchinson River.

After hiding her clams, the young maiden crept along the waterfront, taking care to remain concealed in marsh grasses. The gunfire continued. The young maiden crept carefully, motivated as much by curiosity as fear.

She came to a spot where she peeled back the marsh grasses and peered into the distance. She saw several men in homespun clothes settled behind a glacial boulder. Occasionally they peered around the boulder and fired ancient flintlocks.

She could smell the pungent smoke of burned powder. She could feel the rough stems of marsh grass scrape her face as the willows waved in the breeze. She could hear distant shouts and commands. Soon she could make out a most frightening sight: thousands of men in red coats carrying rifles with bayonets. Leaders shouted commands. Redcoats dropped to their knees, lifted their rifles, and fired at the handful of men behind the boulder.

Figure 3.1. Glover's Rock, used as cover by American militia men as they fired the first shots of the Battle of Pelham on October 18, 1776. Photograph by the author taken March 2, 2002.

Behind the men in red coats, she could see a forest of ship masts and low wooden barges bobbing in the waters of the bay behind Pell's Point. Though she knew something terrible had begun, she did not know that the Battle of Pelham, fought on October 18, 1776, was under way.

Tears involuntarily welled in the maiden's eyes. She watched as the men in homespun clothes broke away from the boulder and ran, hunkered over, to retreat from the wave of redcoats advancing on them. Each running man fumbled with his old flintlock. Occasionally, each turned, dropped to a knee, lifted his musket, and fired at the advancing redcoats before standing and running almost stooped to retreat further and repeat the process. A couple were shot and fell heavily to the ground. The redcoats were ferocious, menacing, and advancing.

The maiden realized that the troops were advancing toward the path that led past the home of Mr. Pell. She wiped her eyes. Crouching, she backtracked through the marsh grasses along Long Island Sound. Her feet remained bare from clam digging, but that mattered little. She crept along the marsh to return to the path parallel to the shore. There she scrambled out of the underbrush and ran.

The maiden's bare feet pounded along the path. Her heart thumped heavily in her breast. She could feel the pounding of her heart in her temples and heard her heavy breathing as she raced. Occasionally, her flying feet stepped on a pebble. The pain did nothing to slow her. She ran as fast as she could as the narrow little footpath turned away from Long Island Sound and became a wider path that headed inland.

The gunfire behind her seemed to have stopped, or at least paused. That mattered none. She had to get to Mr. Pell's house. She never slowed. Her bare feet pounded the path, occasionally frightening grouse and quails from adjacent vegetation, sending the terrified birds fluttering and flapping into the sky. Still, she ran.

As she ran, the gunfire began again. This time it seemed more sustained. This time there were no pauses. The sustained gunfire seemed to energize the young woman. She ran harder, listening to her own feet pound the path and raise puffs of dust behind her.

Soon the path swung along the little river some locals called Hutchinson's River. The young woman could see in the distance the beautiful little farmhouse that stood where the path along which she ran crossed the pathway called Old Boston Post Road. The farmhouse was the home of Colonel David Jones Pell and his family. It was known to local folks as "Pelhamdale."

The young woman did not even know Mr. Pell's full name. Nor did she know he was an American patriot. She only knew that he and his family were kind to her and her family and had been kind for many years. Indeed, her family had told her stories of how Mr. Pell's ancestors had allowed her ancestors to plant corn on Pell's Point, and had allowed them to store their canoes there during something called King Philip's War when settlers fought with Indigenous Americans to the north. She knew that Mr. Pell and his family provided corn and kindness during particularly brutal winters and allowed them to drink freely from the family's wells.

Breathless, the maiden reached the doorway of Mr. Pell's home. Her heart raced. Her feet were bruised and bleeding. She was wild-eyed and wet with sweat. Adrenaline throbbed through her veins. She used much of her remaining strength to pound on the farmhouse door. She pounded and pounded, slapping her palms against the rough wood to wake the family.

David Pell threw open the great door, still pulling on a rough linen blouse. As he did, the young maiden crumpled to the stoop and fell through the doorway onto the floor. The young Paul Revere used David Pell's leg to pull herself up enough to warn breathlessly, "Men in red coats! Guns! Many, many men!" She collapsed, panting and exhausted.

Pell's family huddled behind him as he finished fumbling with the buttons of his blouse. He kneeled and tenderly placed his hand beneath one of the young maiden's cheeks. He lifted her exhausted head slightly and looked into her eyes as if to say, "Thank you!" before bolting out the door and leaving her to the care of his family.

Pell set off in a boat on the Hutchinson River. He rowed upriver to the settlement of Eastchester to warn American troops there that the British had landed and were marching up Split Rock Road toward the Old Boston Post Road (today's Colonial Avenue in Pelham). Clearly the British hoped to overwhelm George Washington and his Continental Army retreating from Harlem Heights toward White Plains.

History may record that American Patriot and Revolutionary War hero Colonel John Glover of the Marblehead Mariners was the first to observe British and German troops disembarking from their ships with a spy glass from a hill near present-day Memorial Field in Mount Vernon, New York, and that he hurried his troop of soldiers forward for a deceptive attack from behind the many stone walls that dotted the Pelham Manor countryside along Split Rock Road. Tradition, however, says that a beautiful young Native American woman ran barefoot for miles along a simple dirt path to provide the earliest warning of the invasion by British and German troops that fateful day.

Are we to believe history or tradition? If the spirit world is any indication, we should believe tradition.

Once the Revolutionary War ended, little was left of the manor of Pelham. Homes and outbuildings had been looted and destroyed by the warring armies. The countryside was barren. Farmland had returned to its native state. The land was devoid of trees, all cut to provide fuel for the warring armies and for the many, many Tories relegated to Manhattan for their own protection. Yet, a few homes had survived.

One of those homes was the little farmhouse of Colonel David Jones Pell. The home was ravaged. Its walls were pock-marked with bullet holes and shrapnel. Of course, not a pane of glass remained in its windows. Its furnishings were gone. A number of its outbuildings were gone, torn down by men for firewood. Yet, the solid guts of the old home remained. Colonel Pell rebuilt the farmhouse and settled there, again, with his family.

After the war, Colonel Pell and his family searched for the young Native woman who had warned them of the redcoats more than a decade before. She was, however, nowhere to be found. Nor were any of her family. Indeed, she and her family either had departed forever or failed to survive the giant conflagration that ravaged their ancestral land. The young maiden was never seen again.

That is not to say, however, that she never was heard again.

Soon after David Pell and his family returned to their home, known today as "Pelhamdale" and located at 45 Iden Avenue, they experienced odd incidents. In the early hours of the morning when they walked the paths and roads near the home that later became Split Rock Road, Wolfs Lane, and Colonial Avenue, they heard strange sounds. Frantic footfalls seemed to pound along the roadways when no one was present. Sometimes those footfalls were accompanied by sounds of heavy breathing.

Others heard the sounds. Indeed, many reported that along the entirety of Split Rock Road and Wolfs Lane to Colonial Avenue, such sounds of footfalls and heavy breathing would begin in the distance, approach, then disappear ahead. In early years, while the paths and roadways were still dirt and unpaved, some reported that the sounds were accompanied by puffs of dust scattered into the breeze from the road surface as an unseen presence raced by.

Even today, if you stand in the perfect spot at precisely the right time in the early hours of the morning each October 18 and you listen very carefully, you will hear frantic footfalls and labored breathing as an unseen presence passes. Unless the howl of October winds masks the sound, you likely will hear those footfalls receding faintly in the direction of the lovely home known as Pelhamdale.

Read More

Bell, Blake A. "Pelham's Ghosts, Goblins and Legends." *Pelham Weekly* (Pelham, NY). October 25, 2002, p. 1, col. 1.

Saunders, James B., ed. *The Pelham Manor Story*, 61. Pelham: Village of Pelham Manor, 1991.

Chapter 4

Dark Spirit of the Devil and His Stepping-Stones

A legend has been told in Pelham for eons. It dates to ancient times when Native Americans populated the region. Famed author Washington Irving, who frequented Pelham as a friend of Reverend Robert Bolton of Bolton Priory, referenced the legend in a book he published in 1824 entitled *Tales of a Traveller*. Although at first blush the legend seems dark and foreboding, it actually is a story of triumph over the darkest spirit ever to visit Pelham.

Long, long ago when Indigenous Americans roamed the region, things turned bad for them—very, very bad. They suffered many misfortunes, including failed crops, poor fishing, brutal snows, and raging storms. The time for action had come.

The Natives understood that the wicked giant devil, known by many names including Habboamoko, long had roamed the region, including today's Pelham Bay Park, Westchester County, and portions of southeastern Connecticut. His giant footprints may still be found in some of the rock outcroppings in places throughout Westchester County and Connecticut. The giant devil was known to create mayhem and to bring periodic misfortune to the Indigenous people.

Concluding that Habboamoko was, once again, the source of their misfortune, Siwanoy warriors and others gathered throughout the region to use strength and wits to chase Habboamoko off the mainland across Long Island Sound and onto Long Island, where he would be left to torment others. The warriors located and rousted Habboamoko and began to battle the giant evil one.

Because Habboamoko was a giant, the battle was difficult and raged for a long time. Slowly, though, the warriors gained the advantage. As Habboamoko retreated, he gathered every glacial boulder he could find in the countryside. He cradled them in his long, menacing arms. He fled to the tip of Pelham Neck and then onto City Island. When he reached the tip of City Island with the warriors in hot pursuit, however, he was not big enough to hop across the deep waters and escape to the shores of Long Island (where today's Steppingstone Park stands).

Though Habboamoko was a giant, Long Island Sound was deep and wide at the point where he needed to cross from City Island. As the warriors closed in, Habboamoko began flinging the boulders he had collected into the sound, using them as stepping-stones to make his escape across the deep waters. Once he had crossed the deep waters, he stood on Long Island and looked back. Warriors lined the shores of today's City Island, Pelham Bay Park, and Pelham laughing at and taunting him. Angrily, Habboamoko took every last boulder still cradled in his arms and, one at a time, threw them across Long Island Sound at the warriors.

The giant boulders thrown by Habboamoko rained down and landed throughout the countryside. Occasionally Habboamoko threw the boulders with such anger that he flung them great distances, covering much of today's Pelham Bay Park, Westchester County, and even lower Connecticut. One giant boulder flung by Habboamoko broke in half when it landed. We know that boulder today as the famous Pelham landmark "Split Rock." Many other boulders likewise have become famous. They became known as Glover's Rock, the Kemble House Rocking Stone, the Priory Rocking Stone, the Grey Mare, and Mishow, to name a few. Many of the boulders were never given names. Nevertheless, they still stand throughout the countryside as silent reminders of the blind anger of the giant devil as he vengefully tried one last time to rain more misery on the Indigenous Americans in and around what became Pelham.

The many boulders that the evil spirit threw into Long Island Sound to use as stepping-stones to make his escape to Long Island became known as the "Devil's Stepping-Stones." As the centuries passed, the Devil's Stepping-Stones became the bane of mariners who navigated Long Island Sound. Countless ships were lost trying unsuccessfully to maneuver around the rocky reefs that skipped across Long Island Sound below the southeastern tip of City Island.

Figure 4.1. Pelham landmark known as Split Rock, one of many glacial boulders of the region thrown by an angry Habboamoko. Photograph by the author taken May 28, 2005.

During the 1850s, the Army Corps of Engineers began blasting away many of the Devil's Stepping-Stones. Not all were removed, however. Thus, the area remained treacherous for mariners. In 1876 and 1877, authorities built Stepping-Stones Light on one of the few remaining Devil's Stepping-Stones. The square-shaped Second Empire–style lighthouse is built of red brick and is one and a half stories high. The lighthouse continues to operate and stands many hundreds of yards off the tip of City Island. It is operated by the United States Coast Guard and is on the National Register of Historic Places.

Thankfully, the Army Corps of Engineers blasted away most of the Devil's Stepping-Stones beginning in the 1850s with a second wave of blasting beginning in 1885. As a consequence, Habboamoko can never return to Pelham. Instead, the devil has had to remain on Long Island ever since. This likely explains a lot about Long Island, including its hellish traffic . . .

Read More

Irving, Washington. *Tales of a Traveller*, 186–87. New York: G. P. Putnam's Sons, 1824. Reprint by the Knickerbocker Press, New Rochelle, New York, 1895.
Skinner, Charles Montgomery. *Myths and Legends of Our Own Land*, 4th ed., 1: 122–23. Philadelphia: J. B. Lippincott, 1896.

PART II
REVOLUTIONARY WAR SPECTERS

Pelham was ravaged during the Revolutionary War. British warships and American gunboats constantly prowled off Pelham shores. Their crews raided Pelham islands and the adjacent mainland. The Battle of Pelham was fought on Pelham soil on October 18, 1776. Moreover, Pelham stood in the midst of the so-called Neutral Ground between the British and American armies and was preyed upon by irregulars loosely "associated" with both sides during the entire war. Consequently, cannonballs and accouterments of the war have been found for many years in and around Pelham and continue to be found.

Certainly, the most significant event to occur in Pelham during the Revolutionary War was the Battle of Pelham. It has been called the "Battle of Pelham,"[1] the "Battle of Pelham Manor,"[2] the "Battle of Pelham Moor,"[3] the "Battle of Pelham Bay,"[4] the "Fight at Pelham Heights,"[5] the "Battle of Pell's Point,"[6] "Colonel Glover's Stand at Pelham,"[7] the "skirmish" of October 18, 1776, and the "Forgotten Battle."[8]

Though historians may not agree on a name, many agree that it was a battle that saved George Washington's Army early in the war.[9]

Background

On October 11, 1776, Washington's army was encamped at Harlem Heights at the northern tip of Manhattan. Americans controlled nearby King's Bridge—a critical means of escape from the island, if necessary.

Washington's army was vulnerable. The British navy controlled the surrounding waters, including the Hudson River, the East River, and Long Island Sound. Washington expected a frontal attack from British troops encamped on the island of Manhattan. He recognized, however, that if British commander Sir William Howe could land his troops on the mainland behind the bulk of Washington's army and race across the mainland from Long Island Sound toward the Hudson River to block the Americans' only overland escape route toward the northeast, General Washington and his army would be trapped and, perhaps, drawn into a fight to the finish. At a minimum, such a move would interrupt transport of critical supplies to the Americans from New England, further weakening the American cause.

The British Landing at Throggs Neck

Washington and his commanders prepared for the possibility that Howe might choose Throggs Neck as a place to land troops behind the American army. Americans placed two groups of twenty-five riflemen at strategic spots where they suspected British forces might attempt to cross an important creek as they marched off Throggs Neck toward King's Bridge. At one spot, commanders ordered the riflemen to take up the planks of a small causeway over which the British troops would have to pass to cross the creek. The second group of riflemen defended a place where the creek could be forded just north of the causeway.

On October 12, 1776, Sir William Howe and his brother, Lord Richard Howe (commander of the British naval forces), oversaw the landing of about four thousand English and German troops on Throggs Neck. The British planned to march up Throggs Neck, cross Westchester Creek, and race toward King's Bridge to cut off Washington's escape and engage the American army.

British commanders sent two columns of troops up Throggs Neck. The first approached the causeway. The second headed toward the ford north of the causeway. As the troops approached the former causeway, the American riflemen lay in wait on the opposite side of the creek behind a large woodpile. When the British and German troops reached what was left of the causeway, the riflemen opened fire and staggered the advance. When the second group of British and German troops arrived at the ford north of the causeway, it also met brisk fire from American riflemen.

In inexplicable and unnecessary caution, the commanders of the British and German forces chose not to fight their way across the little creek. Rather, they withdrew to a nearby hill where they erected earthworks and a battery. American commanders rushed nearly two thousand reinforcements to the area. Sir William Howe's invasion of the mainland via Throggs Neck stalled.

In a critical delay, Howe and his troops encamped in the area for the next six days awaiting additional supplies and reinforcements. In the meantime, Washington and his commanders began withdrawal of the bulk of the American army toward White Plains.

Americans understood they were in a race against time. At precisely the time preparations for the American withdrawal from Harlem Heights toward White Plains began on October 17th, British commanders prepared their own troops for a second landing attempt—this time at Pell's Point in the manor of Pelham.

The situation was bleak for the American army. The next day nearly thirteen thousand American troops would be strung along narrow roads toward White Plains as the British marched across the mainland to attack the vulnerable line. As one scholar of the battle has written: "If the enemy should attack the defenseless and straggling column before it reached White Plains, disaster was certain for the American army and the flickering light of the Revolution totally extinguished."[10]

The Landing at Pell's Point

At about 2:00 a.m. on October 18, 1776, British and German troops were ordered into flatboats to move from Throggs Neck across the mouth of the Hutchinson River to Pell's Point (now known as Rodman's Neck) opposite today's City Island. British ships moved up the sound to protect the troop movement.

In the early morning hours, American reinforcements at the causeway and at the ford near the top of Throggs Neck saw the British and German soldiers moving out of their entrenchments. Commanders at both locations thought that they were about to be attacked by the British in an effort to fight their way across Westchester Creek. But the British and German troops were actually departing for nearby flatboats for transport to Pell's Point. Confusion reigned among the Americans. According to one account:

> The [Commanding Officer] at the causeway rushed an express to General Heath . . . notifying him of an expected large scale British attack on his front. Gen. Heath rushed there with a large number of troops. On his way he was met by another express from the [Commanding Officer] of the troops at the ford. The report this time was that the British were marching northward toward the post [at the ford] for an attack in force. (Actually they were marching to the eastern shore of Throggs Neck to board the ships there for the passage across to Pell's Neck.) Heath turned his forces around and began marching them more toward the southeast, that is, toward the ford.[11]

As Dr. Alfred M. Franko, former city historian of Mount Vernon, noted in his book *Pelham Manor: The Forgotten Battle of the Revolution Near Mount Vernon, New York*, at this moment, General Washington arrived on the scene. After assessing the situation, he ordered General Heath to return with his troops to Valentine Hill to await an impending attack on Morrisania. Washington feared that the movement of the British and German troops in front of the causeway and ford at the top of Throggs Neck was intended to deceive him.

Dr. Franko wrote, "Washington had guessed wrong again. Instead of ordering troops to Pell's Neck where the invasion was actually taking place at that very moment, he sent his troops to the opposite direction, that is to Valentine Hill to be prepared for an attack on Morrisania which never came and was never planned by Howe."[12]

General Washington's move meant that the only thing standing between the British army and the total destruction of the American army was a stocky little colonel named John Glover and the 750 men of the four regiments (including his own Marblehead Mariners) that he temporarily commanded during a brief absence of his commanding officer.

The Battle of Pelham

As dawn broke on October 18, 1776, Colonel John Glover stood on a hill near today's Memorial Stadium on Sandford Boulevard across the street from Glover Field. He gazed through a telescope toward the mouth of the Hutchinson River. What he saw must have sent a chill up his spine. His own account written six days later reads:

> I arose early in the morning and went on the hill with my glass and discovered a number of ships in the Sound under way; in a very short time saw the boats, upwards of two hundred sail, all manned and formed in four grand divisions. I immediately sent Major Lee express to General Lee, who was about three miles distance, and without waiting his orders, turned out the brigade I have the honour to command.[13]

Glover left his own regiment of about three hundred men on the hill with artillery. He ran with the remaining 450 men of the brigade over the wooden bridge across the Hutchinson River. Once across, he had some of his men take up the bridge.

The layout of the principal roads that existed at the time, of course, was different than today's roads. The men essentially ran down the hill and crossed the Hutchinson River along today's Colonial Avenue and onto the roadway now known as Wolfs Lane. They moved southeastward along that roadway to Split Rock Road (not its name at the time). In the eighteenth century that roadway extended across today's Interstate 95, through today's Pelham Bay Park, and across today's Split Rock Golf Course until it met Pelham Road (now known as Shore Road).

In the meantime, British and German troops were approaching from the opposite direction. After they landed on Pell's Point, they marched along roughly what is known today as Orchard Beach Road, then Pelham Road (today's Shore Road) toward Pelham until they reached what later became known as Split Rock Road. Split Rock Road branched away from today's Shore Road in an area roughly near today's Pelham Bay and Split Rock Golf Course entrance and led toward Prospect Hill and Colonial Avenue (the Old Boston Post Road).

Glover and his men soon heard the crackle of gunfire. There is anecdotal evidence that other Americans who were not associated with the men led by Colonel Glover skirmished with the British and German troops shortly after the enemy landed on Pell's Point and that a party of American militia fell back along the road we know today as Orchard Beach Road, specifically using the large glacial boulder known today as Glover's Rock for cover.

According to family tradition within the De Veaux family, on October 18, 1776, an American militia unit of which Abel De Veau Jr. (also known as Abel Deveau) was a member, was on Pelham Neck when British and German troops landed in advance of the Battle of Pelham.

Some accounts say this militia unit was the first to engage the British and Germans, firing on the advancing enemy from "behind the large rock standing on the City Island road"—that is, today's Glover's Rock. According to one account:

> When the Army of General Howe started on their march from Pelham Neck a party of Militia, of whom Abel De Veau—the Grandfather of Capt. John D. De Veau—lay behind the large rock standing on the City Island road and fired upon the British Army. The British followed them up and they retreated, keeping up the fire along Pelham Lane [i.e., Split Rock Road], and lost two men before they got to Prospect Hill. There they were joined by a large party of Militia, and then they had a brisk fight. They then fell back to the hill of Mrs. Ronalds, and there they stood and had another brush. As the British advanced they kept up the fire as long as possible, and only retired when compelled by the numbers of the British to do so. They made a gallant defence.[14]

As members of the American militia fired at the advancing enemy and fell back, Glover and his men raced to meet the enemy. Glover observed the British army's advance guard—a group of about thirty men sent ahead of the main body of troops. He immediately sent his own advance guard of forty men to meet them and to buy time to deploy his own troops to fight the impending battle.

Glover deployed his three regiments of troops en echelon. This is a military formation in which each unit is positioned successively to the left or right of the rear unit to form an oblique or steplike line.[15] In addition, he made certain that each unit was deployed hidden from view behind stone fences that lined the road and crossed the small fields along the roadway.

From Col. Glover's perspective (located along Split Rock Road and facing toward today's Shore Road), he deployed a regiment commanded by Colonel Joseph Read forward and to the left of the roadway. Next, he deployed a regiment led by Colonel William Shepard some distance behind Col. Read's and to the right of that regiment. Next, he placed a third regiment commanded by Colonel Loammi Baldwin some distance behind Colonel Shepard's and, once again, to the right of that regiment. A letter written by Col. Baldwin to his wife in which he touched on troop placements reads: "I immediately joined the [regiments] and found them posted on each side of a road behind a cross fence finely situated to annoy the enemy as they approached."[16]

Col. Glover's term "cross fence" is a reference to a type of fence. Cross fences are built within a larger fenced area and allow multiple uses of land within the larger area bounded by a perimeter fence (with some areas used for livestock and others for growing forage, for example).

Col. Baldwin's reference makes clear that two of the regiments were posted on one side of the roadway and a third was posted on the opposite side of the roadway. While Glover's account of the battle makes clear that Read's men were posted forward and to the left of the roadway from the Americans' perspective, it is not possible from known eyewitness accounts to ascertain whether one or both of the two remaining units were on the other side of the road (although at least one of them was, if Col. Baldwin's account was accurate).

The British and German troops had marched about one and a half miles from their landing into an area in the midst of today's Split Rock Golf Course. As the British advance guard met the American advance guard, Col. Glover rushed forward to direct his troops. His letter, written shortly after the battle, tells the story:

> I rode forward—to the advance guard, and ordered them to advance, who did, within forty yards, and received their fire without the loss of a man; we returned it and fell four of them, and kept the ground until we exchanged five rounds. Their body being much larger than mine, and having two men killed and several wounded, which weakened my party, the enemy pushed forward not more than thirty yards distant, I ordered a retreat which was masterly well done by the Captain that commanded the party. The enemy gave a shout and advanced; Colonel Read's, laying under cover of a stone wall undiscovered till they came within thirty yards, then rose up and gave them the whole charge; the enemy broke, and retreated for the main body to come up.[17]

Glover's men waited in place for an hour and a half before the British and Germans "appeared" with "about 4,000"[18] troops and seven pieces of artillery, advancing on the Americans. Glover and his men remained under the cover of the stone walls until the enemy troops were within fifty yards. Then, according to Glover, the Americans "rose up and gave them the whole charge of the battalion."[19] The British returned the fire "with showers of musketry and cannon balls" until the two sides had exchanged seven rounds.[20] Col. Glover and Col. Read's regiments then retreated to the rear of Col. Shepard and on his left.

The British shouted and advanced, thinking the Americans were on the run. Instead, Col. Shepard and his men rose from "behind a fine double wall"[21] and began firing until he and his men had exchanged seventeen rounds with the British "and caused them to retreat several times."[22]

The British kept coming, however. Slowly the Americans were being pushed back along Split Rock Road toward the large hill that, today, includes much of the grounds of the Prospect Hill Elementary School and surrounding areas.

At about this time, according to a letter that Col. Baldwin later wrote to his wife, he and an aide noticed that the British were engaged in a flanking maneuver and were approaching the place where the Americans planned to recross the creek under cover of the artillery pieces Col. Glover earlier had placed on the hill near today's Memorial Field from which the American troops had started.[23]

Col. Glover, together with Read's and Shepard's regiments, retreated behind Col. Baldwin's regiment. According to Col. Glover's letter:

> [British and German troops] then came up to Baldwin's but the ground being much in their favor, we could do but little before we retreated to the bottom of the hill, and had to pass through a run of water (the bridge I had taken up before) and then marched up a hill the opposite side of the creek where I left my artillery.[24]

Once again, the British became overly cautious and unwilling to cross a stream in pursuit. Glover says, "The enemy halted, and played their artillery at us, and we at them, till night, without any damage on our side, and but very little on theirs."[25]

The British and Germans camped along the Old Boston Post Road (today's Colonial Avenue) from the area around today's Pelham Memorial High School grounds nearly all the way to the New Rochelle border. Only about 450 Americans, commanded by Col. Glover, had delayed some four thousand British and German troops for a day as the bulk of the American army struggled to escape from Harlem Heights to White Plains. The ferocity with which the Americans embraced their duty may best be exemplified by the later testimony of Sir Henry Clinton, a British commander, who testified he thought they were facing fourteen thousand American troops.

Yet, the toll resulting from the battle may have been surprisingly light. Deserters suggested that hundreds of British and German troops died in the battle. This seems an exaggeration. Though the records are admittedly confused and, in at least one case, missing, it can only be said with some degree of certainty that Col. Glover recorded that he had "eight men killed and thirteen wounded"[26] (although official returns list only six dead Americans). The British, in turn, reported a total of only twenty-five casualties, although no firm figures have ever been uncovered for the German troops under British command. A family history records that two members of American militia also were killed[27] (which may account for the discrepancy between Glover's account and official returns). Additionally, recent research suggests that at least five Hessian troops were buried on the grounds of Saint Paul's Church (which was used as a hospital by British and German troops) after the battle.[28]

Conclusion

The two warring armies left detritus throughout Pelham, including musket balls, cannonballs, uniform accoutrements, and more. That is not all they left, however. According to many, spirits of many of the dead were left as well and still haunt Pelham as the following five chapters of this part demonstrate.

Chapter 5

Shrieking Ghosts of Execution Rocks

In Long Island Sound, nearly midway between the town of Pelham on the mainland and Sands Point, Long Island, on the opposite shore is a lighthouse known as "Execution Rocks Light." The lighthouse sits atop a rocky outcropping in a busy shipping lane that grows all the more dangerous when the rocks are exposed during low tides. On March 3,

Figure 5.1. Execution Rocks Light and keeper's house. Photograph by the author taken August 21, 2005.

1847, Congress appropriated $25,000 to build Execution Rocks Light. The structure was designed by Alexander Parris, a prominent American architect and engineer who designed a number of lighthouses located along the coastline of the northeastern United States.

Construction of the lighthouse was completed in 1849, but Execution Rocks Light did not begin operations until the following year. For more than a century, the position of lightkeeper of Execution Rocks Light was considered one of the loneliest posts in the service. In 1979, however, the lighthouse became fully automated.

The lighthouse is listed on the National Register of Historic Places and is designated a "Historic Civil Engineering Landmark" by the American Society of Engineers. On May 29, 2007, the United States Department of the Interior designated "Execution Rocks Light Station" as surplus under the National Historic Lighthouse Preservation Act of 2000. The island is under the authority of the United States Coast Guard and, for the most part, is off-limits to the public.

When traveling on Long Island Sound and nearing Execution Rocks Light, a strange sound sometimes can be heard. At first, from an extreme distance, the sound pierces the silence somewhat like the distant shrieks of clownlike gulls cartwheeling in the skies above the water as they swarm above seething schools of baitfish. Something, however, seems a little different about the sound. It doesn't have the high-pitched optimism of the ubiquitous and nettlesome gulls as they feed on fish. Instead, it evokes more of a primeval chill that makes the hair stand on the back of one's neck.

As a visitor nears Execution Rocks Light, particularly on bright nights when the moon is full, the chilling sounds become unmistakable. They seem possibly human, though they may best be described as inhuman. At first, it seems almost as though the sounds are echoing from some unknown nearby surface. Soon, however, an awful realization washes over the visitor that those are no echoes—only the inhuman cries of several simultaneous vocalists.

Near the jagged rocks of the desolate and forsaken island, the sounds grow unnatural and nigh impossible to describe. Each starts in a way that evokes a guttural groan, then slowly rises in pitch and terror to a crying shriek—not a scream but a shriek seemingly born not of pain but of sheer terror. Occasionally, there is mixed among the cries something that sounds like the clinking of metal. It is difficult to hear over the shrieks, but it is unmistakable. Instinctively any listener recoils. Indeed, the sound evokes a visceral impulse to flee, a primeval fear promoting flight, not fight.

Inevitably, the cacophony of shrieks bespeaks terror, dying, and death. It continues unabated for what seems an eternity until suddenly, and without warning, the sounds die. Indeed, the abruptness of the eerie silence always startles. Such an abrupt silence is as chilling as the cacophony that preceded.

The story behind these unearthly sounds is just as chilling. Locals have long maintained that during the Revolutionary War, the British captured American soldiers and rousted rebel civilians from their settlements on the mainland and on Long Island and transported them to the rocky ledge that came to be known as "Execution Rocks." There the British tortured these unfortunates and executed them. The story is told that the British sought such a desolate location in the middle of the sound to reduce the risk that anyone might witness and reveal their atrocities.

According to the legend, among the many brutal ways the British tortured and killed their captives was to chain them to the rocks at low tide. As the tide rose inexorably, the chained prisoners strained at their chains, causing horrifying clanking sounds as the iron banged against the boulders. Invariably the prisoners groaned at their fate and shrieked to attract the attention of anyone with an ounce of compassion within the sound of their screams. Finally, as the moon labored to drag the tidewaters higher, the prisoners no longer could keep their contorted faces above water. The horrific shrieks typically ended abruptly as the water overwhelmed the poor souls, leaving a startling silence broken only by the sounds of waves crashing against Execution Rocks.

The next time you find yourself along the shores of Long Island Sound or boating on its waters, you will hear what you may think are the shrieks of gulls. Listen carefully. Listen for the clanking of metal. Listen for anything that resembles a guttural groan followed by shrieks. Better yet, stop and assess whether the hair on the back of your neck is standing or whether you feel a chill. If so, those shrieks you hear are likely not those of gulls.

Read More

This legend of the Shrieking Ghosts of Execution Rocks has been told for so long and has gained such notoriety that it recently was the subject of a television investigation by *Ghost Adventures*, a program aired on the Travel Channel. See "Execution Rocks' Haunted History," in *Travel Channel Shows: Ghost Adventures*, https://www.travelchannel.com/shows/ghost-adventures/articles/execution-rocks-haunted-history.

The legend also has been mentioned in numerous books. Here are examples:

Jones, Ray. *Haunted Lighthouses: Phantom Keepers, Ghostly Shipwrecks, and Sinister Calls from the Deep*, 196–97. Guilford, CT: Globe Pequot Press, 2010.

Wood, Maureen, and Ron Kolek. *A Ghost a Day: 365 True Tales of the Spectral, Supernatural, and Just Plain Scary*, 91–92. Avon, MA: F+W Media, 2010.

Chapter 6

Ghostly Cow Rustlers of Pelham Road

"Pop" Doty was proud of his family heritage. Born Girard Post Doty, he was a descendant of Mayflower passenger Edward Doty. In 1912, Pop was seventy-nine years old and living with his nephew, Warren Doty, in a home on Pelham Road. The home stood about a half mile from a monumentally large ancient oak tree. Known variously as the "Haunted Oak," the "Skinners Oak," the "Spy Oak," and the "Haunted Spy Oak," the giant tree was a landmark for centuries along that part of old Pelham Road we know today as Westchester Avenue in The Bronx. The tree was "said to be the largest of its kind east of the Rockies."[1]

Pop's family had owned lands in the area of the giant tree since before the American Revolution. Indeed, as Pop often said, he had played beneath the branches of the Haunted Oak as a child, just like his mother and her mother had.

Pop Doty's maternal grandmother, whom he called "Grandmother Baxter Stuyvesant," was 105 years old when she died. She knew the story of the Haunted Oak better than anyone since she lived much of her life in a home just "across the way" from the tree. Grandmother Baxter Stuyvesant often told Pop and other members of the family a chilling story about the Haunted Oak.

When she was a young girl, Grandmother Baxter Stuyvesant's father and her brothers fought with General George Washington during the American Revolution. At about the time of the Battle of Westchester Creek and the Battle of Pelham that followed, the area was overrun with British. Some were deserters from the British army. Others simply

Figure 6.1. Haunted Spy Oak shown in a photograph published in 1913.

wandered the region, up to no good. Indeed, it was the very beginning of the "Neutral Ground" period during which so-called "Cowboys and Skinners" marauded throughout the region during the war, decimating the manor of Pelham.

"Cowboys" were members of a loosely organized British light horse battalion led by Colonel James De Lancey. American Patriots slapped the unit with the derisive name for its propensity to rustle cattle during raids. The unit operated throughout the Neutral Ground, including the Pelham region, during the entire war. "Skinners," on the other hand, were Americans, though unattached to any particular military unit. Cowboys plundered and tortured local residents who sympathized with the Patriot cause. The Skinners, in contrast, likely consisted of irregulars and terrorized locals in Pelham and in the remainder of the Neutral Ground often without regard to whether the victims were Tories or Patriots.

Early in the war, a group of seven hungry Cowboys schemed to rustle the Stuyvesants' family cow. During a temporary absence of the

Stuyvesant men who were serving the Patriot cause, the seven Cowboys brazenly stole the cow in broad daylight from the family matriarch in front of her young daughter. They butchered the cow and feasted on its remains. Among those who participated in the theft was a young fellow—a handsome boy that the young girl would never forget.

As fate would have it, the very evening of the theft, the young girl's father and two of her brothers returned home to check on their family. When they learned of the assault, the three men organized neighbors, including a few local Skinners, and went after the rustlers. In short order they captured all seven of the Cowboys, including the young Englishman.

In the final years of her life, the once young girl became the family matriarch. All knew her as Grandmother Baxter Stuyvesant. She often thought of the terrible fate of the young Englishman and his six confederates. She recalled that the seven captured Englishmen were dragged to the foot of the giant oak near her home and told they would be hanged. She watched as the young Englishman broke down and asked for paper and pencil to write a final letter—to whom we'll never know. He sat forlornly under the giant oak, gathering his thoughts and writing his last words, knowing that soon he would meet his maker.

The Americans then strung up all seven Englishmen from a giant limb of the ancient oak, forever after known as Gallows Limb. For the rest of her life, Grandmother Baxter Stuyvesant told all who would listen that she never would forget the young English fellow seated beneath the tree writing what most assuredly was a despondent letter to a loved one in the last moments of his life.

After the hanging, the girl who grew to become Grandmother Baxter Stuyvesant and others in the neighborhood began seeing strange things at the giant oak, particularly during exceptionally dark nights. They saw spirits of seven ghosts hanging from the Gallows Limb. In addition to Grandmother Baxter Stuyvesant, there were plenty of old folks who admitted they had seen the same sight on many occasions.

One moonless night was different, though. As she passed the great oak, Grandmother Baxter Stuyvesant had the fright of her life. There, seated beneath its branches, was the luminous ghostly spirit of the young English fellow, writing his despondent letter again. The luminous spirit looked exactly as she remembered so many years before, writing his letter just before he was hung.

The Haunted Spy Oak along Pelham Road long since has died and disappeared. To this day, however, the spirits of seven English Cowboys wander the region, back and forth along the road, forever tied to the place where each of their lives ended. One of those spirits, however, can still be seen, flitting from tree to tree on particularly dark nights. It is the luminous spirit of a young fellow, carrying foolscap and a pencil, searching endlessly for the missing Haunted Oak beneath which he intends to write his last letter.

Read More

Evening Telegram (New York, NY). "Cut Off 'Gallows Limb' of Westchester's Noted Spy Oak—'Pop' Doty Says Grandmother Baxter Stuyvesant Predicted Loss Seventy Years Ago—Hanged 7 Englishmen from Bough for Killing Cow—Children Feared the Weather-Beaten Trunk, Which Was Said to Be Inhabited by Ghosts." September 16, 1912, p. 4, cols. 3–5.

Chapter 7

Specter of the British Spy

The mammoth Haunted Spy Oak and its Gallows Limb have been part of Pelham ghost lore for nearly 250 years. The seven Revolutionary War Cowboys whose spirits haunt the region to this day were not the only ones hanged from the Gallows Limb of the tree. Another who was hanged there during the war was a captured British spy.

Only weeks after the seven English Cowboys died hanging from Gallows Limb, soldiers of Washington's Continental Army were on patrol in the same area along Pelham Road. The patrol moved quietly and slowly through the fields adjacent to the road. The soldiers nearly had to feel their way in the inky blackness of the cloudy, moonless night. Occasionally the men stopped simply to listen for anyone traveling the roadway.

As they stood quietly in the darkness beside the road, they heard in the distance an approaching horse. Members of the patrol waited as the horse and its rider approached. As the horse neared, three members of the patrol leaped onto the roadway to block the horse and grab its reins. Others remained concealed in the shadows along the side of the road.

The rider was a tall young man who rode proudly in the saddle. Clearly startled, his face turned ashen when he realized the men who blocked his way were American "Rebels."

The young man wore a great overcoat that the Americans opened. Beneath, he wore ordinary garb and seemed to be carrying nothing of note. He protested that he was merely passing through on return to his family homestead in Mamaroneck. He explained that he had been on Throggs Neck hoping to buy livestock or chickens, though he had found none for sale.

Members of the patrol questioned the young man about his family, his homestead, and its location. The young man answered each question without hesitation and with complete confidence. As the questions slowed, the leader of the patrol stepped out of the shadows at the side of the road where he had remained concealed while listening. The leader of the patrol had lived in Mamaroneck all his life. He knew the young man was not from Mamaroneck. He declared, rather unceremoniously, that the young man had to be a British spy. He ordered the patrol to arrest him and hang him from the giant oak tree the patrol had passed earlier in the evening.

The patrol tied the young man's hands and dragged him along the roadway to the mammoth oak that stood along Pelham Road. When they arrived at the foot of the tree, they tossed a rope over Gallows Limb. Without words or ceremony, they hanged the poor soul from the massive branch of the ancient oak.

Some may wonder whether such a snap judgment and summary execution resulted in the death of an innocent man. Evidence suggests otherwise. Within days, locals near the great oak began seeing a spirit dressed in full British military garb traveling the roadway near the great oak.

The spirit struck fear in the hearts of all who saw it. The horse glowed. Its luminescent rider had an angry, vengeful countenance. The horse and its rider charged all they encountered as if to run them down. Some claimed the redcoat rider drew his saber as he charged and galloped his luminous horse right through them into the darkness beyond as a cold chill gripped them almost from within.

The specter of the British spy seems to patrol the area most frequently when the moon is full. In death, the spirit parades back and forth along Pelham Road in his redcoat uniform with a long coat and heavy cape. Indeed, according to one account,

> his spirit patrols the roadway near the scene of his ignominious death at frequent intervals, and . . . his spectral form, its haughty carriage made more impressive by its military garb of long coat and heavy cape, may be seen particularly on nights when the moon is full and unhidden.[1]

The Haunted Spy Oak is gone. Yet, the Specter of the British Spy remains. It continues its vengeful search on moonlit nights for those who murdered its corporeal form, haughty and defiant. Take care when next you travel the region on such a night so that you are not mistaken as an object of the specter's vengeance.

Read More

Cook, Henry T., and Nathan J. Kaplan. *The Borough of the Bronx 1639—1913: Its Marvelous Development and Historical Surroundings*, 130–31. New York: Published by the authors, 1913.

Chapter 8

Death March of a Vanishing Spirit

Silas was an old Pelham farmer. Ancient in every sense, he looked and felt his age. Yet, he remained remarkably quick-witted.

Silas also had pride. A son of a son of an ancient Pelham farmer, he had worked the family farm along Split Rock Road since the age of eight. When his grandfather passed, Silas squared his shoulders. When his father died, he comforted his mother and continued to work the land like his Pelham ancestors. Unlike his ancestors, though, Silas succeeded handsomely.

Silas pandered to a voracious market. Silas marketed and delivered Pelham produce to behemoth New York City, barely a dozen or so miles away.

He grew the family farming business as Gotham's population burgeoned during the mid-nineteenth century. Weekly, during the season, Silas loaded a massive wagon with the best produce he could harvest. He then hitched to his massive wagon a team of the most magnificent driving horses money could buy. Old Silas knew that good horses were important when traveling the treacherous roads of the countryside near New York City, but he also understood that friends, neighbors, and passersby would marvel at his success with such magnificent driving horses hauling a massive wagon filled with his treasure.

Silas paired his driving horses carefully. Both were exactly seventeen hands high. One was milk white with midnight black grease spots. The other was midnight black with milk white smuts. Both had flowing white manes that needed no breeze. The pair epitomized equine magnificence.

Late one autumn evening, old Silas loaded his massive wagon with another load of produce for market and climbed aboard. Though the sun had fallen below the horizon and twilight had faded into the purple heavens, a full moon rested heavily on the eastern horizon, working its way skyward. Silas hoped to make it to lower Manhattan in time for early market the next morning. He knew he could doze along the way. No one would be out during the night to admire him, his treasured harvest, and his magnificent steeds.

Soon the throbbing clip-clop of the horses combined with the gentle jostle of the wagon lulled old Silas asleep at the reins. The horses plodded along Pelham Road as they had hundreds of times. They needed no guidance from old Silas, who nodded dreamily as the team crossed Pelham Bridge.

Soon the horses neared the famed Haunted Spy Oak as they had countless times. This time, however, seemed different. As the pair plodded past the ancient tree, their nostrils flared. Oblivious, old Silas continued to doze.

One of the pair reared and cried in a whinny that startled Silas awake. Instinctively he tightened the reins as the horses lunged forward

Pelham Bridge in 1865.
From a sketch by W. J. Wilson.

Figure 8.1. Horses and wagons crossing Pelham Bridge in 1865.

in fear. Even with the full moon, he struggled to see in the darkness. As he settled his horses, his heart leapt into his throat.

A dark figure with an old rifle emerged from the growth along the roadway and stepped toward the wagon. "Highwayman!" Silas thought and reached instinctively for the revolver he kept next to him on the wagon seat. It was gone; it must have slid off the seat as he dozed.

Silas snapped the reins and attempted to flee. The horses refused. Instead, they stomped, snorted, and pawed as the deathly silent figure reached the side of the wagon. Silas looked for anything to use as a weapon but had only a whip. He grabbed and raised it.

It was then that he first looked at the figure. The whip fell from his raised hand. Even his harnessed horses turned their heads to look at the figure. There, next to the wagon, stood the dark form of an eighteenth-century British soldier with a look of desperate dread on his face. He had a long rifle with bayonet, but he did not threaten with it. He kept it shouldered smartly as though standing at attention.

Though colors were muted in the moonlight that bathed the scene, Silas could see that the figure wore a blue cocked hat with light piping. It also wore a red wool coat with dark blue facing. Visible beneath was a fitted white waistcoat. It wore slim-fitting buff breeches that ended in a buttoned cuff just below the knees with white stockings and black leather boots. Silas had learned of such things as a young schoolboy, but had never seen the uniform of a British soldier from the Revolutionary War. What he saw simply did not make sense.

Silas shouted at the man: "Be gone or stand back!"

As if he had received a command from a superior officer, the figure responded with a smart right turn, clicking his heels as he came to and facing the roadway in the direction the wagon traveled. The figure made no other sound and merely stood as if awaiting direction.

The horses seemed to settle. With wide staring eyes, Silas snapped the reins and his wagon moved forward.

So did the apparition.

As the wagon began rolling again, the soldier marched professionally and silently along the right side of the wagon with his rifle rested against his left shoulder. "Hup!" shouted Silas to the horses to speed them along. As if the figure were directed by the command, it began marching double time and kept up alongside the wagon in complete silence. Silas looked at the face of the figure. It retained a look of desperate dread, almost terror. Yet, there was a determination and steeliness in the way the figure moved.

Silas snapped his team to a full gallop. This time the horses obliged and plunged headlong down the roadway. Though, to the eye, the apparition seemed only to be marching double time, it remained immediately alongside the racing wagon as Silas bounced it at breakneck speed for hundreds of yards before finally giving up and shouting, "Whoa!" to rest his team. The figure halted abruptly as well. It executed a smart right turn, then marched off the roadway. As it stepped off the roadway, it dissolved until it had vanished completely without a sound.

Silas sat in the wagon in disbelief. He knew he had not dreamed what he had seen. Nor could he ignore his own senses. There had been no British soldiers in the region since the war ended more than seventy years before. Yet, Silas knew what he had seen. He continued to market in Manhattan where he told not a soul of his experience that night.

A week later, Silas prepared for market again. For the first time, he felt trepidation about the weekly trip. He knew again he must pass the Haunted Spy Oak in the night, this time without a full moon. He cleaned, oiled, and loaded his revolver. This time he slipped it in his belt.

As twilight disappeared, Silas began his trip down Split Rock Road to Pelham Road where his team plodded toward the oak. This time Silas did not doze. This time, Silas watched every shadow and listened for any sounds. Occasionally he fingered the butt of his revolver to make certain it remained in his belt.

As the horses neared the Haunted Spy Oak, Silas's senses heightened. He laid his right hand on the grip of his revolver. His eyes darted as he scrutinized the fields and shrubbery adjacent to the roadway. As he watched, the dark figure with its old rifle appeared from nothingness and emerged from the darkness.

This time, things were different. The horses paid the soldier no mind. Worse yet, this time the figure advanced aggressively toward the wagon with rifle raised.

Silas panicked. He fumbled for his revolver as the figure reached his wagon. Raising the pistol, he shouted, "Halt!" The figure seemed to ignore him. Silas raised his revolver and emptied it into the soldier's breast. The soldier stopped abruptly, executed a smart right turn clicking his heels, and seemed to stand at attention as Silas whipped his team to a frenzy. As the wagon raced down the roadway, the apparition marched double time next to it until the wagon passed the Haunted Spy Oak.

There, the soldier executed a smart right turn, then marched off the roadway. As it stepped off the roadway, it dissolved until it had vanished completely without a sound.

To this day, travelers in the region near Westchester Avenue and Middletown Road in The Bronx as well as Pelham Road and Pelham Bridge in Pelham Bay Park claim to see the apparition of a British soldier that marches along the roadways until it vanishes into thin air. When you next travel there, do not linger as the spirit of at least one British Revolutionary War soldier seems to be fighting the war for eternity.

Read More

Pryer, Charles. *Reminiscences of an Old Westchester Homestead*, 116–19. New York: G. P. Putnam's Sons, Knickerbocker Press, 1897.

Chapter 9

Another Vanishing Soldier

The two young girls were sisters. They lived with their parents in a home near Pelham Bridge in the town of Pelham. They looked alike, with long brown hair and rich green eyes that twinkled when they laughed.

They were good girls. They helped with the family chores. They played together. They cared for each other and for their parents. They were part of a happy Pelham family that lived in a lovely farm cottage near Eastchester Bay.

Late one autumn evening, as the sun set, their mother realized that the water pitchers in the cottage were almost empty. She asked her daughters to take the family's two wooden pails and fetch water from the farmstead's nearby well. The two girls happily picked up the buckets and skipped out the door toward the well.

Swinging their pails, the sisters held hands and picked their way along a shaded narrow path to the well. They approached the well just as the sun sank below the horizon and twilight hung over the land.

The leaves of the trees that stood around the well had not yet fallen and were splotched with color. Once the sun set, the heavy foliage made the area particularly dark. In fact, the two little girls had trouble seeing what they were doing. They had to take great care around the deep well because it was little more than a stone-lined hole in the ground marked at ground level by a simple ring of stones. In such darkness it would be easy to fall into the inky waters.

The sisters tied a small rope lying next to the ring of stones to one of the pails so they could lower it into the well and pull up a pail of sweet water. As they tied the rope, they heard an eerie sound. Both glanced up.

In the murky darkness, they saw a misty luminance. It coalesced into a small glowing puff of smoke that seemed to be floating toward them. As it neared, its brightness seemed to pulse. The girls were transfixed by what they saw. Almost involuntarily, they grasped and held each other.

As the glowing puff floated closer, it seemed to transmute from a luminous cloud to something that resembled a nebulous, indistinct figure. Though the figure was hazy in form, both girls could see what looked like a man that glided toward them without taking steps. Both blinked as if to clear their eyes just as the luminous figure resolved into a terrifying personage.

Gliding toward them, only yards away, was the luminous figure of a man dressed in military garb. The glowing figure wore a great cape like those worn by military men in the late eighteenth century. The figure remained perfectly silent. However, it seemed to consider the appearance of the young girls at the well as an unwelcome intrusion. The gliding apparition scowled as it moved ever closer to the girls.

The specter's angry scowl frightened the girls. They continued to hold each other, frozen in place, as the specter glided closer and closer while remaining deathly silent. The ghostly soldier seemed to pulse in luminosity as if seething with anger.

The girls were transfixed by the specter. As it approached, they held each other tighter. When the apparition was only a few feet away, the sisters prepared for the worst. Too horrified even to scream, the pair trembled. As the specter reached them, it vanished into thin air before their eyes. The black darkness returned. The ghostly soldier had vanished without a sound.

The two girls left the pails at the well and ran in the darkness toward their home. The faster they ran, the more terrified they became. They stumbled on the narrow path and constantly looked over their shoulders, searching for the specter and fearing it would chase them down before they could get home. The sisters burst into the house in terrified tears, hopefully safe from whatever they had seen.

What had the girls seen at the well near Pelham Bridge? Perhaps it was the specter of the British spy hanged on Gallows Limb of the Haunted Spy Oak or the spirit of the British soldier engaged in an eternal march toward death. Maybe it was one of the seven English Cowboys who were hanged from the same Gallows Limb. Perhaps it was the spirit of one of the British troops killed during the Battle of Pelham fought nearby.

A nineteenth-century Pelham author and storyteller named Charles Pryer briefly recounted the eerie incident of the vanishing soldier.[1] In telling the story, he noted that nearby stood the "Skinners' Oak"—also known as the "Spy Oak." He wrote:

> What had they seen? Was it simply some farmer's boy a little late in driving home his cows, whom their excited imagination had endowed with all these peculiar appearances? Or was it the spirit of one of the unfortunates who perished upon the oak as they always confidently asserted? I would hardly dare to venture an opinion upon such an occult subject, still we can scarcely see how any condition of the human mind short of positive lunacy, could change an innocent farm boy in his country garb, into a soldier with a military cloak. Again, were they the only ones who saw sights and heard mysterious sounds there, our conclusion might be different, but the place has always borne a bad reputation, and many others a little late in passing the old tree have experienced phenomena just as queer and weird, even down to our own time.[2]

Did the girls see the Specter of the British Spy that night? For now, all that can be said is that they saw a Vanishing Soldier spirit.

Read More

Pryer, Charles. *Reminiscences of an Old Westchester Homestead*, 104–09. New York: G. P. Putnam's Sons, Knickerbocker Press, 1897.

PART III
GHOSTLY TREASURE GUARDS

Gold! Silver! Treasure! For almost as long as youngsters have let their imaginations run wild, words such as these have prompted them to dig in their backyards in search of riches. Some parents may smile and shake their heads at the naivete of youth. Others may angrily instruct their offspring to fill their trenches. Perhaps parents who reside in Pelham, however, should let their youngsters explore, for treasure has been found throughout Pelham.

Treasures Discovered in Pelham

On one occasion, a laborer working in the cellar of Elisha Guion's home near Pelham Bridge unearthed an old iron pot filled with roughly thirty ounces of Spanish gold coins worth about $600 at the time[1] and more than $55,000 at today's gold prices. On another occasion an entire safe was discovered in a backyard in Pelham Manor. When broken open, a stunning set of sterling silver flatware beautifully chased and lined with gold lay inside.[2] A cache of valuable ancient pewter plates that predate the Revolutionary War has been unearthed in another Pelham yard.[3]

Residents Buried Treasure to Protect against the Ravages of Marauders

Such long-forgotten treasure should come as no surprise. Some of it may have been buried long ago as the Cowboys and Skinners ravaged the local population during the Revolutionary War when Pelham was part of the Neutral Ground. Indeed, it is well documented that the local population buried valuables to keep them from falling into the hands of marauding scavengers during that war.

For example, according to one account, during a service at Saint Paul's Church on the Village Green of Eastchester during the Revolutionary War—the principal church attended by Pelham residents at the time—a man burst in and warned that Skinners were coming. The congregation removed the church bell, filled it with their gold, silver, and other valuables, and buried it. The same account states that as the preacher finished his sermon that day

> scarcely had the last words died upon the lips of the speaker, when the doors of the church were violently burst open and a man, in semi-military apparel, rushed in, shouting: "Save your lives and property! The Skinners will soon be upon us!" The poor fellow was evidently much wearied from his exertions, and sank down in the nearest seat exhausted. The people gathered round him with a storm of questions: "How long before they will be here?" "Where did you see them?" etc.; but they did not waste much time in idle curiosity, and in a moment or two had decided upon a plan to save some of their effects. A few of the strongest went up into the belfry, unhung the bell, and let it down outside the church by means of the rope, then they scattered to their several houses and in an incredibly short time collected all their valuables of gold and silver and returned to the church. These articles, with all the coins in their possession, they put into the bell, and then a couple of the strongest men carried it, not without some difficulty, to a neighboring orchard, where with picks and shovels they dug a hole and buried their treasure, being careful to replace the snow on the spot, so that in the night and at a little distance, it looked as white as the rest of the ground. Scarcely had they returned to their homes before the marauders were upon them and many of the houses were searched, but as we know few things of value were found, so the desperadoes had to content themselves with taking all the horses and cattle they could get in the vicinity, and driving them to their camp.[4]

Treasures likely remain buried in the Pelham countryside. Indeed, as local residents fled the ravages of the Neutral Ground during the war that lasted nearly a decade, it is not inconceivable that some never returned or forgot, with the passage of time, precisely where they had hidden their treasures.

William Kidd

In addition to such treasures hidden during the war, other treasures that may be hidden remain in Pelham. Indeed, it is well documented that pirates roamed the region and sailed in waters off the shores of Pelham. Of course, hope springs eternal that where there once were pirates, there may be buried pirate treasure.

William Kidd (1645–May 23, 1701) was a Scottish sailor who became infamous as "Captain Kidd," a notorious pirate. Some, however, believe Kidd was a privateer and never deserved his reputation as a pirate. Kidd became infamous as a pirate due to his questioning before the English Parliament and the sensational trial that followed.

As Kidd neared the end of a lengthy career as a privateer, he made his way to the New York region. According to one account:

> Prior to returning to New York City, Kidd learned that he was a wanted pirate, and that several English men-of-war were searching for him. Realizing that *Adventure Prize* [a ship he was returning with as a captured prize] was a marked vessel, he cached it in the Caribbean Sea and continued toward New York aboard a sloop. He deposited some of his treasure on Gardiners Island, hoping to use his knowledge of its location as a bargaining tool. . . . Kidd found himself in Oyster Bay, as a way of avoiding his mutinous crew who gathered in New York. In order to avoid them, Kidd sailed 120 miles around the eastern tip of Long Island, and then doubled back 90 miles along the Sound to Oyster Bay. He felt this was a safer passage than the highly trafficked Narrows between Staten Island and Brooklyn.[5]

Oyster Bay, of course, is due east of Pelham a short distance across Long Island Sound.

Kidd's efforts were to no avail. He was arrested and imprisoned in solitary confinement in Stone Prison until authorities sent him to England for questioning by Parliament. Thereafter, he was tried in the High Court of Admiralty in London on charges of murder and piracy on the high seas. He was convicted and, on May 23, 1701, he was hanged at Execution Dock in London. During the execution, the hangman's rope broke and Kidd had to be hanged a second time. His body was gibbeted over the River Thames for three years as a warning to would-be pirates.

Nineteenth-Century Reports of Kidd's Treasure Buried on Huckleberry Island

There is no doubt that Captain Kidd sailed in Long Island Sound and the waters of New York during the late seventeenth century. Of more dubious reliability are the long-whispered rumors that Captain Kidd buried part of his storied treasure on Huckleberry Island off the shores of Pelham.

Huckleberry Island, once known as "Whortleberry Island," lies in Long Island Sound about a mile east of Davids Island. It is about ten acres in size.

As early as 1876 and 1877, newspapers across the country were reporting rumors that part of Kidd's buried treasure was hidden on Huckleberry Island in Long Island Sound.[6] Clearly, even before then the rumors had been around for years. Indeed, the *Kansas Chief* noted that the entire island had been dug up many times over the years in search of the treasure. According to the report:

> [Captain Kidd] usually provisioned his vessel in this vicinity, and many men of desperate fortunes from the neighborhood flocked to him, hoping by so doing to secure great treasures. It was reported that he had buried great treasures in the islands in the sound and the shores around, and consequently almost every part of land and island has at some time or other been dug up by infatuated treasure seekers. Every few years this mania is revived, and we hear of those that are in search of the pirate's hidden gold, but, as yet I believe none has been discovered. Huckleberry island was a favorite resort of the renowned freebooter—almost every inch of the soil of which has been turned up. Kidd's Point, on the opposite shore of

Long Island, has also received attention in this way, much time and labor having been expended there.[7]

Conclusion

As one might suspect, with reports of gold and silver treasure discovered in Pelham over the years as well as reports that Captain Kidd may have buried treasure on an island off the shores of Pelham, there are ghost stories about hidden treasure in Pelham. The two chapters of this part of *The Haunted History of Pelham, New York* relate two such tales.

Chapter 10

Ghost of Captain Kidd

Bitten long ago by the gold bug, during the 1870s a bedraggled old treasure hunter hopped from island to island off Pelham shores in search of the storied pirate's treasure of Captain Kidd. He and others of his ilk (and greed) tore up nearly every nearby island in Long Island Sound. They explored and dug up virtually every inch of a host of islands off Pelham shores, including Huckleberry Island, High Island, Rat Island, The Blauzes, Goose Island, South No Nations, East No Nations, Twin Islands, Middle Reef Island, Cuban Ledge, Big Tom, Green Flats, Hunter's Island, Davids Island, and many, many others.

One day, the bedraggled old treasure hunter was tired after another day-long search on Huckleberry Island, still called Whortleberry Island by old-timers. The sun sank. Daylight faded. But the old man refused to give up his hunt. With the fading light, he squinted as he poked among rocks and boulders on the island. His bronzed face was deeply etched with the wrinkles of a long and hard life. His tattered clothing was speckled with patches, some of which were worn through and in need of patching themselves. His unkempt gray hair waved in a light breeze as he used an old, bent shovel with a weathered and cracked handle to poke at the island rocks and boulders. Occasionally the old fellow ranted, though no one was there to hear.

Though it would be easy to dismiss such an odd codger, there was something fascinating about him. It could be seen in his eyes (had there been anyone there to stare into them). He had brilliant blue eyes that flashed brightly as they searched for gold. These were not the vacant,

Figure 10.1. Detail from 1867 map of Eastchester, Pelham, and New Rochelle showing Whortleberry Island (today's Huckleberry Island), far right.

unfocused eyes of a demented man. They were the clear eyes of a driven man burning with greed. They darted back and forth, up and down. No crevice, rock, boulder, stone, or even speck of ground escaped their searching gaze while the old man was on the prowl.

That evening, the old man's bright blue eyes locked on to an oddity among the boulders and stones of the island. Two large boulders rested against one another, but seemed odd. Though they were separate boulders, they rested together with such a perfect, matched fit that it did not seem possible that even a sheet of paper would fit between them.

The bedraggled old man tried to stick the blade of his shovel between the two stones. Only a fraction of an inch of the blade made it. The boulders seemed fitted together.

Like a predator circling its prey, the old fellow began walking around the two boulders. On the opposite side there was a cascade of large stones resting against the two boulders. It looked as though an ancient rockslide had piled the stones in that spot. Something, however, was amiss. There was nothing above the two large boulders from which such stones could have slid.

The old man had a hunch. He leaped onto the pile of stones and began tossing them aside. They were large and heavy. That made no difference. A surge of strength electrified him as he shoved, pushed, and threw aside the stones from top to bottom until . . .

Eureka! Beneath the pile of stones was a large flat stone nearly three feet square. Clearly, it covered something.

The old man scrambled to remove the heavy, flat stone. He pried at it with the blade of his shovel as the sun rested on the western horizon momentarily, before beginning to sink below. With Herculean effort, the frenzied treasure hunter pried the stone up enough to get a grip on it. He dragged it away. Beneath was a dark hole that extended downward several feet and sloped underneath the two giant boulders.

The old man had no light, no matches or candles. Sweat dribbled down his forehead and into his eyes. He licked his lips and climbed into the chilly blackness of the hole.

He could sense a fairly large open area under the two boulders above him. His bright eyes darted back and forth but could see little until, slowly, they adjusted to the darkness. Indeed, it was a race against time. While his eyes adjusted, the light outside grew dimmer and dimmer, offering little hope that the old man could explore the cave-like area.

As his eyes searched, he thought he could make out a stack of something in the darkness. He could not see what it was when he looked directly at it, but when he glanced to the side, his peripheral vision perceived something—a stack of something.

The old man stepped forward slowly, sliding his feet carefully and holding his hands before him to feel his way in the dark. He approached the stack and stumbled into it. He felt with his hands all over the stack. Old wooden crates! Heavy old wooden crates! Wet, moldy, and stinking old wooden boxes! Was this what he had sought for years? Was it Kidd's treasure?

As the old man's brain swirled, a flash of light illuminated the room. He spun around and there before him—between him and the only escape—was a large, luminous spirit. The luminescence lit the cave. The old man now could see that the area was small and was filled with a stack of wooden boxes, some of which at the base of the stack had rotted and were crushed by the weight of those above. The glint of gold and silver could be seen amid the debris of the rotted crates that had settled under the weight of the crates stacked above.

The bedraggled old man knew in an instant he had discovered Kidd's treasure. Torn between exhilaration and terror, though, his attention fixed instantly on the apparition. Though the spirit made no sound, it began to float around the old man, circling him as its prey. The spirit was dressed in seventeenth-century seaman's clothing that, like the clothing of the old man, was bedraggled and torn. The old man turned slowly with the spirit as it tried to circle him. The old man never let the spirit get behind him and never turned his back on the ghastly ghost. As the spirit circled, it soon was between the treasure and the old man. That meant the ghost no longer floated between the old man and the only exit from the tiny cave.

The old treasure hunter backed toward the exit. As he did, the ghost became agitated, then enraged. In a flash the spirit raised a ghastly luminous saber that sparkled in the dim light as though made of solid steel. The ghost darted forward and slashed at the old man with the blade.

The old man stumbled backward and fell as the saber struck a stone where he had stood. A shower of sparks burst from the blade as it struck the rock. A ringing of steel on stone echoed in his ears! Before the spirit could slash again, the old man scrambled out of the hole and ran for his life. He left his old bent shovel in the cave and never looked back as he stumbled over the rough ground in the dim twilight toward his ancient rowboat on the island's shore. He leaped into the decrepit vessel and took off for the mainland. As he looked back, he could see the luminous ghost of Captain Kidd floating above the shore of the island. The angry specter held the flashing saber over its head triumphantly. Occasionally the spirit pointed the tip of the saber directly at the old man rowing away as if to threaten him. The old man rowed for his life, never to return to the island.

Had the old man returned to the island even as soon as the following day, he would have seen that everything was exactly as it had been the day before, as though nothing had happened. The flat stone was back in place, covered with a pile of large stones at the back of the two boulders. The only thing that would have seemed out of place on the island was an old bent shovel with a weathered and cracked handle that was broken into pieces lying on the shore from which the old man had fled.

Read More

Bolton, Robert, Jr. *A History of the County of Westchester, from Its First Settlement to the Present Time*, 1: 435–36. New York: Alexander S. Gould, 1848.

Buffalo Commercial Advertiser (Buffalo, NY). Untitled. July 11, 1876, vol. 45, no. 15018, p. 1, col. 6.

Evening Telegraph (New York, NY). "Captain Kidd's Treasure Will Be Unearthed Soon by 'King of High Island'—'Jim' Murphy 'Too Busy Digging Clams,' Anyway, to Begin Search at Once—Has Known for 75 Years Where It Lies, He Says—Half Breed Indian, Whose Father Saw Pirate Horde, Pointed Out Place to Him." September 22, 1912, p. 4, cols. 6–7.

Kansas Chief (Troy, KS). "The Huguenots—The Settlement and History of New Rochelle." January 18, 1877, vol. 20, no. 31, p. 1, cols. 4–5.

New-York Tribune. "Huckleberry Powwow—Indians and Flub Dubs—Treasure of Captain Kidd Comes to Light at Last." September 19, 1904, p. 9, col. 5.

Sun (New York, NY). "Col. Kane's Coach Route—Extending a Pleasant Drive to Historical Grounds." July 6, 1876, vol. 43, no. 297, p. 1, col. 2 (discussing legend of Captain Kidd's treasure buried in Pelham).

Tennessean (Nashville, TN). "A Crusoe of the Sound—Capt. Jim Murphy the Old Inhabitant of High Island." September 27, 1909, p. 10, col. 5.

Chapter 11

Elegant Lady of the Old Stone House

Splintering wood and a massive crash startled the old woman awake in her bed on the first floor of her old stone house on that warm summer night in 1879. Groggy from sleep in the middle of the night, the Widow Mary Parrish's senses sharpened as she realized someone had smashed open the door of the home in which she lived alone.

The seventy-year-old widow was terrified. Even though twenty-eight years had passed since the tiny little settlement of Pelhamville had been founded in 1851, there had been little development in the area. Her old stone house sat forlornly on First Avenue. Her nearest neighbor lived a hundred yards away and likely was sound asleep at 1:00 in the morning. She knew her screams would not be heard by anyone who could help.

Feeling utterly alone, the widow next heard prying at her bedroom door. The door burst open and a strange man wearing a mask stood before her. According to news accounts, the bandit held up one hand in a gesture of "stop!" and whispered hoarsely, "Now, keep quiet, old lady; don't be afraid; we're not going to hurt you so long as you don't give no alarm."

The masked man stepped into the room followed by two other masked strangers. The three addressed each other as "One," "Two," and "Three" as they moved about the room emptying drawers and rifling through the wardrobe.

Finding nothing of value, the robbers commanded Mrs. Parrish to get out of bed. She did. The men used knives to rip her featherbed mattress to shreds, searching unsuccessfully for hidden treasures.

One of the men found a satchel and ripped it open with his knife. Inside was $100, which the man pocketed. The bandits then moved to the dining room where they took up the carpet, ripped drawers out of the buffet, and ransacked closets all to no avail.

One of the masked men shouted at the woman: "Where are the bonds?" Mrs. Parrish repeatedly denied having bonds or any other securities in the house. According to a news account of the robbery published a few days later, the following next occurred:

> "Have you a Bible!" they then asked her.
> "Yes," was her response.
> "Then get it," said the leader.
> The Bible was produced, and the villains administered to her in the very words of the court from an oath to the effect that, in declaring she had no convertible securities, she told the truth, the whole truth, and nothing but the truth. She could not be shaken in her denial. The robbers, evidently much disappointed, led her back to the bedroom. Here they laid her upon the bed and tied her limbs to the bedposts, just as Chastine Cox did those of Mrs. Hull [a then-recent crime that led to the death of the female victim]. They told her to beware of making any noise, and threatened to return immediately if she gave an alarm before they had been gone a sufficient time to render certain their escape.[1]

The masked men left poor Widow Parrish tied to her bed for two hours as they searched the house high and low for valuables, all to no avail. Chastened and disgusted by the lack of booty in the old stone house, the burglars left the old woman tied to her bed and fled into the night.

It may have taken Mrs. Parrish hours to escape from her bindings. For much of the remainder of that terrifying night she must have feared that she never would escape the ties and might die in her bed from lack of water and food. By the end of the night, however, she had freed herself.

During the early morning hours, local residents who knew Mrs. Parrish began receiving messages from her to come to her home. Three of them hurried to her home and discovered the woman in such a state that they questioned her sanity and even the veracity of her account. According to one news report:

Early in the morning, Mrs. George Pearson, a neighbor, received a message from Mrs. Parrish that she desired to see her. On going to her house, Mr. and Mrs. Pearson were met at the door by Mrs. Clark, wife of the postmaster of the village. They entered and found Mrs. Parrish in a most excited state. When asked how she had gotten loose from her bonds after the departure of the burglars, Mrs. Parrish said she did not know, and nothing at all could be learned from her on this point. This reply was so inconsistent with her statement that she had been tied by the burglars that it has caused a good deal of wonder among her neighbors. Many of them, however, seize the occasion to declare that they have for a long time suspected her of being unsound in mind on certain subjects, and that she has of late read and talked a great deal about the murder of Mrs. Hull. They hint, therefore, that the whole occurrence as related by her may be an illusion, the result of monomania. Not only does the circumstance of the binding remind one strongly of the Hull tragedy, but a candle, half consumed, which was found in her room and which, according to her, was used by the robbers, forms another singular coincidence. On the other hand, another burglary which took place on the same night at Pelhamville points to an organized plan of plunder on the part of a band of thieves, who were very well acquainted with the locality. An hour or so earlier than the robbery of Mrs. Parrish the Episcopal church was entered, and a large and valuable carpet was taken away. Several dogs belonging to neighbors barked warningly, but did not cause alarm.[2]

Mary Parrish was never the same after that night. The poor woman had suffered for years after losing her husband, James Parrish. Mr. Parrish bought the old stone house that still stands at 463 First Avenue in Pelham on October 15, 1855, from a man named Alexander Diack who built the home in the early 1850s. According to tradition, James Parrish had a business in which he employed a truckman named Adams. Parrish and Adams reportedly began a local express business as a sideline. The business did very, very well. When James Parrish died, his widow, Mary Parrish, grieved his death for years. Her departed husband, however, ensured that after his death Mrs. Parrish received dividend payments from the successful express business paid in gold.

News accounts published shortly after the home invasion at Mrs. Parrish's old stone house on First Avenue clearly indicate that the widow did, indeed, own securities in the firm of Adams Express. According to one account that appeared in the July 18, 1879, issue of the *Chronicle* published in Mount Vernon:

> The victim of the crime is Mrs. Mary Parrish, a widow about seventy years old, who lives entirely alone in a stone house, and is reputed to be the possessor of a considerable sum of ready money. Quite recently she had at least $600 in her purse. Whether this was still in her possession at the time of the burglary cannot be ascertained. It is known that she had a large amount of Adams Express stock.[3]

After the incident that frightened Mary Parrish so terribly on that night in 1879, she began hiding the gold she received as dividends from the express business somewhere on the property of the old stone house. From that day on, the Widow Parrish was not known to spend—only to save and to keep to herself with her doors and windows locked and, some said, barricaded. During the remainder of her life the neighborhood rarely saw the Widow Parrish. Occasionally she was seen in the windows of her home dressed elegantly in beautiful but older clothes that had grown out of style. She typically could be seen peeling back otherwise drawn curtains to peer from windows. Indeed, according to tradition, whether she was robbed or not on that fateful night, Mrs. Parrish never truly recovered her mind. She lived in constant terror that bandits would return. She hoarded her gold and hid it on the grounds of the old stone house. The old woman constantly peered from her windows searching for any threat to her gold.

Upon the death of Mary Parrish, Pelham tongues wagged. Many said that the old woman who never spent any money had accumulated more than one million dollars in gold in her later years. With gold valued at about $18.94 an ounce in those years, that would be about 52,798 ounces (nearly 3,300 pounds) of gold. Today, with gold trading at about $1,800 an ounce, Mrs. Parrish's gold would be worth more than $95 million in today's dollars.

Figure 11.1. The old stone house at 463 First Avenue, Pelham, New York. Photograph by the author taken in early 2000.

Shortly after her death, local residents were shocked to see the elegantly dressed Mary Parrish in broad daylight peering from windows of the old stone house. Residents of the home over the last 125 years repeatedly have reported that the ghost of Mrs. Parrish can be seen within the home going about the business of guarding its gold even in broad daylight.

In his seminal history of the town of Pelham published in 1946, Lockwood Barr wrote of the ghost of Mrs. Parrish:

> It is said that a million dollars in gold is hidden in the house, or buried in the gardens. Search has been made of the house, and grounds excavated, but without result. However, underneath a hearthstone in the basement kitchen, a hundred small coins of early date were found by one of the owners—but no pot of gold.

It is tradition among the old-timers that the house is haunted by the ghost of a beautiful lady who appears in broad daylight dressed in the height of fashions of the 1850s. Edward Everett Horton, of cinema fame, is a descendant of one of the Diack family, and some years ago he visited the home of his ancestors. The owner, who had seen the beautiful lady, related her story, describing in detail her costume and its color; whereupon Horton told her that the description fitted exactly a daguerreotype of one of his great-grandmothers.[4]

In addition to coins beneath a hearthstone in the basement kitchen, one owner found a silver comb and a gold ring while digging in a garden of the home.[5]

Some claim that even today the ghost of Mary Parrish may be seen peering from windows of the old stone house during the day. If you happen to pass the home, look carefully. Even if you don't see an elegantly dressed spirit peering from a window, you will see a gorgeous stone house that was among the first few built in Pelhamville in the early 1850s.

Read More

Barr, Lockwood Anderson. *A Brief, but Most Complete and True Account of the Settlement of the Ancient Town of Pelham Westchester County, State of New York Known One Time Well and Favourably as the Lordshipp and Manour of Pelham Also the Story of the Three Modern Villages Called the Pelhams* (Richmond, VA: Dietz Press, 1946), 135–36.

Bell, Blake A. "Pelham's Ghosts, Goblins and Legends." *Pelham Weekly* (Pelham, NY), October 25, 2002, p. 1, col. 1.

Chronicle (Mount Vernon, NY)."Burglaries in Pelhamville." July 18, 1879, vol. 10, no. 513, p. 2, col. 1.

Rochester Daily Union and Advertiser. "Almost Another Hull Case—Singular Circumstances of a Masked Burglary—An Old Lady Tied to Her Bed as Was Mrs. Hull—Daring Villain." July 18, 1879, vol. 54, no. 169, p. 1, col. 3. Reprinted from July 17, 1879, issue of *New York Herald.*

Valenti, Ken. "Spooky Legends Are Part of Town's History." *Journal News*, October 31, 2004, p. 4B, cols. 1–5 (Local News—South Edition, Section B).

Village of Pelham—Centennial Celebration Walking Tour 1896–1996, 19–20. Pelham, NY: Village of Pelham, 1996. Softcover.

PART IV

PHANTOM SHIPS OFF PELHAM SHORES

Though difficult to imagine, the little town of Pelham has a long maritime tradition. For many years it was principally a shipbuilding, oystering, and fishing community. Indeed, until the latter decades of the nineteenth century, the bulk of the town's population lived on City Island, then part of Pelham.

Even before the Revolutionary War, people such as Benjamin Palmer recognized that the island known today as City Island was ideally situated to attract and service vessels sailing to and from nearby New York City. Indeed, Palmer devised a grandiose plan to rename the island (then known as Minneford Island) as "City Island" and to develop it as a deep-water harbor town intended to rival, and compete with, New York City's port of New York Harbor. That plan, of course, ended ignominiously with the onset of the Revolutionary War.

Nevertheless, during the nineteenth century, City Island became an important ship repair, shipbuilding, and yachting center. Famed City Island resident George Washington Horton seems to have played an instrumental role in the birth of the ship repair and shipbuilding industry on the island.

During the mid-1850s, George Washington Horton and members of his family owned a large swath of City Island, including a tract at the foot of the eastern end of what is known today as "Pilot Street."

Horton was a maritime entrepreneur, of sorts, involved in a host of money-making ventures on the island.

In 1856, Horton or members of his family apparently sensed an entrepreneurial opportunity to repair and service the many local sloops, skiffs, ships, boats, and all manner of local vessels that frequented the island not far from the notoriously treacherous rocks of Hell Gate and the Devil's Stepping-Stones. They arranged for a New Rochelle man named Underhill, under the supervision of George Washington Horton Jr., to construct and oversee a short marine railway at the east foot of what was known then as Pilot Avenue (today's Pilot Street). Typically, at the time, a "marine railway" was a railway with a rolling cradle for hauling ships out of water onto land for work and returning them into the water when the work was complete.

The marine railway was intended to permit short-hauling, servicing, and maintenance of local watercraft and vessels from elsewhere that suffered distress locally. Underhill, however, seems to have operated this early shipyard (or simple marine railway) for only a brief time since a man named Samuel Hart soon replaced Underhill. Significantly, Samuel Hart was from Northport, Long Island, New York.

According to City Island shipyard specialist Tom Nye of UK Sailmakers LLC at 175 City Island Avenue in City Island, Bronx, New York:

> Hart at that time operated a shipyard in the Northport area and was in the middle of a lease dispute with the town of Huntington and during the long litigation found the opportunity to take over the railway at City Island. Sam Hart along with another Northport shipbuilder James Ketcham ran a small business advertising for the repairing, painting, cleaning, caulking, and building of vessels of a limited size on their railway.[1]

Thereafter, Samuel Hart (according to an account published in 1900) began to do a "large business in repairing vessels injured by striking the rocks in Hell Gate or getting ashore around Hart's Island."[2]

At about this time, or at least by 1859, David Carll and his brother, Jesse, were operating a shipyard in Northport. (According to a letter written by David Carll in 1875, he began working as a shipbuilder in 1854, although it is not yet known if he began his work at that time with his brother in Northport.) Be it sibling rivalry, business differences, or something else, in 1859 David Carll decided to leave the shipyard in Northport and explore an opportunity with two friends on City Island: Samuel Hart and Northport shipbuilder James Ketcham who were operating the marine railway and tiny shipyard at the foot of Pilot Avenue.[3]

That year, David Carll built the thirty-seven-foot sloop *Bell* for James Sackett using the Pilot Street railway on City Island. Shortly afterward, Carll bought the business and established David Carll's Shipyard.[4] David Carll remained partners with his brother, Jesse, in the Northport shipyard venture until the pair settled on a buyout of David's interest in 1865.[5]

Given City Island's strategic location, it should come as no surprise that the island was used for ship repair many years before the first marine railway was established on the island in the 1850s. Indeed, as early as 1821, a sloop from Newport, Rhode Island, was hauled out at City Island for repairs.[6] In short, Pelham's long tradition of ship repair and shipbuilding is two centuries old—at least.

Moreover, before New York City annexed City Island and Pelham Bay Park from Pelham in 1895, Pelham had a long shoreline overlooking Long Island Sound. Because the sound, during the seventeenth, eighteenth, and nineteenth centuries, was the principal shipping lane for vessels traveling up and down the northeast coast of the United States, tens of thousands of ships have passed the shores of Pelham, continuing to this day.

Given such a maritime history, it should come as no surprise that over the centuries there have been so many sightings of phantom fire ships and other phantom ships off the coast of New England and in Long Island Sound from Hell Gate to Gardiner's Island that famed American poet Henry Wadsworth Longfellow penned an important work entitled "The Phantom Ship" in 1850 that described the phenomenon elegantly. He wrote, in part:

> On she came, with a cloud of canvas,
> Right against the wind that blew.
> Until the eye could distinguish
> The faces of the crew.
> Then fell her straining topmasts,
> Hanging tangled in the shrouds,
> And her sails were loosened and lifted,
> And blown away like clouds.
> And the masts, with all their rigging,

Fell slowly, one by one,
And the hulk dilated and vanished,
As a sea-mist in the sun!
And the people who saw this marvel
Each said unto his friend,
That this was the mould of their vessel,
And thus her tragic end,
And the pastor of the village
Gave thanks to God in prayer,
That, to quiet their troubled spirits,
He had sent this Ship of Air.[7]

As one might suspect, Pelham ghost stories include a number of phantom ships that haunt the waters off Pelham shores. The three chapters included in this part tell the tales of three such phantom ships.

Chapter 12

Fiery Phantom Ship of Long Island Sound

Long, long ago when three-masted merchant sailing ships plied the waters of Long Island Sound, one such ship departed New York Harbor for Newport, Rhode Island. Ominous clouds hung over the region. The air was thick. Experienced seamen knew a storm was brewing.

The captain intended to sail his fully loaded ship into Long Island Sound despite any storm. He had sailed the sound in bad weather countless times. He viewed this time as no different. He wanted to make it to Newport on time. His ship not only carried a heavy cargo of lumber, but it also transported a few horses. One of the horses was a magnificent, high-spirited, white thoroughbred that even the crew stopped to admire as the handsome beast was loaded.

His experienced crew went about their tasks with professional precision. Soon, the captain gave the order to let go and haul. The ship maneuvered through Hell Gate and the Devil's Stepping-Stones into Long Island Sound. The winds, though, became violent. The sound grew angry. Evening faded. Darkness enveloped the ship.

Neither captain nor crew were alarmed. Instead, the captain sought a sheltered area where his ship might ride out the storm. He thought of City Island, Hart Island, and Eastchester Bay at Pelham Bridge. The captain gave the order to come about just as the lookout in the crow's nest shouted, "Ship ahoy!"

The captain and his crew turned and could see a large ship advancing on the stern of the merchant ship. Something seemed terribly odd. Despite the darkness, the ship had no navigation lanterns lit.

The captain had no stern chaser to fire a warning. His was a merchant ship. Indeed, only a few of his crew likely had any personal firearms. Now the captain became alarmed.

The large ship advanced quickly on the merchant ship and pulled alongside. "Pirates!" one of the crew members shouted. As quickly as he shouted, a shot rang out and a musket ball dropped him, dead. The captain of the merchant ship shouted, "All hands!" but was shot as well before he could complete his command.

Grappling hooks flew and in a moment the heavily armed pirate crew boarded the merchant ship. There was no fight to the death. The crew of the merchant ship were surprised and promptly overwhelmed.

As the storm intensified, some of the pirates rounded up their victims and tormented them while others rampaged throughout the merchant ship and looted all valuables they could find. Though not interested in the cargo of lumber and horses, the pirates found many valuables among the possessions of the captain and his crew as they pillaged the merchant ship.

As the storm blew, both ships rolled in the high waves. The pirates tied the merchant ship crew tightly to masts and other parts of the ship as the howling wind intensified and the storm displayed peculiarly terrific violence. Most of the pirates disembarked with their loot to their ship. A pair, however, slipped to the cargo hold of the merchant ship.

Moments later the two pirates scrambled out of the hold and leaped back aboard their ship. Within seconds, the orange flicker of flames could be seen creeping from the hold. Smoke billowed. The anguished screams of horses, sounding almost human, filled the air. The merchant ship was rolling in the heavy seas from side to side as the flames consumed the lumber and the ship.

The poor souls tied to the masts and other parts of the ship struggled frantically to free themselves to avoid the advancing conflagration, to no avail.

Had the wind not howled so loudly and the rain not pounded so heavily, those along the shores likely would have heard the piteous screams of the merchant ship crew as the flames reached them and slowly burned them to death. The screams seemed unearthly as burning debris cascaded onto the deck of the ship. Soon, the shrieks and screams gave way to nothing but the sound of the howling wind.

Since that terrible night long ago, mariners and landlubbers alike have reported that during storms on Long Island Sound of "peculiarly terrific violence" a luminous three-masted ship fully enveloped in a glowing fire may be seen plowing through the waves of the sound with a magnificent white horse stamping and pawing at the heel of the foremast of the ship and a ghostly phantom crew assembled at quarters. As the fiery ship passes, long comet-like streaks of flames and sparks stream from it and unearthly screams and shrieks can be heard, though the ghostly crew remains motionless and statue-like, assembled at quarters.

For two centuries, at least, the Fiery Phantom Ship of Long Island Sound has been seen from Block Island at the eastern end of Long Island to Hell Gate at its western end. Indeed, as early as 1843, there was a published report referencing sightings of the fiery phantom ship. That report stated:

> There are few countries where traditions and legends are handed down from generation to generation with more fidelity than in New England, more particularly along the sea-coast and the shores of the Sound. The "fire ship" is supposed even now by the old fishermen to be seen cruising occasionally in the vicinity of Block Island in the furious storms of thunder and lightning. The tradition is, that she was taken by pirates—all hands murdered, and abandoned after being set on fire by the buccaneers. Some accounts state that a large white horse which was on board, was left near the foremast to perish in the flames—and in storms of peculiarly terrific violence that she may be seen, rushing along enveloped in fire, the horse stamping and pawing at the heel of the foremast, her phantom crew assembled at quarters.[1]

Local historian Robert Bolton Jr. mentioned the account of the fiery phantom ship in his *History of Westchester County*, the first edition of which was published five years later in 1848. He noted that throughout the waters of the sound the fire ship has been seen glaring in the darkness, "her phantom crew like red hot statues, standing at their quarters, as rushing onwards, in the furious storm . . . leaving comet-like long streams of flames behind."[2]

Should you happen to be near Pelham shores during any storm of peculiarly terrific violence, look across the waters of the sound and listen. Like so many others, you may see the Fiery Phantom Ship of Long Island Sound and hear the unearthly shrieks and screams of its crew standing at quarters while the wildly terrified ghost of a magnificent white horse stamps and paws at the heel of the foremast of the great ghost ship.

Read More

Bell, Blake A. "Pelham's Ghosts, Goblins and Legends." *Pelham Weekly* (Pelham, NY). October 25, 2002, p. 1, col. 1.

Bolton, Robert, Jr. *A History of the County of Westchester from Its First Settlement to the Present Time*, 1: 434–35. New York: Alexander S. Gould, 1848.

Silliman, Augustus E. *A Gallop among American Scenery: Or, Sketches of American Scenes and Military Adventure.* New York: D. Appleton, 1843).

Valenti, Ken. "Spooky Legends Are Part of Town's History." *Journal News* (White Plains, NY). October 31, 2004, p. 4B, cols. 1–5 (Local News—South Edition, Section B).

Chapter 13

Ghostly Gunship of Long Island Sound

The manor of Pelham was desolate, almost ghostly. Warring armies were battling across the region and left little standing in their wakes. The Revolutionary War fought between American Patriots and their British oppressors had begun only a year or so before. The so-called Neutral Ground of the manor of Pelham, in those days, was nearly ground zero in the midst of the conflict.

Few souls could be seen in Pelham. Nearly all had fled or had learned to spend their days and nights in hiding to avoid the brutal sadism of the rogue Cowboys and Skinners who scoured the region looting, burning homes, and torturing residents.

Off the shores of Pelham large British naval ships prowled the waters. Occasionally American patriots known as "whaleboat men" would pilot long rowboats with small cannons among the massive naval vessels. The whaleboat men fired at the British vessels and their crews with the tiny cannons and small muskets. These whaleboat men worried the naval gunboats like pesky mosquitoes. They often were swatted away with massive cannonades and hails of musket fire from the decks of the large British ships. Occasionally, though, the pesky little mosquitoes drew blood.

On one such occasion, the winter evening was particularly dark and biting. A thick fog shrouded the waters and the mainland of the manor of Pelham. Not far from Locust Point on today's Throggs Neck, near the southern tip of City Island, a hulking British naval vessel rested silently on the black water. With no moon and soupy fog, the black night hung thickly. The fog muffled noises across the water, distorting the sounds of lapping water until the sounds became unearthly.

American Patriots on the mainland knew the hulking gunship skulked off their shores. Word of the ship and its anticipated movements had spread quickly among the Patriots even before the vessel departed New York City and made its way to the sound. Americans were hiding along the shores of Pelham and Long Island surveilling the gunship despite the thick fog. A few courageous Patriots dragged a long whaleboat fitted with a small cannon into the inky black waters off the shores of Pelham and slipped silently into the darkness in the direction of the massive gunboat.

The entire region was in the midst of the famed "wood famine" of 1777. For more than a century, settlers had leveled forests in the New York City region for farmland and chopped every tree in sight for firewood. Matters worsened as the two warring armies battled and camped throughout the region in the early months of the war. Troops fell what few trees remained.

On that dark, foggy night, the crew of the British gunship skulking off the shores of Pelham was low on wood. They needed wood for cooking and warmth. They also knew that their local garrison always needed firewood. Their captain was concerned enough to detail his men to proceed ashore to scrounge for wood despite the wood famine. Knowing wood would be hard to come by and assuming neither man nor beast would be afoot on such a black, biting, and foggy night, the captain foolishly detailed nearly all his crew ashore to scavenge.

The large group of British sailors slithered off their gunship under cover of fog and darkness and made their way by small boats to Locust Point on Throggs Neck. They muffled their oars with rags wrapped around the oarlocks and remained silent as they eased ashore.

As the British sailors left their ship thinking they were undetected, they failed to observe a group of armed Patriot whaleboat men who were skulking silently in their long boat only yards away from the British ship, hidden in the inky blackness of the foggy night. The Patriots heard their enemies depart the ship and formed their plan.

The whaleboat men waited silently in the fog and darkness until the British sailors seemed long gone. Remaining deathly silent, they maneuvered their whaleboat alongside the British vessel and scaled it, springing onto the deck with boarding axes, pistols, and muskets to the shock of the guard left aboard to protect the vessel. The surprise was so complete that not a shot was fired. The guard was quickly tied and stowed below while the Americans prepared to sail their massive prize into the night and northward to Connecticut.

Slowly the Americans got the great ship underway. They knew the waters off the manor of Pelham like the backs of their hands. They steered the Leviathan northeast and slowly made their way around City Island into the inky black night. Had any been left behind, they would have seen the dark hulk of the giant vessel slithering slowly into the fog until the black night enveloped it.

Once the ship disappeared into the foggy night, neither it nor its Patriot crew were ever seen again. Its disappearance was complete. It vanished without a trace. No word ever was heard from any of the brave whaleboat men who steered the vessel into the maw of darkness that night.

Since that night, according to veteran sailors on Long Island Sound, on dark foggy nights, a ghostly British naval vessel may be seen gliding along the water with a crew of specters dressed in eighteenth-century sailing garb staring silently with ghostly eyes from the rails of the deck. Though the ship seems luminescent, there are no lights aboard. It glides silently. Indeed, some say that as the ship passes in the fog, waves calm, the waters of the sound grow eerily quiet, and even the wind seems to pause as the ghostly Patriot sailors continue to make their silent getaway with their British prize for all eternity. As one account published in 1897 stated:

> Day after day, day after day, and still no tidings of the captured ship, until the heart was weary, and the eye was dim with watching. At last the skipper of a coaster gave the somewhat startling report: "While lying-to off New London, in a fearful gale, he saw a small war-ship approach, apparently of English build, with every stitch of canvas set, even to her royal studding-sails. She heeded neither bar, shoal, nor rock, but kept steadily on her course, until nearly abreast of him, when sail after sail and mast after mast began to vanish, until nothing but the hull of the vessel with her open ports, through which the guns were projecting, was visible. Slowly and silently the outlines of the ship became less and less clearly defined, until nothing of the majestic vessel was left. "What this vision of another world portended nobody ever knew, but even to our

own time many old salts are willing to swear that often, before the most terrific storms, when their vessels were compelled to lay-to under reefed topsails, they have distinctly seen an old-fashioned war-ship, under a cloud of canvas, approach near to them, and then gradually vanish into air. Some go so far as to say they could see the crew on her deck, and plainly recognized the knee-breeches and cocked hats of the last century. But, be this as it may, the vessel or crew, so far as I am able to learn, never reached port in this world, and was probably lost in one of the severe spring gales, so prevalent in this latitude at that season.[1]

The Ghostly Gunship of Long Island Sound still glides silently past Pelham on the Long Island Sound on dark and foggy nights. The valiant Patriots sailing the ghostly ship continue, to this day, to try to deliver their prize to its destination all in the cause of American liberty.

Read More

Gumpert, Bert. "The Bronx Bandwagon . . . Ghost Ship." *New York Post*. August 12, 1959, p. 13, col. 1.

Pryer, Charles. *Reminiscences of an Old Westchester Homestead*, 65–74. New York: G. P. Putnam's Sons, Knickerbocker Press, 1897.

Chapter 14

Ghost Ship *Palatine* and Its Mad Specter

The shrieks are undeniably horrifying. They begin in the distance, difficult to hear over the rumbling surf crashing onto the shores of Pelham and Pelham Bay Park and pounding the rocks around Shore Park in Pelham Manor. As the shrieks and screams intensify, usually there is a glow in the distance—many say a greenish glow. Those willing to remain at water's edge despite the unearthly shrieks and the terrifying, constantly growing glow typically must strain to focus into the distance until they can make out the profile of a large eighteenth-century ship sailing on Long Island Sound enveloped in flames. As the burning ship nears, the unearthly screams become louder until it is clear they are the demoniac screams of a mad woman in hellish agony.

Those who have seen the apparition report that the luminous, green, glowing ship is entirely afire, with flames even climbing the masts of the vessel. In the midst of the flames can be seen the specter of a woman screaming and writhing in agony as the fire envelopes her until the burning deck seems to collapse beneath her and she disappears into the conflagration below, screaming preternaturally as she falls, while the burning ship sails into the distance and disappears.

Those who have seen the horrifying spectacle have witnessed the Ghost Ship *Palatine* and Its Mad Specter that plies the waters of Long Island Sound. It can be seen from Hell Gate to Block Island and beyond. Indeed, mariners and coastal dwellers have seen the apparition as far north as Boston and beyond. The specter is so widely known and has been seen in our region for so many centuries that even famed American poet

John Greenleaf Whittier wrote a gripping poem entitled "The Palatine" about the terrible eighteenth-century tragedy involving the *Palatine* and its apparition that sails Long Island Sound. The poem ends as follows:

> For still, on many a moonless night,
> From Kingston Head and from Montauk light
> The spectre kindles and burns in sight.
>
> Now low and dim, now clear and higher,
> Leaps up the terrible Ghost of Fire,
> Then, slowly sinking, the flames expire.
>
> And the wise Sound skippers, though skies be fine,
> Reef their sails when they see the sign
> Of the blazing wreck of the Palatine![1]

There is a well-founded history of the actual shipwreck of the *Palatine* on Block Island at the northeast entrance to Long Island Sound that led to the terrifying apparition that has been seen—and reported—by thousands since the mid-eighteenth century. The shipwreck of the *Palatine* led to investigations and even depositions intended to get to the bottom of the matter. Nevertheless, several versions of the story since have evolved.

One of the most widely told legends of the *Palatine* involves pirate "wreckers" on the shores of Block Island. Eighteenth-century "wreckers" used "false lights" to lure ships to rocky shores where the ships wrecked and, then, were plundered.

In the mid-eighteenth century, so the story goes, the *Palatine* was carrying a shipload of Dutch immigrants from Holland to Philadelphia but was blown wildly off course by a terrible gale. As the gale intensified, the captain of the ship saw onshore lights on a small island indicating safe harbor shelter. The captain sailed toward the lights only to sail into the trap set by pirate wreckers on Block Island.

The ship was wrecked and many of the hopeful immigrants drowned. The wreckers climbed onto the wreckage and killed others as they plundered. One of the Dutch women witnessed the carnage from the hold and lost her mind from both the butchery she witnessed and the fear she would be next. She secreted herself in a wrecked niche below and listened to the screams of her fellow immigrants until, finally, all grew silent.

As the storm intensified, the wreckers looted all they could from the wounded vessel. Once their dastardly slaughter and thievery were completed, they set fire to the ship to destroy as much evidence as possible and slithered off the burning wreckage back ashore with their booty.

To the surprise of all, however, the rising torrents of tide and the massive waves raised by the gale lifted the burning wreckage from the rocks and washed it offshore, burning all the way. As the wreckers watched the sight they began to hear in the distance, quite difficult to hear over the waves crashing onto the shores, undeniably horrifying shrieks. Those shrieks and screams intensified and the glow of the burning ship shimmered on the frothing waters and lit the demonic faces of the wreckers straining to focus into the distance to watch the burning ship. As the deck burned and the flames climbed the masts of the ships, the wreckers could see a single Dutch woman standing on the burning deck screaming demoniacally, in hellish agony, as she burned with the ship. As the burning ship rolled into the distance on the massive waves, the burning deck collapsed and the mad Dutch woman disappeared into the flames below, her screams soon ending.

Any time you are near Long Island Sound during the blackness of night, pause and stare across the distant waters. Search for a greenish glow on the horizon. If you see it, watch closely. You may join the ranks of thousands of coastal dwellers and mariners on Long Island Sound who have witnessed the ghost ship *Palatine* and its mad specter.

Read More

Mancelona Herald (Mancelona, MI). "Ghosts of the Sea." December 19, 1912, vol. 34, no. 18, p. 6, cols. 1–3.

Olean Times Herald (Olean, NY). "Lights of Ghost Ship Reported Seen Again Off New England." May 5, 1951, p. 7, cols. 4–5.

Whittier, John Greenleaf. "The Palatine." In *Personal Poems—Occasional Poems: The Tent on the Beach by John Greenleaf Whittier with the Poems of Elizabeth H. Whittier and an Appendix Containing Early and Uncollected Verses*, 274–78. Boston: Houghton, Mifflin, Riverside Press, 1888.

PART V
GHOSTS OF THE MURDERED, INSANE, AND SUICIDAL

The little town of Pelham is particularly safe with little crime, most of it petty. Like any community with a history that extends hundreds of years into the past, however, the town has experienced its share of heinous crimes. Over the last three hundred years or so there have been murders,[1] robberies, and shootings by armed highway bandits on lonely Pelham country roads,[2] safes that have been dynamited,[3] and even home invasions.[4]

One of the most heinous and horrifying crimes ever committed in Pelham occurred on November 23, 1855. During foul weather the *Eudora Imogene*, a schooner laden with coal and bound east, anchored for shelter between City Island and Hart Island. Once the weather cleared, City Island residents observed a man leave the ship using one of its small skiffs and make his way toward shore. As they watched, the entire schooner capsized and sank as the man rowed away. When the City Islanders screamed for the man to return to the ship in his skiff and help the crew, he turned the skiff away as if fleeing.

Two of the islanders, one a town constable, hopped in small boats and rowed to the skiff where they found the man with an ax, butcher's knife, and the money and possessions of several people. The constable arrested the man.

After the ship was salvaged, it was determined that the man, George Wilson, was the cook on the *Eudora Imogene*. No body was found in the ship once it was raised, but bedding and a flag in the captain's quarters were soaked in blood and a small piece of a human skull was found on the ax in Wilson's possession when he was arrested. The captain of the ship, William Palmer, was missing. Nearly six months later, Captain Palmer's body washed ashore on Hunter's Island. Its skull was slashed open and its jaw was broken.

Wilson was held in the White Plains jail until he was tried and convicted of the terrible crime. He was hanged from gallows in front of the White Plains jail. Hundreds of newspapers throughout the United States reported on the gruesome murder, the subsequent trial, and the hanging.[5]

In a particularly gruesome twist, after the hanging Wilson's body was decapitated and his head was pickled in a large jar. The pickled head was displayed for nearly thirty years afterward in a tavern on City Island.[6]

Though the *Eudora Imogene* murder was particularly heinous, it is not as well known as one of the most infamous Pelham crimes: the murder of Anne Hutchinson and members of her family in August 1643.

Born in England in 1591, Anne Hutchinson traveled to Boston with her husband, their children, and some of her husband's relatives in 1634 seeking greater religious freedom. She was a strong-willed, charismatic woman with intense religious beliefs. Massachusetts religious leaders found her and her beliefs threatening.

She developed her own following. Consequently, in late 1637 clergy and local leaders accused her of religious teachings that were inconsistent with the tenets of the local church. They issued a decree of banishment from the Massachusetts Bay Colony. In early 1638, she and her family left for the colony of Rhode Island and Providence Plantations.

Longing for the widely renowned religious tolerance of the Dutch in New Netherland, in 1642 she and members of her family migrated from Rhode Island to an area known as Vreedlandt controlled by the Dutch that later became part of the manor of Pelham. On about August 20, 1643, she and members of her party met tragedy.

That year, the native Lenape population in the region rose against the Dutch of New Netherland led by Director-General Willem Kieft. After months if not years of escalating violence against local Indigenous Americans, Kieft ignored the wishes of his colonists and, without approval of his council, authorized an attack against nearby Lenape. Kieft's War, also known as the Wappinger War, followed from 1643 until 1645.

On about August 20, 1643,[7] Anne Hutchinson and her family were working about their tiny new home in the wilderness of Vreedlandt. A Lenape native arrived and feigned peaceful intentions. He used hand signals to indicate fear of the large family dogs on the grounds and prompted the settlers to tie the dogs to secure them. Once done, the Lenape signaled, and a large band of other Lenapes descended on the settlement.

The band murdered Anne Hutchinson, Francis Hutchinson, William Collins, several servants, a Hutchinson daughter (also named Anne), and the younger Hutchinson children: William, Katherine, Mary, and Zuriel. As one of the daughters tried to flee, she reportedly was captured "as she was getting over a hedge, and they drew her back again by the hair of the head to the stump of a tree, and there cut off her head with a hatchet."[8]

The murderers dragged the bodies into the house and burned all structures including those with cattle. One youngster of the family, nine-year-old Susanna Hutchinson, was away from the house picking berries and was discovered by the Lenape after the attack. The natives kidnapped the youngster and held her for several years until she was ransomed and returned to distant family members in Boston.[9]

That day, Anne Hutchinson and most of her family were massacred by Native Americans. Today Anne Hutchinson is revered as a symbol of religious freedom—a strong-willed and courageous woman who lived up to her principles.[10]

Where in the Pelham region did Anne Hutchinson and her family settle and die? There has been confusion for centuries prompted by a legend that it was near the Pelham landmark known as "Split Rock."

It is difficult to identify the origins of the myth that Anne Hutchinson and her family settled at Split Rock, a giant glacial boulder cleft in half that stands near the Hutchinson River Parkway entrance ramp to northbound I-95. The assertion was first documented in print by Robert Bolton Jr. in his seminal work entitled *A History of the County of Westchester from Its First Settlement to the Present Time* published in 1848. There he asserted:

> The residence of Anne Hutchinson appears to have been situated on Pelham neck, formerly called *Ann's hoeck*, literally, Ann's point or neck, hoeck being a Dutch name for a neck

or point, for, up to a very late period, her farm was distinguished as the *Manor of Anne hooks neck*. A small stream that separates this town from Eastchester on the west still retains her surname *Hutchinson's* river.[11]

"Pelham Neck"—referenced by Bolton as "Ann's hoeck"—is the area on the mainland near today's City Island now known as Rodman's Neck, where the New York City Police Department maintains a firing range.

Bolton, or his editor, seems to have refined the research a little by 1881 when the second edition of his posthumous two-volume history of Westchester County was published. That work asserts:

> This colony [established by Anne Hutchinson] was situated on Pelham Neck formerly called "Annie's Hoeck," and was long distinguished as the "Manor of Anne Hoock's Neck," and nearly adjoined the Dutch district of "Vredeland" or the "Land of Peace." Yet no patent or ground-brief appears on record for these lands, and why? for [sic] the simple reason that Mrs. Hutchinson was cut off before the purchase had been completed.[12]

Research must have raised some doubts in the mind of Robert Bolton Jr. or his editor over the accuracy of the tradition regarding the location of Hutchinson's home. The same text includes another reference stating: "It appears that . . . this noble, generous and tender-hearted woman settled down her little colony of sixteen persons, *either on Pelham Neck or somewhere in close vicinity thereto* . . ."[13]

If one delves into the footnotes of the 1881 edition of Bolton's work, it seems that Bolton, or his editor (C. W. Bolton), was nibbling around the edges—perhaps beginning to suspect that Anne Hutchinson's homestead stood near Pelham, but not within the boundaries of the town of Pelham at the time (which included Rodman's Neck). One footnote in the 1881 edition states:

> In the grant of the "Ten Farms" by Thomas Pell, to James Eustis and others, in 1664, there appears to be a direct allusion to the first house erected in the vicinity of Reed's mill, on the "old planting ground," viz., "at Hutchinson's; that is, where the house stood, at the meadows and uplands,

on Hutchinson's river." This was just twenty-one years after the massacre. Close by Reed's mill is a small rivulet, called "Black Dog Brook," and, sometimes, "Hutchinson's Brook." Perhaps the Black Dog had some kind of connection with the massacre of Mrs. Hutchinson in 1643. Tradition asserts, however, that Anne Hutchinson's residence was located on the property of George A. Prevost, Esq., of Pelham, near the road leading to the Neck, on the "old Indian Path." Certain it is that the ruins of an old house on the Prevost estate, near Hutchinson's river, are still to be seen, a little south-west of the "Split Rock"; also, some ancient apple trees and shrubs; while close by is a fine spring of fresh water; all of which are claimed to have been associated with the history of this remarkable woman.—[Editor.][14]

Regardless of how the story that Hutchinson lived near the Split Rock arose, by the late nineteenth and early twentieth centuries, it was firmly entrenched. Stories were told of Hutchinson's children scrambling over Split Rock as they tried to escape from Indigenous Americans. Split Rock was widely believed to be the location of Anne Hutchinson's home at the time of her death.

During the 1920s, a local historian named Otto Hufeland worked hard to locate the place of Anne Hutchinson's home. In 1929, the Westchester County Historical Society included in its annual publication an article considered to be a seminal work on the location of Anne Hutchinson's residence.[15]

The article, entitled "Anne Hutchinson's Refuge in the Wilderness—The Second Settler in Westchester County—Where She Settled in 1642 and Died in the Following Year," referenced the "tradition," stating:

> The tradition . . . placed [her home] near the Split Rock, a great cloven boulder in Pelham Park on the west side of the road running over Prospect Hill, connecting the newer Boston (Turnpike) Road with the Shore Road . . . the Hutchinson house is supposed to have been near it . . .[16]

In his chapter, Hufeland painstakingly pieced together passing references to Hutchinson, Hutchinson's house, and local landmarks contained in land grants and deeds from the seventeenth century. Historians since have agreed that his work "very definitely determined"[17] the location of the house to be near the old "Eastchester Planting Ground"—quite a distance southwest of Split Rock. Hutchinson's home was located within Eastchester—not within the boundaries of today's town of Pelham.

But the town of Eastchester was carved from Thomas Pell's original purchase that became known as the manor of Pelham. On June 24, 1664—almost ten years to the day after Pell purchased his lands from local Indigenous Americans—Thomas Pell executed a land grant to James Eustis, Philip Pinckney, and others acting as agents for the now legendary "Ten Families" from Connecticut who settled the area that later became the town of Eastchester. Significantly, as noted by Otto Hufeland, Pell's land grant states:

> Know all men, that I, Thomas Pell, have granted unto James Eustis and Philip Pinckney, for themselves and their associates to the number of ten families, to settle down at Hutchinson's, that is where the house stood, at the meadows and uplands to Hutchinson's River.[18]

And if such a reference were not sufficiently definitive, only one year later the Ten Families made even clearer that the lands sold to them by Thomas Pell from his original land purchase included the place where Anne Hutchinson's home stood. In the famous "Eastchester Covenant" prepared by the settlers in 1665, the following statement appears:

> Imprimis—that we, by the Grace of God, settle down on the tract of land lying between Hutchinson's Brook, where the house was, until it comes unto the River that cometh in at the head of the meadow.[19]

Nearly one year later, Governor Richard Nicholls issued a confirmation of a royal grant dated March 9, 1666, describing the same lands as follows:

> [land] bounded to the east and ye north east by a certain river commonly called Hutchinson's River, which runs in at ye head of ye meadow, and is ye west bounds of Mr. Pell's patent, to ye south by a certain creek, the mouth whereof openeth to ye south east, including ye meadows heretofore

called Hutchinson's Meadows and ye upland, to ye now known and common path coming up from Westchester, to take in also of ye upland between Hutchinson's and Rattlesnake Brook, from said path to ye extent of half a mile north west from ye path—moreover, I do hereby grant and confirm unto ye said patentees—That their plantation shall continue and retain ye name of Eastchester.[20]

Such descriptions help identify the location of Anne Hutchinson's tiny settlement. This is because the earliest known maps of Eastchester, on file with the Secretary of State's Office in Albany, include several of the landmarks referenced in the grant. One such map, created in 1708, is referenced as Map No. 163, p. 19 Catalogue of Maps and shows "Planting Land of East Chester" wedged between "Rattle Snake Brook" and "Hutchinsons Brook" bounded to the southeast by "Hutchinson Meados [sic]."[21]

A second map of the area created at or about the same time in 1708, once again in connection with a grant of land by Queen Anne to William Peartree and Associates, also shows "Rattle Snake Brook" and "Hutchinsons Brook." More significantly, however, it also shows a path coming up from the town of Westchester.[22]

Hufeland, in his seminal work, analyzed the location of the path and considered it in connection with more recent maps of the area, suggesting that the path evolved into Mill Lane which, in turn, was the site of a well-known structure that had been documented through photographs known as the Miller Reid's House in Eastchester. Considering all this evidence, Hufeland was able to place the location of Hutchinson's house within a very small area, although no physical evidence of the wood frame structure built in 1642 has ever been found. Hufeland concluded:

> A most diligent search has not discovered any documentary evidence that would connect the Hutchinson name with Pelham. From this summary it would seem that the tradition has no basis in any tangible evidence and that the cumulative evidence presented here would justify the statement that Mrs. Hutchinson settled on the land occupied twenty years later by the Eastchester settlers. Not only does this evidence lead to that belief, but the location at the Split Rock was so unsuitable to all the requirements of new settlers, that its

selection for this purpose by an intelligent company seems almost unbelievable.[23]

The location of the Hutchinson settlement since has been obliterated by development and construction in the area of New York City's famed Co-op City that towers above the Hutchinson River and stands near Pelham Bridge.

Though Anne Hutchinson's home never stood within the boundaries of today's town of Pelham, it stood within the boundaries of the original manor of Pelham purchased by Thomas Pell from Indigenous Americans only a few years after the murder of Anne Hutchinson. It should come as no surprise, then, that the ghost of Anne Hutchinson wanders the Pelham region. The Anne Hutchinson haunting is one of a number of Pelham ghost stories that center around disturbing events involving murder, insanity, and suicide. This part includes three such tales.

Chapter 15

Ghost of Anne Hutchinson

A brisk August breeze blew from Long Island Sound across Vreedlandt on the mainland that bright day. Salty gusts billowed the plain black cotton dress of a graceful woman who stood in the doorway of her crude log home with split cedar shingles. Though the day was warm, the woman had a shawl draped across her shoulders, her only adornment.

Anne Hutchinson and her family had built the cabin and planted their tiny settlement only months before in late 1642. Hutchinson had lived for years in Boston where she served her friends and neighbors as a midwife and herbalist. There she held weekly meetings in her home to discuss the local minister's sermons. She freely shared her interpretations of the teachings of Puritan John Cotton and gathered followers whom she taught could achieve God's grace directly through faith.

As Hutchinson's flock of followers grew, local religious figures whispered that her views were heretical and deviant. Despite intense pressure to conform, Anne Hutchinson refused. The controversy became known as the Antinomian Controversy. Local magistrates labeled Hutchinson a danger to the community. Finally, Massachusetts Bay Colony governor John Winthrop had enough and charged Anne Hutchinson with sedition and heresy.

Colony leaders tried Hutchinson in November 1637. Winthrop interrogated her, but she answered each of his questions defiantly with challenging questions of her own intended to emphasize his hypocrisies and those of the magistrates and local religious leaders. During the trial, Hutchinson claimed that the bases for her beliefs came directly from

God—an assertion Massachusetts Bay Colony Puritans deemed heresy. The trial concluded with the banishment of Anne Hutchinson from the colony.

Hutchinson was excommunicated from the church in Boston on March 22, 1638. She and her husband fled to join a colony in what is now Portsmouth, Rhode Island, where her husband died in 1642. Late that year, after continued persecution by English Puritans, Anne Hutchinson fled once again to an area in New Netherland outside of the control of English authorities. The area was known by the Dutch authorities at Fort Amsterdam as "Vreedlandt"—an area that later became part of the manor of Pelham.

Now, only months after her family's arrival in Vreedlandt, Anne stood in the doorway of her tiny home and enjoyed the wash of the breeze. She felt her plain cotton dress and white shawl billow in the wind. She smelled the tangy salt air. She heard the happy barks of her pair of large, playful dogs. She listened joyously to peals of laughter from several of her children and watched one of them, nine-year-old Susanna, skip along with a small basket as she headed into the brush to pick berries. She watched as servants, her children (including little Anne, William, Francis, Katherine, Mary, and Zuriel), and a family friend named William Collins scurried about the little home caring for animals and engaged in the business of life. As she savored the scene about her, she smiled and nodded approvingly.

Anne thought of new beginnings. In Vreedlandt she and her family were building a new life. Officials in New Netherland were far more forgiving and tolerant of diverse religious views than the English Puritans across the northeast. Life, she thought, would be good in Vreedlandt.

As Anne contemplated the future, she observed a man approaching. Dressed in skins, he was a local Native.

Anne expected to welcome the man. She had grown comfortable with Narragansett Natives during her time in Rhode Island. She stepped toward him warmly as he approached.

He seemed nervous as the two large family dogs circled him and barked. He signaled, through gestures, that he wished the dogs to be restrained. One of the Hutchinsons tied up the dogs.

As quickly as the dogs were restrained, the man fell upon the family with a knife. Other Natives sprang from the undergrowth. They first seized and killed Francis Hutchinson and William Collins, even scalping them as the settlement erupted in screams. The Natives grabbed family members and servants, murdering each in cold blood. One of Anne's daughters nearly escaped but, as she climbed over shrubbery, she was caught. The poor soul was dragged by her hair to a stump nearby where she was beheaded in a terrible act of evil.

Little Susanna was away in the underbrush picking berries when the attack began. She watched through the brush in terror as the Natives dragged her family's bodies into the tiny log home and set it on fire. Her stifled crying caught the attention of a Native who plunged into the brush and seized her. The Natives carried the poor youngster away and held her captive for years until Dutch authorities successfully ransomed her and returned her to distant family.

Given the horrific fate of those in the Hutchinson settlement on that August day in 1643, one might expect that their ghosts wander the Eastchester Bay and Pelham Bridge region once known by the Dutch as Vreedlandt. The ghost of Anne Hutchinson, however, haunts elsewhere in Pelham.

Figure 15.1. Nineteenth-century engraving of *Massacre of Anne Hutchinson* from William Cullen Bryant's *Popular History of the United States*, published in 1878.

International public relations expert Le Roi Layton Elliott and his wife once owned the famed Pelham Manor home known as "Pelhamdale," located at 45 Iden Avenue in the village of Pelham Manor. The home is on the National Register of Historic Places. One bright August day when the family owned that lovely property, their son, Bradford, arose early.

He walked to the kitchen and started the coffee pot. He turned from the kitchen toward the pantry. As he passed the door that opened to the dining room he was startled. Inside that doorway stood a woman in her fifties dressed in a plain black cotton dress that seemed from another time. She had a white shawl about her shoulders, her only adornment. For a moment, she seemed lost in thought. She smiled and nodded approvingly while seemingly staring vacantly into the distance as her dress and shawl billowed despite no breeze indoors.

Bradford Elliott looked about to determine if anyone else was present and could see the woman. When he looked back, the woman was gone. She had disappeared.

Bradford Elliott woke his parents and told them what he had seen. His father, Le Roi, smiled. He had heard the local legend that the ghost of Anne Hutchinson still wandered the region where she and her family had been murdered. He knew from his son's description of the plain black cotton dress from another time and the simple shawl the woman wore that his son had seen the ghost of Anne Hutchinson.

Read More

Texaco. Legend of Pell House. *Texaco Westchester*. April 21, 1978 (unnumbered page from an internal publication of Texaco distributed in the Texaco Westchester facility in Harrison, New York; original in collection of the Office of the Historian of the Town of Pelham).

Chapter 16

Ghost of the Murdered Traveler at Bartow-Pell Mansion

The blackhearted crime was dastardly and brutal. Worse, it was murder.

No reliable account of the murder exists. Likely a cruel and remorseless highwayman accosted a hapless colonial traveler returning from Pelham Neck toward New Rochelle along the ancient colonial road known today as Shore Road. The highwayman committed his crime near a very special giant oak.

The name of the murdered traveler is unknown. His dastardly murderer fled after fiendishly robbing and killing the poor soul beneath the spreading branches of the Pell Treaty Oak. That giant oak once stood along Shore Road on the grounds of today's Bartow-Pell Mansion Museum.

Since that black day in the mid-eighteenth century, the ghost of the murdered traveler wanders the region in the darkness. He can be seen near the place the grand oak once stood.

To this day, late in the night, those who pass Bartow-Pell frequently report a strange sight: an angry specter that seems to be searching vengefully for the murderer who sentenced it to an eternity of wandering. The ghost is dressed in rough homespun clothing with a beaten, broad-brimmed hat and a crude knapsack slung so that it rests low on his back. He wears what look like homemade, rough hide boots and walks with a long carved wooden staff that is almost as tall as he. Long, wild, and matted hair cascades from beneath his hat. He seems to scan the countryside and shakes his staff in anger as he picks his way along

Figure 16.1. Pell Treaty Oak from an article published in *Scribner's Magazine* in 1892.

the roadway and through the woods in the area. All who encounter the specter report a foreboding sense of sadness as he approaches and passes. He seems to acknowledge anyone he encounters and seems to let them pass, suspiciously, as if in begrudging recognition that they are not the focus of his vengeance.

The grounds of the Bartow-Pell Mansion Museum where the specter may be found are among the most ancient historic spots in all of the manor of Pelham. An Indigenous American village once stood near the gated driveway entrance to the grounds. Indigenous American remains and artifacts have been excavated near the water's edge on the sound side of the mansion grounds. Oyster midden left long ago by Indigenous Americans still can be seen at the water's edge near the mansion.

On the grounds of the mansion is a circular iron fence that once protected the Pell Treaty Oak that stood near the mansion. Beneath that oak, according to legend, Thomas Pell and other Englishmen met with Native Americans on June 27, 1654, to sign the deed by which Pell acquired the lands that became the manor of Pelham. In the early 1670s, Pell's nephew and principal legatee, John Pell, built a manor house not far from the Pell Treaty Oak and lived there until his death in the early years of the eighteenth century. The home is believed to have stood until it burned either during or immediately after the American Revolutionary War.

The Pell Treaty Oak once stood near today's Shore Road, which passes the Bartow-Pell Mansion. Shore Road runs along an ancient Indigenous American footpath that traversed the region parallel to, and only a few yards away from, Long Island Sound. It likewise has an ancient pedigree as a roadway. It is one of the few roads in the area that existed during colonial times. By the mid-eighteenth century, the well-traveled road had widened from a simple footpath to a comparatively busy roadway used by many as they traveled along the coastline back and forth between Pelham Neck, New Rochelle, and other settlements along Long Island Sound.

Figure 16.2. Bartow-Pell Mansion in 1917.

No record of the dastardly crime that forms the basis for the legend of the Ghost of the Murdered Traveler has been located. There are, however, countless recorded accounts of highway robbers who preyed on travelers along the lonely, unlit roadway known variously as Pelham Road, the road to New Rochelle, the Westchester Turnpike, and Shore Road. Many such accounts describe violent confrontations and brutal robberies by highwaymen who attacked local residents and others merely passing through the region even as late as the last years of the nineteenth century.

When you next find yourself on the grounds of the Bartow-Pell Mansion Museum (or driving past it on Shore Road), particularly late at night, pay close attention to the wooded areas near the roadway. Look and listen carefully. You may see the Ghost of the Murdered Traveler who wanders the region seeking vengeance against its murderer. Make certain to pass quickly, though. You would not want to be mistaken as the one for whom the ghost searches.

Read More

Sun (New York, NY). "Fire in the Pell Oak—The Historic Tree Incurs a New Peril—Once Struck by Lightning." April 9, 1906, p. 4, col. 2.

Chapter 17

Ghost of the Insane Pelham Lover

The young Pelham man was madly in love with a beautiful woman. Both lived in the tiny settlement of Bartow that once stood along Shore Road in the town of Pelham in the last half of the nineteenth century not far from today's Pelham Bit Stables (the Bronx Equestrian Center) in Pelham Bay Park. Now, appropriately, it is a ghost town.

Yes, the young man was madly, madly, madly in love. All he could ponder was his beautiful belle. He spent every waking hour thinking of her and planning his next opportunity to be with her. He spent every sleeping hour dreaming of the lovely object of his affections. It seems, however, that the object of his adoration did not share his feelings. Yes, she flirted lightheartedly with the young man, but she flirted with others in Pelham. She simply did not share the young man's insanely intense devotion.

When the beautiful Pelham belle tired of the young man's attentions, she simply ended all contact with him. The young beau was crushed. For weeks he made every attempt to recapture the flirtatious attentions of his beautiful belle. With each passing week of failure, the young man grew ever more despondent. He watched as the object of his mad love continued to flirt with others. His despondency sank into a gloomy sadness that could not be shaken.

The young man's family grew ever more concerned as he began wandering the halls of the family's dark home at night. He muttered as he shuffled up and down hallways and stairs, though the only mutterings his family could understand were his repeated mumblings of the name of his young belle.

Concerned for the young man's safety, members of the family stayed with him day and night. They sat with him as he rocked back and forth, muttering as tears streamed down his face. The weeks turned to months and it became clear that the young man's mind had departed. He had descended into madness.

Exhaustion set in. At night, the young man's family simply could not handle him. His mind may have left him, but his youth and strength had not. When his mutterings seemed to turn suicidal, the family began locking him inside the unfinished attic of their Bartow home with nothing but a mattress on the floor each night.

The walls of the attic were unfinished. Its rafters hung heavily above. At night the room was exceedingly dark since the family was unwilling to leave a burning lantern with the young man. Even worse, the home stood in an infinitely lonely and silent spot on the outskirts of the tiny Bartow settlement that consisted of only a handful of homes and commercial buildings near the old Bartow Station on the New Haven Branch Line railroad tracks. The family put a strong bolt on the outside of the door that led to the attic room to keep the young man locked inside. They also put strong iron bars across the attic window to prevent his escape. Soon, the young man had to be kept in the room around the clock rather than only at night.

Thankfully, the young madman was not violent. He was fed, clothed, and cared for, but his madness worsened.

The insane lover's mental state seemed to worsen during each thunderous storm that swept over Pelham from Long Island Sound. When torrents of rain beat upon his roof, lightning crackled above, and thunder shook the house, the young man became nearly uncontrollable. With each thunderbolt he wailed in despondency and even pounded his fists on the floor and walls of his attic cell. It was as if each thunderous blast drove him deeper into the dark depths of insanity.

During a terrible storm on All Hallows' Eve, lightning pierced the skies all over Pelham. Thunder blasted the region and shook the homes. After one nearby lightning strike that was followed instantaneously by an ear-splitting crack of thunder, the young man wailed and pounded so violently that his family feared for him. They scrambled up the stairs and unbolted the attic door hoping to do something—anything—to settle and console him.

As the door opened, the young man bolted through it and bounded down the dark stairs as his family gave chase. Down the stairs and through the house he ran. He threw open the front door and plunged into curtains of rain. As the family ran into the torrential downpour behind him, he began outdistancing them until the family could no longer see him through the rain. Only because occasional flashes of lightning illuminated the entire region were they able to follow the fleeing madman from a distance as he ran toward Long Island Sound.

The howling wind drove the rain into wet needles that felt as though they would pierce the skin. The family was not certain if all the howling they heard that night was only that of the wind as they ran after the young man.

He ran with insane purpose straight to Flat Rock. He looked directly into the howling wind and driving rain over the frenzied waters of the sound, whipped to a froth by the storm. He squinted for a moment as the needles of rain blinded him. Just as members of his family arrived at Flat Rock, the young man turned and stared at them wild-eyed, then leaped into the churning waves, drowning himself. His body never was recovered.

The insane lover's body was never seen again, but soon his spirit was. Each night, after darkness descended, the ghost of the anguished young man wandered the rooms and halls of the old house in which he had been held captive during his final months. All in Bartow soon knew that the home was haunted by the ghost of the insane lover.

Soon no one in the settlement of Bartow would go near the house. As one published account noted, "no villager can be found who will venture near the spot at night."

The family moved out of the sad house, leaving it to the spirit of the mad lover. The isolated frame structure sat forlornly on a hill at the edge of the settlement for years until a New York City charity named the Little Mothers Aid Association decided to use the home and its grounds as a summer camp for "Little Mothers." These Little Mothers were young girls whose family circumstances required them at a tender young age to serve as substitute mothers to care for even younger siblings.

Though the haunted house at Bartow sat empty throughout the fall and winter each year, it became a cheery summer camp center for happy Little Mothers from New York City during the spring and summer. Despite the happy occupants of the home, the anguished mad specter of the insane Pelham lover continued to stalk the hallways and rooms of the home after dark.

Wise camp counselors and experienced campers made certain to warn new campers of the ghost of the insane Pelham lover as each new wave of campers arrived. Each new wave of little campers who arrived, after hearing the terrible story, ventured to the top of the attic stairs, pulled back the heavy bolt on the outside of the door, and peered timidly into the dark attic room where they could see the heavy iron bars at the window of the room that once housed the captive. Of course, the little campers only ventured to the top of those stairs during bright, sunny days.

During the mid-1890s, on a cold winter day when, of course, the Little Mothers camp was not in session and the haunted house sat empty, a New York City policeman patrolling in Pelham Bay Park stopped by the house to check on it.

The first thing Officer Gilmartin noticed as he approached the house was an outside cellar door that had been broken in leaving the basement open. The officer climbed into the cellar and groped about in the semi-darkness. When he reached a rear corner of the dark room, he felt an odd, irregularly shaped bundle that "rattled as if in protest as he dragged it out into the air."

Tied up in what evidently had been a bed sheet was a human skeleton. The policeman recoiled in horror, tucked the bundle under his arm, and raced on foot to the nearby police station that once stood near the Bartow Station on the New Haven Branch Line. There officers at the station contacted the local coroner and wired a report to New York City.

Word in the little settlement spread quickly regarding the skeletal remains at the police station. Nearby residents began crowding into the tiny police station to view the skeleton. According to one account: "much alarm was felt . . . [t]hat a horrible crime had been committed." Was the skeleton that of a camper or counselor? Had the ghost of the insane Pelham lover finally turned violent in the afterlife?

Thankfully, the skeleton was not that of a little camper. Rather, it was "that of a full-grown man of large stature."

It took a reporter for the *New York Herald* to solve the gruesome mystery. According to a newspaper account, the ghost of the insane Pelham lover had not turned to murder. The reporter visited an official of the Little Mothers Aid Association, told her about the alarm in the settlement of Bartow, and inquired about the origins of the skeletal remains.

After the official finished laughing, she explained that the skeleton was a medical specimen that belonged to Dr. William Percy who had practiced for many years in New York City but since had moved his practice to Elmira, New York. According to the official, Dr. Percy became fascinated with the many accounts of the ghost of the insane Pelham lover and decided the previous summer to try to frighten the ladies who ran the Little Mothers Aid Association.

He sneaked up to the attic, known to all as the "Haunted Room," and strung up the skeleton like a marionette puppet, rigged for motion when anyone entered the room. One night he enticed the ladies who ran the camp up to the Haunted Room, expecting to frighten them. Instead, according to the *New York Herald*, "his effort failed ignominiously." The women were neither frightened nor amused by the amateurish efforts to scare them.

Dr. Percy bashfully wrapped up the skeleton and hid it in a corner of the basement so as to not frighten the little campers. He forgot, however, to remove it when he departed and, despite numerous requests from the staff that he remove it, he never did before the camp ended for the summer. Only a short time later, the Little Mothers Aid Association seemingly could take the ghost no more and moved its camp to the Hunter Mansion on nearby Hunter's Island off the shores of Pelham.

The ghost of the insane Pelham lover murdered no one of which we know (at least no one whose remains have been found). The settlement of Bartow is now simply a New York City ghost town with all structures gone except the stone remnants of the once-bustling Bartow train station. In this case, the Bartow area is a true ghost town as the Ghost of the Insane Pelham Lover who once was banished to an attic cell can still be seen during violent storms running from the area to the Long Island Sound where he howls and leaps from Flat Rock and disappears beneath the inky waters.

Read More

New York Herald. "Spoiled a Fine Ghost Story—Accounting for the Mysterious Skeleton Found in Bartow's Haunted House—It Belonged to a Physician—Neighborhood Residents Feared That It Might Be Evidence of a Dreadful Crime—Merely Part of a Joke." March 21, 1894, no. 21030, p. 13, col. 6.

Chapter 18

Suicidal Specter of Manger Circle

There once stood a magnificent elm that rose above the Manger Circle neighborhood in the village of Pelham Manor. It stood at 5 Manger Circle. An ancient elm, it towered as a solemn sentinel.

By 1953, the once-magnificent sentinel was at the end of its days, victimized by Dutch elm disease. That dastardly disease, first reported in the United States in 1928, was in the midst of its relentless and brutal spread across the nation. The disease was killing the giant elm of Manger Circle.

The owner of the property was saddened by the imminent death of the ancient tree. The dying elm cast sadness over the neighborhood. Bare, gnarled limbs hung heavily from its wrinkled, twisted, and decaying trunk.

Its owner noticed that never a day passed without at least one passing traveler stopping to stare forlornly at the stricken tree. Each time such a passerby stared, a look of sadness seemed to cast a pall across the staring face. Often it seemed as if a painful memory was welling within.

The owner knew. It was time. He had to take down the dying elm.

The heartsick owner and his son (who tells this story even today) were on hand for the gloomy event the day the ancient elm was felled. That day, the heaviest limbs of the gnarled tree hung lower, slumping like broad but defeated wooden shoulders resigned to a sorrowful fate.

As the task of taking down the giant elm began, neighbors poured into the yard. Each was alarmed. Each arrived and asked the same question: If the old elm is destroyed, what would happen to the ghost of the man who hung himself from its limbs?

Shocked by the revelation, the owner and his son listened to a despairing tale that explained the sense of sadness that pervaded the area and the constant forlorn stares of passersby. Years and years before, a sadly desperate man had chosen a heavy limb of the magnificent elm. From that he hung himself.

Neighbor after neighbor came forward to say that ever since that terrible event, on particularly gloomy nights, the ghost of the man could be seen wandering near the tree, just as gloomy and just as grief-stricken as the specter's living predecessor had been in his desperate final hours. The phantom confined its wanderings to the area around the tree, somehow still tethered to the ancient elm that was used to end the living days of the specter's predecessor.

The owner's son remembers to this day how the neighbors seemed genuinely concerned about what would happen to the forlorn ghost once the tree was removed. Yet, the owner of the property had no choice. The old tree came down.

Today the Manger Circle neighborhood is one of the loveliest places in Pelham. For those who live there and others who visit, however, care should be taken on particularly gloomy nights. Pay close attention to the darkness for it may be possible even now to see the Suicidal Specter of Manger Circle wandering the area in search of the giant elm whose gnarled limbs once hung heavily from a wrinkled and twisted trunk as it stood at 5 Manger Circle.

Read More

Bell, Blake A. "The Suicidal Specter of Manger Circle." *Historic Pelham* (blog). http://historicpelham.blogspot.com/2016/10/the-suicidal-specter-of-manger-circle.html, accessed October 29, 2019.

PART VI
WAILING GHOSTS OF PELHAM

Pelham ghosts, truth be told, are a raucous and loud lot. Be they shrieks, wails, or guttural moans, the sounds of Pelham ghosts have filled the air of our region with frightening dins for centuries.

Researchers who dismiss ghostly encounters have suggested that many such instances can be explained by spiking electromagnetic fields from nearby equipment or even infrasound, extremely low frequency sound waves that typically cannot be heard but can be sensed by some people.[1] According to one researcher:

> The most reported experience with hauntings is sound. The noises can be rapping noises coming from within walls, floors or ceilings, musical sounds, mumbled voices (singing, conversations), the sound of furniture being moved across the floor even though after checking the room in question, nothing is out of place. Sometimes a ghost will call out a name or seem to direct a question or comment to the person living in the "haunted house." Other times, no apparent heed is taken to anyone living or present in the room when the voice is heard. It is almost like the ghost is simply in another time frame and does not know that anyone else, living or dead, is in the same area. The sound of objects or glass breaking is often reported even though nothing is ever found broken or destroyed. Some large heavy objects may fall and hardly a sound is heard while quite small objects may drop and a thunderous noise is reported.[2]

Other researchers focus on why some people seem more prone than others to hear the shrieks, wails, and noises made by spirits. Indeed, a recent study released by researchers at Durham University concluded that some people are more prone to hearing "clairaudient communications" (ghostly sounds). Such people, in contrast to the general population, are more prone to a personality trait known as "absorption," a trait "linked to one's tendency to become immersed in experience or thought."[3]

Many Pelham ghost stories include spirits that make rackets to frighten witnesses. Whether it is the Moaning Ghost of Hart Island or the Shrieking Ghost of Wolfs Lane, it seems that some ghosts in Pelham simply cannot keep their spectral mouths shut.

Chapter 19

Moaning Ghost of Hart Island

Hart Island lies off the shores of Pelham. It is adjacent to City Island in Long Island Sound and, like City Island, once was part of the town of Pelham until New York City annexed both islands and the adjacent mainland in 1895.

The island is small. It is about one mile long and about a third of a mile wide, even after centuries of landfill projects designed to increase its size.

During the Civil War, Hart Island was used as a mustering-in site and a training facility for Union troops. Fifty thousand such troops passed through the island on their way to fight Confederates during the American Civil War. In addition, the Union Army operated a Confederate prisoner of war camp on Hart Island late in the war. Though the camp was open for only about four months at the end of the war, it lost seven percent of its Rebel prisoners to death due to harsh conditions, lack of shelter, and extreme overcrowding.[1]

Since 1869, Hart Island also has served as New York City's public cemetery for the burial of indigents and the dead whose bodies remain unclaimed. The remains of more than one million people are buried on the tiny island. In view of its history, it should come as no surprise that Hart Island is a focal point of the tortured spirits of many who died in horrific circumstances or who now lie there in anonymous graves, still unclaimed.

Hart Island, it seems, was haunted before it became New York City's pauper's cemetery. Indeed, Union troops stationed on the island during

Figure 19.1. View of Hart Island in 1864.

and shortly after the Civil War were frightened by the island's tortured spirits. One such instance involved the moaning ghost of Hart Island.

Shortly after the Civil War ended, Hart Island remained crowded with military men and their families, housed in a variety of buildings constructed on the island during the war. One such family was a young military couple: an officer of the Fourteenth Regiment Regular Infantry and his wife.

The young officer and his wife lived in a tiny building on the grounds of the military post. Though the couple added lovely touches to the outside and inside of their little home, it would be embellishing things to describe the home as a cottage. It was more of a repurposed military shack, a tiny frame structure with simple wood sideboards on its exterior and split wood shingles with a very small stone and mud chimney poking through the roof. Though it was an ordinary structure, the young couple were proud to make it their home and thankful for the opportunity to remain together in it while the young officer and his wife served their nation.

Then it began.

On a late September evening in 1865, the wind picked up. Waves gnawed at Hart Island's shores. An autumn tempest brewed over Long Island Sound.

The frothing waters of the sound were not all that was restless. The young officer and his wife churned restlessly in bed. The sticky air of the unusually warm night seemed oppressive despite the wind that bellowed outside their tiny home. The young officer lay awake in bed as his wife slept fitfully.

Late that night, despite the howls of the wind outside, a different sound startled the young officer. It was a gruesome noise, distinct and utterly unmistakable. It was the sound of a person struggling for breath. To a seasoned military man like the young man, the breathing sounded exactly like that of one who had been wounded through the lungs. The raspy, labored gasps sounded painful. Worse yet, the sounds were accompanied by horrid "suppressed groans."[2]

Alarmed, the young officer leaped from his bed and lit a lantern. The flickering flame lit the room. Dark shadows danced on the walls. The young man searched the tiny building for the source of the relentless,

Figure 19.2. Military housing on Hart Island in 1864.

awful noises. As he searched, the sounds seemed to drown the howls of the wind and even pulse within his head. It was a sound of death. It chilled the young man to his very soul.

The young officer searched frantically, but could find nothing. Each time he approached what he thought was the direction of the sounds, they seemed to emanate from elsewhere—sometimes, from everywhere. As he rumbled about the little home, his wife awoke and heard the gasps and groans. The sounds terrified her.

The officer's searches proved fruitless. The groans and gasps continued as he tried to soothe his frightened wife. Soon, exhaustion set in, but the couple could not sleep. Indeed, according to a later-published news account, the pair "passed the night in sleepless anxiety."

The next day, the officer and his wife wandered Hart Island and told others of their horrific, sleepless night. They described the horror of listening for hours to the suppressed groans and the raspy, labored gasps of the last hours of a dying person struggling to breathe. They begged authorities to move them anywhere else on the post—anywhere away from their little home.

An older officer of the post volunteered to switch places with the couple and stay overnight in the house. Late that night, once again, the awful sound of raspy gasps, groans, and labored breathing rattled the very foundations of the home. Try though he did, the older officer similarly could not identify the source of the horrific sounds. The officer noticed, however, that during the night he stayed in the home, the horrid gasps and groans seemed to emanate from only one side of the small building.

Neither the young couple nor the older officer would return to the haunted home of Hart Island. Finally, the quartermaster of the post, Lieutenant Dana, "determined to make a thorough investigation" of the ghostly matter. The quartermaster had troops remove the entire side of the building from which the sounds seemed to emanate the night the older officer stayed in the building. With the sideboards of the building removed, careful search revealed . . . nothing!

The quartermaster had the side of the building restored. That very same evening, the terrifying gasps and groans returned but were even "louder and more painful" than before. This time, the sounds could be heard outside the haunted home.

The haunted house of Hart Island became an object of curiosity. Indeed, the *New York Evening Express* published an entire article on the ghostly gasps and groans in its September 25, 1865, issue. That article noted: "The haunted house is an object of considerable curiosity among the officers—whose families carefully avoid it—and by the soldiers who cluster around it, anxious to learn the cause of so singular a condition of affairs."

Some tried, with straight faces, to suggest that the painful gasps and dying groans heard each night in the house were the "nocturnal serenades" of some unidentified and unseen bugs within some of the decayed timbers of the home. Those who had spent sleepless nights in the home knew better, however. The sounds were not the hum or buzz of munching bugs. They were the sounds of a person gasping and struggling for breath as though wounded in the lungs. They were the sounds of pain and suppressed groans of a dying person. Indeed, they were the very sounds that made the haunted house of Hart Island one that military families avoided dutifully from that day until the abandoned structure was demolished.

Demolition, however, did not end the gasps and groans. It only seemed to make them more anguished. Indeed, on windy nights when the waves of Long Island Sound gnaw at the shores of Hart Island, the ghastly gasps and groans of the moaning ghost of the haunted house of Hart Island still may be heard.

Read More

New York Evening Express. "Spooks on Hart Island." September 25, 1865, p. 4, col. 6.

Chapter 20

Shrieking Ghost of Wolfs Lane

Daylight died late that Monday evening in 1905. Darkness shrouded North Pelham. The desolate area between Pelham Reservoir and Wolfs Lane was bleak and lonely. Virtually none of the residences and buildings that stand in the area today had been built. The Hutchinson River Parkway did not yet exist. The area was still rural pastureland.

On clear moonless nights, the Milky Way and stars provided the only light. On cloudy moonless nights, it was nigh impossible to see a hand in front of one's face. On such a night one could stumble about in the darkness far from any residence. That particular Monday evening, after daylight died, was cloudy and moonless.

John Kenny, a Mount Vernon resident, was walking near a pumping station at the Pelham Reservoir that still stands along today's Hutchinson River Parkway. Two women were nearby.

As Kenny walked in the darkness, an ear-splitting hiss roared from the darkness. The horrific sound terrorized the poor man. His eyes desperately searched the darkness for the threat. Unsure of the direction in which to flee, he next heard a horrifying screech that echoed in the darkness and convinced him that he shortly would meet his Maker.

John Kenny fled for his life. As he ran, he looked over a shoulder in abject fear. Only then did he observe a white apparition in the form of a "human figure" chasing him. He ran even faster across the rough ground in the inky blackness.

As he ran, the apparition gained on him until it was only "five or six feet away" according to a local news report. As Kenny ran, he realized that running ahead of him were the two women who had been nearby, likewise fleeing for their lives. The white apparition chased Kenny and the two women all the way to Wolfs Lane.

When the trio reached the roadway and looked back, the apparition had vanished. The night, once again, was deathly silent.

The trio escaped with their lives to tell their stories of their near-death experiences. As always, however, cynics and disbelievers were quick to debunk the tale.

Cynics said the "apparition" was no ghost but, instead, "a white horse in pasture somewhere on Vernon Heights." No one, however, had seen such a horse and no one could say where it might be after the spooky events of that evening had ended. Nor, as one published account noted, could anyone explain how it could be that "Kenny could not tell the difference between a horse and a human figure five or six feet away."

Other skeptics advanced the theory that Kenny had heard a hiss of steam from the pumping station near Wolfs Lane, had seen the wispy steam rise from the station, and had heard the scream of a screech owl startled by the hiss of the steam. No one, however, could explain claims for weeks afterward that the ghost was "seen elsewhere in Pelham."

For several weeks afterward, Pelham residents reported hearing "a hideous and unearthly shriek" at night. "Almost daily," according to the *New York Times*, "some one [sic] came forth with a fresh story of having seen the ghost while walking through Wolf's [sic] Lane at night."[1] Intriguingly, the report noted that some Pelhamites "went so far as to give minute descriptions" of the shrieking ghost.

The shrieking ghost of Wolfs Lane became "the principal topic of conversation for several days," according to the *New York Times*, after John Kenny and the two women had fled from it late in the evening on August 14, 1905. People speculated that "in days gone by there [had] been suicides in the lane" and this may have played some role in the appearance of the ghost.

Eyewitness accounts of the shrieking ghost of Wolfs Lane soon became so numerous that townspeople organized a "posse" of men to hunt down the ghost. After midnight on August 20, 1905, the posse "hid on the property of James D. Connor and waited for the ghost to stalk forth." At 2:00 a.m., the members of the posse were startled by "a hideous and unearthly shriek." According to the *New York Times*, "At first several of the posse were frightened, but regaining their nerve decided to run down the noise."

Again came the awful sound. This time it was described as "like the laugh of a maniac."

The posse raced in the direction of the noise only to discover that the town's "ghost" was a "screech owl with a cracked voice" sitting in a tree. Given those days of less sensibility to the cruelty of such acts, the newspaper reported in a rather satisfied tone that "the posse caught the bird and wrung its neck, and now the villagers are resting easier."

Thus, cynics and skeptics finally were satisfied. John Kenny and the two women, however, knew what they had seen. It was not a horse. It was not a puff of steam. It was not a bird. Rather, they had seen and heard the Shrieking Ghost of Wolfs Lane.

Read More

Bell, Blake A. "More Ghosts and Goblins of Pelham." *Pelham Weekly* (Pelham, NY). October 13, 2006, vol. 15, no. 40, p. 10, col. 1.

Daily Argus (Mount Vernon, NY). "Steam and an Owl—Thus Is the 'Ghost' at Wolfs Lane, Pelham, Explained." August 21, 1905, p. 1, col. 3.

Daily Argus (Mount Vernon, NY). "Pelham's Ghost." August 22, 1905, p. 2, cols. 1–2.

New York Times. "Posse After a Ghost—Many Pelhamites Had Heard It and Some Said They Had Seen It." August 21, 1905, vol. 54, no. 17376, p. 7, col. 2.

PART VII
PELHAM POLTERGEISTS

Pelham poltergeists are among the most disturbing spirits of Pelham lore. The German origins of the term "poltergeist" are the words *poltern* (to rant or to crash about) and *geist* (ghost or spirit). The term, of course, describes noisy ghosts that enjoy making sounds by moving or destroying objects.

Believers claim that there are five levels of poltergeist activity:

- Level One: characterized by strange noises or smells, a feeling of being watched, and frightened pets

- Level Two: marked by increased activity over Level One with more defined noises, humanlike whispers, shrieks, moans, or giggles, cold rushes of air, and even the launch of small objects

- Level Three: characterized by moving furniture, turning appliances and equipment on or off, opening and closing doors and windows, and feelings of being touched or grabbed

- Level Four: marked by an even more violent movement of objects, sounds that seem violent or threatening, feelings of being physically attacked, and more

- Level Five: considered a "Danger Level," it reportedly can involve bites, scratches, punches, launches of knives or other items as weapons and activity that could lead to bodily harm

Thankfully, believers would say, Pelham poltergeists are comparatively gentle spirits and seem never to rise beyond Levels Two or Three. Thus, Pelham poltergeists include the Melancholy Apparition in the Old Pelham Farmhouse, who opens and slams doors and bumps in the night; the Phantom Bell Ringer of Christ Church, who rings the church bell repeatedly even when guarded and inaccessible; the Whispering Bell of Saint Paul's Church that involves an unhappy poltergeist who moans and rings the church bell on a certain grim anniversary; the Petulant Preacher Poltergeist, who seemed angry until his lost grave was found and moved; and the Poltergeist of Pelhamdale who moves furniture during the night. These stories are told in this part.

Chapter 21

Melancholy Apparition of the Old Pelham Farmhouse

The withered old man was a simple gardener. He was a happy old fellow with a creased face and features darkened by years in the sun toiling at his humble job as a caretaker for an affluent Pelham landowner. He was a simple man who had little, longed for little, and led a contented life with his wizened wife and small family.

The old gardener was particularly happy that day in March more than 175 years ago. Indeed, that very day he and his little family had moved into a small Pelham farmhouse that he rented for a song.

Though a recent snow blanketed the countryside thickly, the elderly gardener spent much of his day toiling on his employer's grounds, clearing thick snow from shrubbery, shoveling paths, and scraping snow from roofs of the home and outbuildings. He was tired at the end of that day and welcomed the roaring fire and the family that greeted him when he reached the little cottage. Though exhausted by age and work, the tired old fellow began toiling again, happily, as he and his wife ordered their few possessions and cleaned the smart little cottage near Shore Road. They were excited to spend the first day in their new home.

As the sun sank at dusk, so did the energy of the little family. Exhausted from moving, cleaning, and—in the case of the gardener—toiling at his employment, the family retired contentedly to their cozy beds as the roaring fire quieted to glowing embers and darkness crept over the cottage.

In the middle of that silent, comfortable night, the snoozing gardener jolted awake. His ancient eyes tried to focus, but the darkness was too thick. Then, he heard something again.

It was a strange noise. Perhaps a thump with a scratch. Maybe it was more of a solid bump followed by creaks that suggested someone or something walking across the floorboards of the cottage. He heard it again. Then he felt a chill, almost a chilly puff of breath.

He swung his feet to the floor and fumbled with the oil lamp to light the room. As the wick burned and flickered, a shadow caught the corner of the old man's eye. He jerked his head around but saw only shadows dancing on the walls of the cottage from the flickering light of the lamp. His wife stirred in the bed and mumbled a question, asking what was wrong. The old man told her the cottage might have mice. He said he would inspect things more carefully in the morning. He rolled down the wick of the lamp and settled beneath the warm covers of the bed where he slept soundly the rest of the night.

The following day was beautiful. The azure sky seemed nearly to sparkle. The temperature turned warmer, almost balmy. Snow melted. There was no breeze, only soul-warming sunshine. The old man left his family behind to continue their work cleaning the little cottage. He trudged up Shore Road to his employer's estate where he toiled the day away, happy to have his family, his home, and the warm sun on his back.

Late that day, when he returned home, he opened the door expecting the welcome of a roaring fire and a warmhearted family. He got neither.

His wife leaped into his arms, trembling. She assailed him with a frantic story that tumbled from her mouth. She cried that precisely at noon that day, every door in the little farmhouse suddenly was "thrown open, and fearful noises were heard to resound through all quarters of the house." Tears tumbled from the wrinkled corners of her eyes as she described the madness she had witnessed and the awful noises that had assaulted the family's ears.

The old gardener thought of the odd noises that had jolted him awake the night before but said nothing of them. Instead, he held his wife tenderly and consoled her with his touch and his strength. He dismissed the events she described as the results of a terrible, gusty "March wind" and drew his chair to the hearth where he poked embers and loaded wood to start a fire to warm the cottage before supper.

As the fire chewed at the oak and hickory in the hearth, the smoky aroma stung the old man's nostrils. He smiled and settled deeply into his chair, extending his feet toward the hearth. As he did, every door in the house popped open and slammed shut violently. The snapping doors startled him. His family ran to his side as he stood and strode to the front door of the cottage.

Thinking that a storm must be brewing, he stepped out of the door only to witness a perfectly serene evening. There was no breeze. He heard chirping songbirds and the drips of melting snow plopping into puddles on the ground. Trees and their branches were perfectly still. The clear sky was darkening to purple-black as twilight ended.

Closing the door to return to his chair at the hearth, the wrinkled old man could not forget his wife's fearful words earlier in the evening when he arrived home. At that moment, he learned the terrible source of the awful noises, slamming doors, bumps, and creaks.

The far wall of the room seemed to dissolve or open almost as if an aperture yawned forth. Something shadowy and almost misty seemed to emerge from the wall. It was a dark, vapory mass that seemed to crawl out of the wall and then take the form of a female figure, at first ill-defined but gradually assuming appropriate proportions and sharpening into view of all in the cottage. Soon, the floating figure stood out in bold relief, nearly as perfect as any living being.

Twenty years old or so, with dark hair streaming over her shoulders and fluttering as though waving and blowing in a nonexistent breeze, the apparition was that of a beautiful young woman who looked pitiable, dejected, and utterly melancholy. All eyes of the family were transfixed on the spirit's face. It looked anguished and sorrowful as if ready to cry. All pitied her.

The piteous apparition seemed to survey the old gardener for several moments, then began to glide across the room. Her billowing gown fluttered and waved like her hair as if blowing in a breeze that only she could sense. The spirit never seemed to stride. It merely floated across the entire room as the gardener and his family watched in horror.

Though the family expected the poor creature to cry out, moan, or wail at any moment, she silently floated across the room without a sound. As she reached the opposite wall, she merely passed through it as if it were not there and disappeared.

It was then that the old gardener and his wife understood why they were able to rent the little cottage for a song. All night the gardener and his family packed. The next day they "took departure," as a nineteenth-century account of the frightening events recounts. They never returned to the little cottage.

Read More

Pryer, Charles. *Reminiscences of an Old Westchester Homestead*, 6–12. New York: G. P. Putnam's Sons, Knickerbocker Press, 1897.

Chapter 22

Phantom Bell Ringer of Christ Church

The lazy, late summer evening hung thickly over the sleepy hamlet of Pelham Manor as the midnight hour approached in early September 1890. The area had not yet been incorporated as a village. The population between Shore Road and the New Haven Branch Line railroad tracks was sparse in those days. The neighborhood grew dark and desolate at night. There were a few homes near the gorgeous little stone sanctuary of Christ Church and a few more nearly a mile away around Manor Circle adjacent to the railroad tracks and the Pelham Manor Depot. Between the two clusters of homes was a dark, primeval forest known by all as the "picnic grounds."

At the stroke of midnight that lazy summer evening, a frantic, incessant clanging of a bell awakened nearby residents. The clamor of clangs echoed throughout the darkness and alarmed all who heard. All feared unknown calamity and assumed the Christ Church bell was being rung as an alarm beckoning all to action.

Residents scrambled to dress. They poured from their neat homes toward Christ Church. Some ran. Some galloped on horseback. A few hitched their horse-drawn carioles and whipped their horses to trot smartly to the scene. Then, as abruptly as the ringing had begun only minutes before, it died. An eerie silence returned, broken only by the clip-clops of trotting horses and the footfalls of residents making their way to Christ Church.

A crowd gathered outside the stone sanctuary. All were surprised that the church was dark. The church bell hung motionless and silent.

Figure 22.1. Christ Church in 1848.

The belfry was empty. No one was within the church. Every door and window remained snugly locked for the night.

Friends and neighbors milled around outside the church. A low murmur rumbled through the group. All speculated over how the church bell had been rung and by whom. All agreed the mystery could not be solved that night. Thus, everyone departed for home and the comfort of their warm feather beds.

The following night, at midnight, the Christ Church bell clanged again. Fewer gathered at the church this time. Once again, those who rushed to the scene found the church dark and unoccupied. Soon, the midnight clanging seemed almost a regular event. The bell did not ring every night, but it rang many nights.

Church vestrymen were angry and alarmed. Although all suspected a prank, there was concern over the ease with which a prankster somehow was able to enter the locked church and gain access to the rope used to ring the bell. The solution, however, seemed simple. The vestrymen had the rope removed temporarily so the bell that hung high in the little steeple of the church could not be rung. When residents learned of the measure, they seemed smugly satisfied the unknown prankster had been thwarted.

That night, at midnight, the Christ Church bell rang more clamorously than before. All who heard it were shocked. The question "Who rings the bell?" was on the lips of everyone in the hamlet.

Church officials were incensed. Next, they secured the area that provided access to the bell. Yet, with the area secure and no rope pull attached to the bell, it continued to ring at midnight.

All were perplexed. The church was locked at night. Access to the bell had been secured. Most significantly, the rope pull for the bell had been removed. Who rang the bell and how?

Church officials hatched a plan. They staked out the church to capture the prankster.

Without fail, each night that officials hid in or near the church to catch the culprit, the bell failed to ring. Virtually every night no one staked out the church, the bell clanged and clanged to the consternation of residents.

Soon residents were beside themselves. One Pelham Manor resident offered a $25 reward for the arrest of the disturber of his dreams.

Despite the reward, the poltergeist known as the "Phantom Bell Ringer of Christ Church" was never caught. Indeed, to this day as you lie awake at the stroke of midnight and hear any clock in your own home chime the hour, listen carefully. You might also hear in the distance the bell of Christ Church clanging.

Read More

Statesman (Yonkers, NY). "Who Rings the Bell?" September 19, 1890, p. 4, col. 2.

Chapter 23

Whispering Bell of Saint Paul's Church

Saint Paul's Church stands on a portion of the old Eastchester Village Green located only a few hundred yards from Pelham on lands once part of the manor of Pelham. The beautiful, ancient church is built of stone and brick and once was a principal church of Pelham residents before construction of Pelham's first church, Christ Church, in 1842.

Construction of the stone and brick Saint Paul's Church building began in 1763 as a replacement for a tiny square wooden meetinghouse used by Eastchester and Pelham residents as a church beginning about 1692. The church grounds include an ancient cemetery where an estimated nine thousand dead are buried in graves with tombstones ranging from the simple to the magnificent and dated as early as 1704. Many of those buried in the cemetery were important eighteenth- and nineteenth-century residents of Pelham.

Construction of the church proceeded slowly and halted during the Revolutionary War. During the war, the unfinished sanctuary was used at various times by British, Hessian, and American troops. Both sides used it as a hospital. A group of Hessians who died at the church are buried beneath a common marker in the church cemetery.

A highlight in the early history of the church, now listed on the National Register of Historic Places, was the presentation to the congregation in 1758 of a beautiful bronze bell by the Reverend Thomas Standard, a longtime rector of the church. The small bronze bell was cast in London at the same foundry as the famed Liberty Bell. The small bronze bell often is referenced as a "cousin of the Liberty Bell."

Figure 23.1. Saint Paul's Church, Eastchester, in 1848.

The beautiful bronze bell, a pride of the congregation for more than two centuries, first hung from the rafters of the square wooden meetinghouse. It reportedly was buried with other valuables during the Revolutionary War to hide it from marauders but later was hung in the magnificent steeple of the stone and brick church building.

The beautiful bronze bell still hangs in the magnificent steeple of the church. It is the subject of the ghostly tale of the Whispering Bell of Saint Paul's Church.

Long, long ago in the earliest years of the nineteenth century, Saint Paul's Church employed an old sexton to dig graves, fill them once occupied, and maintain the cemetery. Though such work might make some gloomy, the old sexton was a delightfully jovial and lighthearted old man. Indeed, he went about his work heartily. One account said, "He had a big heart throbbing in his bosom, a heart that did not throb for one alone, but all, and was as light and happy at the 'worst of times' as at the best."

One cold December afternoon, the old sexton was walking the grounds with a member of the congregation. The pair approached the church and started up the short cascade of steps to the stone porch of the main entrance. As the old sexton fumbled for the keys to unlock the church, an eerie moan echoed across the cemetery. The moan sounded as if someone lay among the graves groaning. Shortly, however, it seemed to float nearer and nearer and transform into something almost melodic, something like the strangely hollow chanting of a church choir. The sound rose higher and higher until it died in soft, sweet whispers as if its melody had been exhausted. Though the church was empty, the moment the eerie sound ended, the bronze bell of the church pealed *one, two, three* times.

The old sexton turned with a look on his face that shocked his companion. There was something "strange and solemn" in the expression of his face. The old sexton asked his companion, "You heard it, did you not?" His companion nodded with a rather frightened look on his face.

"'Tis the anniversary," said the old sexton. "How strange that I did not think of it before." His companion replied, asking, "The anniversary of what?"

"'Tis a long story," said the sexton, who walked his companion down the little knoll leading from the church to the old sexton's cottage where the pair greeted the sexton's wife and sat before the warm fireplace. There, the old sexton related a terrible saga.

During the Revolutionary War, this region was part of the so-called Neutral Ground between lands controlled by American troops and sympathizers to the northeast and lands controlled by British and Hessian troops and their sympathizers to the southwest. The Neutral Ground was ravaged by the "Cowboys" and "Skinners." They terrorized the local population. They tortured citizens and plundered their livestock and property throughout the war.

In the midst of a wartime service in the partially built Saint Paul's Church, a militiaman burst in and shouted a warning that Skinners were on the way. He warned the churchgoers, "Save your lives and property!"

Members of the congregation scrambled to action. They pulled down the prized bronze bell of the church and filled it with their valuables. Some scurried home to gather additional valuables and returned to add them to the cache. The congregants then hoisted the heavy load and carried it to a nearby orchard where they buried the treasure near a large apple tree.

Among those who helped bury the bell and its contents was a pair of strapping young brothers known as the Wilson brothers. Henry and Harry Wilson were poor handymen who performed odd jobs about the neighborhood. Both were knaves. A propensity toward drink, however, made Henry much worse than his younger brother Harry.

Henry had a wife named Mary and a three- or four-year-old daughter. The younger brother, Harry, was engaged to be married to a young woman who also lived in the village of Eastchester.

Henry Wilson was an alcoholic known for binges that turned him into a raving madman and caused his wife, Mary, all manner of suffering. Henry's younger brother, Harry, never drank. Indeed, even he was troubled by his brother's binges and told him so frequently. This caused great friction between the two and drove Henry to a dark, evil hatred for his younger brother. Indeed, during his drunken rages Henry Wilson often threatened that if his younger brother ever crossed him "it should cost him his life."

Henry and Harry Wilson scrambled with their neighbors that December afternoon to haul the bronze bell filled with treasures to the nearby orchard where the group buried it three feet deep and about two feet from the trunk of an old apple tree. Once buried, the group spent time covering their tracks, then scurried to their homes to await the onslaught of the terrible Skinners.

For days, as he drank himself into another stupor, Henry could think of little but the church bell and the treasures it held. He thought of leather coin purses filled with coins. He thought of gold and silver, candlesticks, silver combs, brushes, and mirrors, and more. His black heart grew darker until he resolved to steal away to the orchard at midnight the following day, plunder the treasures, and flee.

At midnight the following evening, Henry Wilson stumbled to the orchard with a rusty shovel by the dim light of an old lantern. He made a beeline for the old apple tree and began his dastardly work. In short order, he dragged the bell and its contents from the hole and sifted some of the treasures through his hands. As he watched the treasures cascade to the ground, he noticed in the distance a dim light bobbing toward him.

Wilson glanced about frantically. There was no time to rebury the bell and its contents. There was no place to hide evidence of his dastardly deed. All he could do was extinguish his lantern and slip behind the apple tree as the bobbing light approached.

As Wilson watched, a dark figure with a lantern skulked toward the apple tree. Wilson wondered if his lamplight had been seen. He wondered if another had hatched the same terrible plan to plunder the treasure he coveted. As he watched from behind the tree, the figure circled the hole and held the lantern near the ground to inspect the scattered treasures and the bell that had been dragged from its hole. As the figure stooped to pick up a coin purse, Wilson sprang from behind the tree.

Wilson leaped onto the back of the dark figure and wrestled it to the ground. The two grasped and wrestled furiously as the oil lantern crashed to the ground and burst into flames. As the small fire raged, the flames illuminated the pair as they grappled and fought fiendishly. Wilson finally gained the advantage. He rolled and pinned the figure on its back. As the flames roared higher Wilson stared into the wild eyes of his foe.

"Harry!" screamed Henry Wilson as he pinned his younger brother to the ground. "You!" screamed Harry Wilson, who could smell the stench of whiskey on his older brother's breath.

Henry Wilson struggled to clinch his younger brother by the throat and growled, "Your time has come." As poor Harry struggled, Henry Wilson tightened his clinch and choked the younger man's life out of his thrashing body.

The following morning, villagers stumbled upon the scene. The body of Harry Wilson lay next to the bronze church bell. Treasures remained strewn about the hole. Only a single bag of gold coins was missing, as though the murderer had fled precipitously. Villagers collected everything and distributed all to its owners. They carried the heavy bronze bell back to Saint Paul's Church and rehung it.

Other villagers carried the body of the younger Wilson brother to the cemetery of Saint Paul's Church where the jovial old sexton shook his head sadly and began to dig another grave. No one said a word to the sexton. Yet the Sexton knew blackhearted Henry Wilson must have followed through on his many threats and finally murdered his younger brother.

As the afternoon waned, the sexton finished his work and filled the grave. He strolled to the church and, with dirty fingers, fumbled with the keys to lock the main entrance. He shook his head sadly, again, and left for the warm hearth of his nearby home.

With the sexton's departure, the dark church and its deserted grounds seemed forlorn as the twilight faded. Though not a living soul was present, an eerie moan echoed across the cemetery. The moan sounded as if someone lay among the graves groaning. Shortly, however, it seemed to float nearer and nearer and transform to something almost melodic, something like a strangely hollow chanting of a church choir. The sound rose higher and higher until it died in soft, sweet whispers as if its melody had been exhausted. Though the church was empty, the moment the eerie sound ended, the bronze bell of the church pealed *one, two, three* times—just as it has every year since on the anniversary of the terrible murder of Harry Wilson by his brother, Henry, who was never seen again.

Read More

Holden's Magazine. "The Whispering Bell; A Legend of Westchester." April 1848, pp. 219–23.

Chapter 24

Petulant Preacher Poltergeist

No one could believe their eyes. The jovial old sexton of Saint Paul's Church had been working hard with two members of the congregation to scrub down the high pews of the ancient sanctuary of the church as the sun waned. As it became too dark to continue their spring cleaning that evening, they filed down the main aisle of the sanctuary to leave via the main door of the church. A glimmer of light, however, stopped all three.

The old sexton rubbed his tired eyes in the dark, yet still he could not believe what he saw. He glanced at each of his two compatriots and saw the looks on their faces. He knew then that they also could not believe what they saw. There, floating along the aisles of the sanctuary was a lit candle. It floated for what seemed like minutes, almost as if some unseen hand holding the candle belonged to a spirit inspecting the work the three men had just performed.

As suddenly as the candle appeared, it snuffed out. Darkness reigned inside the church. The sexton was the first to speak. He blurted, almost involuntarily, "The Reverend!"

The three men almost tumbled out the main door of the church and down the front steps to the Village Green outside. They were animated but not fearful. One asked the sexton: "So you saw it too?"

"Yes," came the reply.

"You said something to it. The Reverend? Is that what you said?"

The sexton averted his eyes for a moment before replying quietly, "Yes, Reverend Standard."

The other two men froze for a moment. They had heard the stories for years. Congregants whispered that the church was haunted by Reverend Thomas Standard.

Reverend Standard, the sexton explained, was one of the most important figures in the early years of Saint Paul's Church. He was the second Church of England Rector of the church. He followed Reverend John Bartow, who served from 1702 to 1725. Though Reverend Standard had a stormy tenure, he served in the role from 1727 until his death in 1760. In 1758 he purchased from a London foundry and donated to the church the bronze bell that still hangs in the church belfry.

When Reverend Standard first arrived in Saint Paul's parish in 1725, he learned that most congregants were committed Puritans who did not follow various tenets of the Anglican faith. His relentless, confrontational efforts to impose Anglican tenets on the congregation led to nearly a full revolt by his flock. After the threatened revolt, he seemed a changed man who grew less rigid and better able to accept his community's worship practices. Though the Saint Paul's Church community refused to embrace the Church of England, Reverend Standard nudged his parish toward its eventual conversion to the Anglican / Episcopal Church. In his last years he was plagued with health problems, but his flock grew to respect him, if not love him.

The old sexton grew somber as he continued his story.

When poor Reverend Standard died in 1760, the grand brick and stone church had not yet been built. Instead, the first church building built about 1692 still stood nearby—a tiny square wood meetinghouse. Reverend Standard's congregants showed great respect by burying him and his wife beneath that church building.

Shortly after the burial, the parish intensified its efforts to replace the tiny meetinghouse with a grand stone and brick church building. Construction began in 1763 but the community was small. Money was tight. Construction was very slow and the new church building remained unfinished when the American Revolution began.

As the Revolution progressed, the unfinished church building was used at various times by both sides as a hospital. Over time, the original, small meetinghouse church building was entirely destroyed, dismantled by troops for firewood. The coffins and remains of poor Reverend Standard and his wife thereafter lay in unmarked graves for decades.

Time passed. Memories faded. The congregation completed construction of the grand new church. Afterward, even older members of

Figure 24.1. The grand stone and brick Saint Paul's Church building completed shortly after the Revolutionary War from an engraving published in 1895.

the congregation could not remember exactly where Reverend Standard and his wife lay in their unmarked graves. That is when it all started.

In the night, Eastchester villagers saw lit candles floating inside the church. Occasionally it sounded as though the beautiful old pulpit was being pounded by angry hands although no one was present. In windstorms, cries and moans rose within the church above the howling winds. Reverend Standard, it seems, had become an unsatisfied and unhappy spirit.

Tongues wagged in the tiny village of Eastchester about the ghost of Reverend Standard. Church elders agonized over what to do. All seemed to agree that something had to be done. To make matters worse, as emotions intensified, so did the activities of the late Reverend Standard.

Finally, the congregation settled on a plan. In 1818, nearly sixty years after the reverend's death, the coffins containing the remains of Standard and his wife were located, exhumed, and reburied in a place of honor beneath the east wing of the grand Saint Paul's Church.

Yet, the hauntings continued.

Lit candles floated in the sanctuary at night. Pulpit pounding continued and echoed throughout the church due to the massive pulpit sounding board. Moans and groans filled the air on windy nights.

For decades longer the congregation and local villagers endured the angry escapades of Reverend Standard's spirit. It was not until 1875 when the church renovated and added a memorial tablet dedicated to Reverend Standard that the hauntings seemed to subside.

Yet, occasionally even today, on stormy nights floating lights may be seen through the windows of Saint Paul's Church as moans, groans, and pulpit pounding echo angrily within the sanctuary. Some might wonder. Might a larger, more prominent memorial tablet help?

Read More

Osborn, David. "Thomas Standard: The Minister Buried Beneath St. Paul's Church." Saint Paul's Church National Historic Site website. December 2009, https://www.nps.gov/sapa/learn/historyculture/upload/Thomas%20Standard_rev.pdf, accessed January 15, 2021.

Valenti, Ken. "Spooky Legends Are Part of Town's History." *Journal News* (White Plains, NY). October 31, 2004, p. 4B, cols. 1–5 (Local News—South Edition, Section B).

Chapter 25

Poltergeist of Pelhamdale

There is a lovely historic home located at 45 Iden Avenue in the village of Pelham Manor. It is known as "Pelhamdale." Portions of the home including the rear basement with entrance and massive fireplace predate the Revolutionary War. The home once was owned by American Patriot David Jones Pell. The structure is listed on the National Register of Historic Places.

The home, known also as the Old Pell Place and the Old Pell Home, is located today on a triangular tract bounded by Carol Place, Iden Avenue, and the Hutchinson River Parkway. The plot on which the home sits was part of a large eighteenth- and nineteenth-century farm that was bounded by today's Colonial Avenue (the Old Boston Post Road), the lane that became known as Wolfs Lane, today's Boston Post Road, and the Hutchinson River.

Colonel Philip Pell III (1753–1811) owned an adjacent farm, the farmhouse of which once stood at the intersection of today's Cliff and Colonial Avenues in the village of Pelham. Col. Pell was a son of Philip Pell II who, in turn, was son of Philip Pell, who was a son of Thomas Pell (so-called Third Lord of the manor of Pelham). The original farm cottage that forms a portion of today's "Pelhamdale" at 45 Iden Avenue was built by Philip Pell II around 1750–1760.

Philip Pell II was the father of Colonel Philip Pell III (often referenced, oddly, as Philip Pell Jr.) and David Jones Pell. Both sons were American Patriots. After the death of the elder Pell, his son David Jones Pell became owner of Pelhamdale. David Jones Pell's brother, Philip Pell

III, built his adjacent farm and farmhouse. That farm included the land on which today's Pelham Memorial High School stands. A memorial marker and date stone of the home built by Colonel Philip Pell III stand next to the front entrance of the high school.

After the death of David Jones Pell in 1823, Pell's widow sold the farm to James Hay, who owned it until his death in the 1850s. Hay extensively expanded and renovated the home, giving it an appearance similar to the home's appearance today. During a renovation of the home, James Hay embedded in its north wall a large block of sandstone on which is carved in relief the Hay family coat of arms.

As one might expect, with a portion of the home now more than 270 years old, there has been a long succession of owners and tenants who have lived there. Also, as one might expect, the home is associated with a number of entertaining and important Pelham ghost stories. One of several such stories associated with the home is that of the poltergeist of Pelhamdale.

Mrs. Garnett Mabel Winslow was visiting Pelhamdale, the stunning home of her daughter and son-in-law, Mr. and Mrs. Le Roi Layton Elliott, many years ago. After a pleasant Friday evening with the family, Mrs. Winslow retired to an upstairs guest bedroom where she slept soundly in the supremely appointed bed.

In the wee hours of Saturday morning, long before sunrise, Mrs. Winslow was startled awake by the screech of furniture being dragged on a floor. Once she cleared the fog of sleep from her mind, she heard, quite distinctly, the banging of chairs and, again, the dragging of furniture in a third-floor studio above her bedroom.

Mrs. Winslow loved her daughter and her son-in-law, but it was a little annoying so early on a Saturday morning that they had chosen to rearrange furniture in the room above her as she slept. To make matters worse, the sounds suggested that furniture was being dragged from one side of the room to another and then back repeatedly!

As the banging and scraping grew almost frantic, Mrs. Winslow realized that she was wide awake and unlikely to slip back into sleep. She lay in bed awake as the bumps and scrapes continued until dawn crept into her room. At that moment, the noise from the studio above ended abruptly. Mrs. Winslow got up, dressed, and wandered downstairs for coffee and to visit with her daughter and son-in-law.

When she made it downstairs, not a soul was present. Pelhamdale was quiet. Neither her daughter nor son-in-law was downstairs. Thinking it odd that they would work so hard in the third-floor studio overnight then return to bed, Mrs. Winslow shrugged, made the coffee herself, and waited for the pair to come downstairs.

Soon Le Roi Elliott and his wife wandered downstairs. Still sleepy, they were surprised to find Mrs. Winslow and a half-finished pot of coffee in the kitchen. The trio sat to enjoy the morning when Mrs. Winslow remarked that the work in the studio in the wee hours of the morning must have been exhausting since it sounded as though her daughter and son-in-law had been rearranging furniture for much of the night.

Mr. and Mrs. Elliott stared at her in disbelief, then glanced at each other. "Mom," Mrs. Elliott said, "we just got up. There was no one in the studio last night."

Mrs. Winslow felt a chill run up her spine. She knew better. Someone had, in fact, been in the studio last night. That someone, it turned out, was the poltergeist of Pelhamdale.

Read More

Texaco. Legend of Pell House. *Texaco Westchester*. April 21, 1978 (unnumbered page from an internal publication of Texaco distributed in the Texaco Westchester facility in Harrison, NY; original in collection of the Office of the Historian of the Town of Pelham).

PART VIII

Haunted Houses and Ghosts of Pelham Mansions

Pelham, among the oldest settlements in the New York City region, long has had a tradition as a place of grand homes and a country retreat for New York society. This, of course, is combined with a written history that extends to the early years of the seventeenth century and a prehistoric record that extends thousands of years before that. As a study of Pelham architecture published in 1975 stated:

> Sheltered among the quiet tree lined streets of Pelham today are many buildings which mark its historic development. As one of the oldest towns in Westchester, the architectural features that have evolved during its growth from orchards, farms and timberland captivate the imagination.[1]

Long before Pelham became a lovely suburb of New York City, many wealthy New Yorkers built grand homes in the region. By the 1890s when New York City annexed from Pelham the lands that we know today as Pelham Bay Park, there were nearly fifty homes on the annexed lands, many of which were grand mansions such as the Bartow-Pell Mansion, John Hunter's mansion on Hunter Island, the James D. Fish mansion on the Twin Islands, Hawkswood (the Marshall Mansion) on Pelham Neck, and many more. Moreover, even within today's town of Pelham, grand mansions once stood throughout the town, including Pelhamdale, the

Bolton Priory, the Martin J. Condon mansion, the Black Family mansion on Pelhamdale Avenue, and many more as well.

Such mansions and homes have many stories to tell, including ghost stories. The five chapters included in this part tell the tales of haunted homes and mansions of Pelham.

Chapter 26

Ghost of the Haunted Hardenbrook House

Marvin R. Clark of New York City was a dyed-in-the-wool skeptic. He did not believe in superstitions. He did not believe in ghosts, goblins, ghouls, or spirits. Indeed, he devoted much of his life to proving that such things are poppycock.

As if to prove himself, Clark was the thirteenth member of the original thirteen members of the famous Thirteen Club of New York City. The club existed in the nineteenth century to flout such poppycock, nay, to disprove it all. Its members met in Room 13 of the Knickerbocker Cottage on Sixth Avenue and 28th Street in Manhattan at 8:13 p.m. each Friday the 13th. Club members broke mirrors, opened umbrellas inside, passed beneath ladders, kept black cats, and forbade the tossing of salt over the shoulder. The club even placed advertisements in the *New York Herald* offering a reward to anyone who could identify a truly haunted house in New York City in which members of the club might dine. They never found one.

Yet, there Clark stood in the garden of a Pelham home at midnight on a cool September evening in 1886 staring into the derisive countenance of a Pelham ghost that seemed to beckon him forward. Frozen in place in abject terror, Clark could only listen in horror as a housekeeper standing behind him let loose a blood-curdling scream.

The story of Clark's amazing ghostly encounter that night on Shore Road in Pelham later warranted nearly half a page of newspaper coverage in the *World* of New York City.[1] Indeed, the article included two images reflecting events of that night, one of which may be the only known image of a Pelham ghost based on an eyewitness account.

The tale of that night of terror is one of the most fascinating Pelham ghost stories. Here is the saga of the ghost of the haunted Hardenbrook house on Shore Road.

On a moonless, breezeless, and cool night in September 1886, Thirteener Marvin R. Clark visited his friend, John A. Hardenbrook, at the Hardenbrook home on Shore Road. Hardenbrook's beautiful cottage was on the Long Island Sound side of the road. The cottage sat on a slope that led to the water. The entry and parlor of the home was at road level in the front of the home. The rear of the cottage was a story lower than the parlor level.

The lower level of the home included a cozy dining room that also served as a comfortable sitting room for after-dinner drinks and smoking. Adjacent to that cozy room was a kitchen. Both the dining room and the kitchen looked out over Long Island Sound. Between the cottage and the sound was a small garden planted with all the vegetables a cook might need, including corn, cabbage, carrots, radishes, lettuce, pumpkins, and much more. Hardenbrook lived in the cottage with his housekeeper, Mrs. Gordon. Mrs. Gordon was a little gray-haired lady with a boundless sense of humor. She was surprisingly active and kindhearted. She adored John Hardenbrook and worked hard at her job to keep the cottage and to cook and clean.

Like Marvin Clark, John Hardenbrook was a journalist. He was a bright, intellectual fellow who had been nicknamed "Doctor" by his journalist peers. That September he invited Marvin Clark to stay with him at his cottage for several days to get away from the hustle and bustle of New York City.

Every evening during Clark's visit, Mrs. Gordon prepared a sumptuous meal for Hardenbrook and his guest. At the conclusion of every meal, after Mrs. Gordon had cleared the table, and cleaned and put away the dishes, the three would sit in the cozy dining room to sip beer while the men smoked their pipes and swapped stories.

Doc Hardenbrook knew his friend was a member of the Thirteen Club. Hardenbrook, like his friend, was a jaded journalist and a skeptic who harbored no superstitions and likewise did not believe in ghosts, ghouls, goblins, or spirits.

On a particularly black night, the threesome enjoyed after-dinner aperitifs and swapped stories in the brightly lit cottage. The kerosene lanterns were unshaded. Their tall wicks burned intensely, casting brilliant light throughout the room and out of the windows of the cottage into the inky night.

Figure 26.1. Newspaper depiction of Mrs. Gordon, Marvin R. Clark, and John A. Hardenbrook as they swapped ghost stories on the fateful night.

As the clock crawled to midnight, Doc Hardenbrook and Mrs. Gordon prepared to retire for the evening. As they busied themselves, Marvin Clark leaned back in his chair to read a little of the *Book of Martyrs* by John Foxe.

Clark became thoroughly engrossed in his book. A deathlike stillness pervaded the cottage broken only by the sound of Doc Hardenbrook and Mrs. Gordon opening the door from the kitchen to the garden to step outside to count chickens and check on the old sow in a nearby pen. Not a breeze stirred.

Remaining absorbed in his book, Clark soon heard a gasp and glanced toward the door. He saw Hardenbrook holding the door slightly ajar as Mrs. Gordon stretched to watch over his shoulder through the crack of the open door. Both had ghastly, horrific looks on their ashen faces with wild-eyed stares directed at something immediately outside.

Paralyzed with fear, Mrs. Gordon whispered hoarsely, "It's a real, live ghost." She urged Doc Hardenbrook, "Lock the doors!"

"Nonsense!" replied Hardenbrook. Yet, Hardenbrook never averted his gaze. He remained wild-eyed, with his stare transfixed on something just beyond the door.

Marvin Clark could see that Mrs. Gordon was shaking with fright. She said with alarm, "See, Doctor, it is moving this way! Oh, what will become of us all! I say, Doctor, don't stay there! I cannot bear to look at it! Come in and shut the door!"

Ever the skeptic, Clark smiled. He assumed the pair was playing a prank precisely because he was a dedicated skeptic and also a member of the Thirteen Club. He remained seated until . . .

Mrs. Gordon let out a horrified shriek and turned toward Marvin Clark with a "ghastly white face." Clark later wrote that the scream "almost curdled the blood in my veins." He realized that whatever the pair saw outside the door had truly terrified them. He stood and "crept cautiously" toward the door. Doctor Hardenbrook was holding tightly to the edge of the slightly ajar door. His knuckles were white and bloodless from gripping the door so fearfully. The housekeeper continued to peek over his shoulder timidly through the crack of the door at something in the garden.

As Clark approached the door, he realized that the pair were quaking with terror. He then understood that it was no prank. The pair could see something, as he later wrote, "a long way out of the ordinary, nay, beyond the extraordinary."

When Clark reached the door, Doc Hardenbrook whispered, "Look there!" and made barely enough room for Clark to step around him just onto the doorstep to look. What Clark saw sent shivers down his spine. He later described his feelings at that moment:

> I gasped when my eyes fell upon the object which had riveted their attention for so long a time while I had sat in the dining-room, under the impression that they were trying to play a joke upon me and frighten a Thirteener. The smile that was upon my face faded away instantly, and was superseded by a look of real alarm. . . . I was suffused with an indescribable fear which was the very extreme of terror. . . . It is the feeling of despair, which surrounds one like a cloud, with the knowledge of a quickly impending and unavoidable doom, and yet more than this. It is the knowledge that this is something supernatural not of the earth, but intangible, and

therefore irresistible. It is the overpowering sensation that the bravest of the brave must go down before it as helplessly as the most cowardly of all cowards. It is the realization that strong and weak alike must succumb to its ghostly influence, as to the avalanche, . . . the hurricane, the mountain torrent and the tidal wave, against which human power of resistance is as a straw.

Outside in the garden Clark saw a luminous, shimmering shape floating above the ground. He later described it as an "awful shape, as plainly defined as ever was mortal man, all gleaming with white, its form perfect and outlined in silvery waves of light, standing out clear and distinct against the ebony darkness of the night for a background." According to Clark, the luminous shape plainly was that of a man from head to foot. Though there was no breeze and not a leaf stirred, Clark later maintained that from neck to floating feet, a shimmery robe-like light seemed to undulate as if it were blowing in a soft breeze that

THE DOCTOR SEIZED ME BY THE ARM.

Figure 26.2. One of the only known depictions of a Pelham ghost taken from eyewitness accounts.

could not be felt in the black night. As Clark described it, it seemed to undulate with "graceful oscillations." In addition, the creature's arms rose and fell with a peculiar motion as if to beckon Clark to approach if he dared. Clark shivered involuntarily as he looked at the face of the creature. As he later wrote, its face was "smiling upon me derisively, as if to say, tauntingly, that I dared not" approach. Even Clark realized that to doubt what he saw before him was to doubt not only the evidence of his own senses but also that of his two friends who likewise stood mute and paralyzed beside him.

Clark later wrote: "I am not exaggerating—not one hair's breadth. There was the image, just as I have described it, and its long, white robe, almost reaching the ground where it stood, softly moving to and fro, while the arms waved and the ghastly head nodded and bowed at me solemnly." Yet, with "more than human effort," Clark took a step forward.

The terrible spirit neither advanced, nor retreated. Clark advanced another step. The shimmering ghost stood its ground, shimmering and undulating in the still night. Clark could stand it no longer. He rushed forward to touch and grab the awful creature.

Mrs. Gordon uttered a soul-piercing scream that rang out shrill and clear in the still darkness. Doc Hardenbrook sprang forward and attempted to grab Marvin Clark by the arm to stop him. Clark grasped at the creature's outstretched arms. He felt utterly nothing. It was as if the apparition was made of light—no substance; no mass; no heft; only shimmering, dancing light.

Marvin Clark was a dedicated skeptic and a loyal Thirteener. Ever afterward he never accepted what he saw that night in the Hardenbrook house on Shore Road in Bartow-on-the-Sound. Indeed, for years he maintained that he and his two companions had seen nothing but dancing light from an unshaded kerosene lantern shining through a cottage window and playing through waving stalks of corn in the garden. He claimed that when he later examined the rows of corn outside the cottage window there were two odd stalks that "stood out distinctly from the others" and were peculiarly shaped just right to filter the light so as to cast an image of "the tall figure of a man" into the night. He claimed that "our fevered imaginations pictured the rest."

Of course, loyal Thirteener Marvin Clark could never explain how the corn stalks swayed to play in the light on a windless night. He could not explain how the apparition was that of a luminous man with its "form so perfect" (as he admitted). Nor could he explain what the lantern light had projected onto to create so perfect an image of a floating man. Perhaps most significantly, he never tried to explain the look of derision on the apparition's face as it beckoned him to approach.

Though Clark's explanation of what he had witnessed that night seemed to satisfy smug members of the Thirteen Club, Clark's explanations and rationalizations fell on the deaf ears of at least two people: Doc John Hardenbrook and his housekeeper, Mrs. Gordon. Those two never stepped into the garden of the Hardenbrook house in the dead of night again. Both knew what they had seen that awful evening: the ghost of the haunted Hardenbrook house on Shore Road.

Read More

World (New York, NY). "All Sure They Saw a Ghost." October 8, 1893, vol. 34, no. 11737, p. 19, cols. 1–3.

Chapter 27

Spirits of Bartow-Pell Mansion

Though a New York City showplace, the imposing Greek Revival mansion on Shore Road known as the Bartow-Pell Mansion almost blends into the inky blackness of each night. During winter months, the gnarled hulks of leafless trees seem to grab at the mansion and even lean with the wind as if attempting to pluck all who come within reach from the very ground beneath their feet.

The mansion and its carriage house stand isolated and distant from any other structure within the darkness of Pelham Bay Park. At night, the shrieks of owls echo throughout the region. Occasionally, the bawling howls of mangy coyotes chill the heart.

Today the mansion serves as the Bartow-Pell Mansion Museum. The mansion, its carriage house, and grounds have quite a history. The estate once was part of the manor of Pelham and, later, the town of Pelham before the area was annexed by New York City in 1895. Scholars believe that John Pell, a nephew and the principal legatee of manor of Pelham founder, Thomas Pell, built a home near today's mansion in the early 1670s. Four generations of Pell family members resided in the home until, according to a variety of sources, it was destroyed at about the time of the American Revolution when Pelham stood in the midst of the so-called Neutral Ground between the warring armies.

The property passed from the Pells to Herman and Hannah Leroy in 1813. Robert Bartow, a New York City merchant, bought the property in 1836. Shortly afterward, he built the Greek Revival mansion of native stone and moved with his family into the home by 1842. The

Figure 27.1. Bartow-Pell Mansion in Pelham Bay Park. Photograph by the author taken March 22, 2003.

Bartow family remained in the home for more than four decades. They attempted to develop an area around the nearby City Island Station on the New Haven Branch Line into a settlement that came to be known as Bartow and "Bartow-on-the-Sound." (The railroad station likewise came to be known as "Bartow Station.")

In 1888, while assembling parcels to create today's Pelham Bay Park, New York City acquired the Bartow estate. (It likewise acquired the lands that formed the tiny little settlement of Bartow nearby.) For nearly the next three decades, mansions in the region acquired by the City of New York—including the Bartow mansion—languished scandalously. They were subject to vandalism, squatters, and municipal corruption involving "rentals" of some of the structures to well-placed city employees for virtually nothing.

In 1914, the International Garden Club was formed "to promote horticultural knowledge and to save the Bartow-Pell Mansion." The organization raised funds and restored the mansion. Today, the mansion and grounds, including the Bartow carriage house built in the 1840s, are owned by the City of New York, overseen by the New York City Department of Parks and Recreation, and operated by the Bartow-Pell Conservancy. The Mansion Museum is a member of the Historic House Trust and is listed on the National Register of Historic Places.

The grounds on which the mansion stands have a recorded history of nearly 350 years. The mansion is more than 175 years old. Of course, it should come as no surprise that such an ancient location with such a grand old structure as the mansion is replete with ghosts in addition to the Ghost of the Murdered Traveler at Bartow-Pell Mansion (see chapter 16). Indeed, as the following suggests, the Bartow-Pell Mansion and its grounds are among Pelham's most haunted spots.

Whose Spirit Sits on the Lannuier Bed?

One of the most magnificent items in the collections of the Bartow-Pell Mansion Museum is the magnificent mahogany French bedstead crafted in New York between about 1812 and 1819 by French émigré furniture craftsman Charles-Honoré Lannuier (b. 1779; d. 1819). Lannuier and his contemporary, Duncan Phyfe, were the leading New York furniture makers of their day. Their work was considered by affluent Americans at the time to represent the pinnacle of sophistication and the height of American cabinetry and furniture craft.

Bartow-Pell's Lannuier Bed includes a rare original crown encircled with classical faces of gilded brass that surround a gilded brass lion's head in the center of the front of the crown. From the crown hang opulent bed curtains. Bartow-Pell's former historian, education director, and curator, Margaret Highland, has written of the bed, in part, as follows:

> [The bed] features a superb and rare original crown encircled by classical faces made of gilded brass with a lion's head in the center. Massive vert antique lion's paw feet, gilded acanthus leaves, and columns terminating in gilded foliate scrolls provide additional classical ornamentation typical of Lannuier's oeuvre from the period beginning in 1812 until his death in 1819. The bed is made of fine figured mahogany veneer with secondary woods of mahogany, yellow poplar, and white pine. Casters allowed it to be moved easily for changing the bed

linens or for cleaning. Although tradition dates the bedstead to around . . . 1810, Lannuier scholar Peter Kenny assigns a date range of 1812–19. This is partly because of the bed's stylistic characteristics, which place it in Lannuier's mature antique style, with its rich classical ornamentation and appearance of monumentality. In addition, the Bartow-Pell bedstead bears the bilingual engraved label that Lannuier used during this period. The label features a cheval glass with the eagle from the great seal of the United States in the pediment. Patriotic symbols were especially popular around the time of the War of 1812.[1]

The Lannuier Bed, it seems, is haunted. For years those who work in, and visit, the Bartow-Pell Mansion Museum repeatedly have observed that after no one has been in the room for a time, an indentation forms on the bed as though someone is seated there. The area is roped off from the public. The indentation often appears overnight when no one is present. Bartow-Pell staff and docents repeatedly smooth the indentation, only to have it recur.

Nonbelievers claim that the down settles within the feather mattress, creating the indentations. Believers, however, know that the bed is haunted. Some have watched as the indentation appears in the form of a backside. Moreover, a few years ago Bartow-Pell arranged for Dan Sturges of Sturges Paranormal (a prominent paranormal investigation agency) to investigate paranormal activity at the mansion. Sturges and his colleagues typically use equipment including environmental gauges and audio recorders to identify and assess paranormal activity, particularly in historic homes. While in the bedroom, Sturges directly confronted the spirit, asking it to identify itself. According to Margaret Highland, he "picked up a voice that sounded like 'Nathan Walker.' We don't know who he was, but we do have a piece of [nineteenth-century] embroidery made by an Abigail Walker."[2]

Does the Ghost of George Bartow Haunt His Bed Chamber?

George Lorillard Bartow (b. 1828; d. 1875) was the eldest son of Robert Bartow and Maria Lorillard Bartow, who were married in 1827. George lived a life of leisure and never married. Not only was he the only son of the family who did not graduate from Columbia College (of today's Columbia University), but he also is believed to have devoted much of his time to horse racing as an avid fan.

George Bartow lived in Bartow-Pell Mansion most of his life, even as an adult. He died at the age of forty-seven in St. Augustine, Florida, and is buried in the cemetery of St. Peter's Episcopal Church at Westchester Square in today's borough of The Bronx.

The reasons that George Bartow never married have not been known—until now, perhaps.

Recently when a group of paranormal investigators, including Dan Sturges, visited Bartow-Pell, they spent a great deal of time in the bed chamber of George Bartow. One of the psychics working with the group was able to contact George Bartow's spirit and learned that, in life, he had experienced a grave "disappointment in love" and that he once had a fiancée who broke off their engagement. More significantly, the group also carried recording equipment while in the bed chamber. Later, upon review of the recording, it was determined that equipment picked up a voice of forgiveness—likely that of George—admitting "it wasn't the girl's fault."

The Child Ghost of the Third Floor

Perhaps the most perplexing apparition that routinely appears in the mansion is that of a lonely child. The apparition always appears on the third floor of the mansion and has been seen repeatedly for years. Though the child whose ghost wanders the third floor has yet to be identified, the most disconcerting aspect of the sightings is the fact that unconnected sightings over many years by people with no connections always result in descriptions of the child ghost that are shockingly similar.

The Haunted Attic

As if all this were not enough, the attic of the Bartow-Pell Mansion is said to be haunted as well. Numerous people have heard footsteps walking above in the attic when the attic was known to be empty. Indeed, the sound of such steps moving back and forth across the dark attic above has been particularly unsettling for those who work in the facility at night.

The Long-Skirted Apparition of the Mansion

One of the mansion's tour guides has seen a figure in a long skirt disappearing quickly. Was it the ghost of Maria Lorillard Bartow slipping away quietly? Could it have been the spirit of Clarina Bartow, one of the Bartows' girls, slipping back to her bed chamber after trying on one of the period dresses that the museum periodically puts on display—often in Clarina's bed chamber? Was it the apparition of one of the many, many elegant nineteenth-century women who visited the Bartow family and toured the mansion enviously?

The Ghostly Music of Bartow-Pell

The Bartow-Pell Mansion Museum periodically hosts beautiful concerts. It has hosted classical guitarists, brass quintet holiday concerts, First Friday music concerts, classical music concerts, woodwind quintets, and much more. Indeed, music remains an important and powerful part of programming at Bartow-Pell just as music once was an important

Figure 27.2. Bartow-Pell Mansion and grounds in 1892.

entertainment in the mansion during the tenure of Robert and Maria Bartow and their family.

Perhaps the importance of such music to the Bartow family is best illustrated by the ghostly strains of music that float throughout the mansion at times when no musical instruments or equipment are present. Reports suggest the music is lilting, lovely, and almost hypnotic. It never is harsh or frightening and evokes a sweetness and happiness that suggest the blossom of youth—perhaps performances by the ghosts of young Bartow family members for the entertainment of their elders.

An Angelic Presence in the North Parlor

The most intriguing and heartwarming tale of the supernatural in the Bartow-Pell Mansion is the oft-told tale that there is evidence of an angelic presence in the North Parlor of the mansion. Some report to have felt the presence. Others claim to have perceived it in some fashion. All seem to agree that the presence leaves those in the room with a supreme sense of peacefulness and contentedness.

Perhaps this angelic presence watches over the many spirits of the Bartow-Pell Mansion!

Read More

Bell, Blake A. "Spirits of Bartow-Pell Mansion." *Historic Pelham* (blog). October 29, 2019, http://historicpelham.blogspot.com/2019/10/spirits-of-bartow-pell-mansion.html.

Highland, Margaret. "Crowning Glory: Bartow-Pell's Lannuier Bedstead." *Mansion Musings* (WordPress blog). June 27, 2016, https://mansionmusings.wordpress.com/2016/06/27/crowning-glory-bartow-pells-lannuier-bedstead/, accessed September 14, 2019.

Villager. "Haunted by Houses." October 22, 2015. https://www.thevillager.com/2015/10/haunted-by-houses-3/, accessed September 14, 2019.

Chapter 28

Ghostly Gardener of Bolton Priory

Bolton Priory, also known as the Priory and Pelham Priory, is a historic home built in 1838 in Pelham Manor by the Reverend Robert Bolton and his family. It still stands and is listed on the National Register of Historic Places. Robert Bolton designed the home in the Romantic idiom, making it appear as if it had been constructed over a lengthy period of time. Stone was used in one section and brick in another. The main section of the home is a two-story block intersected by a gabled two-story wing with a crenellated four-story octagonal tower at the northern angle of that junction and a crenellated three-story square brick tower at the southwestern end of the main block. The home evokes a Gothic Revival style and resembles an ancient residence deep in the English countryside. Each evening, as the sun sets, the towers of the home appear almost defensive. The silhouette of the structure seems spooky.

For many decades, Jules Martin served as the caretaker and gardener of the Priory and its grounds. Martin was a surprisingly patrician, white-haired man with a hearty laugh and a twinkle in his eye. He was French and spoke perfect English with a strong French accent.

Growing up in Pelham Manor in the early 1960s, a Pelham youngster named Peter got to know Jules Martin, a friend of his mother. "Mr. Martin," as young Peter knew him, had been the caretaker and gardener of the Priory for more than thirty years (at least since the Priory was owned by Frederick Hobbes Allen and Adele Livingston Stevens Allen in the 1930s).

Mr. Martin often regaled young Peter with entertaining stories of the Priory and its occupants. Jules Martin was the Priory caretaker who

Figure 28.1. Bolton Priory in 1844, shortly after construction.

telephoned the fire alarm to the Pelham Manor Fire Department when the Priory burned in 1932.[1] He confronted a prowler on the estate on one occasion and had a knife pulled on him before he led police to the man who was jailed for the incident.[2] Jules Martin also led tours of the estate and answered questions about its history during events hosted at the Priory.[3] Jules Martin would tell his stories, laugh heartily, and wink at young Peter with profound joy.

As a youngster, Peter was inspired by the Priory. It was massive, ancient-looking, and labyrinthine. He enjoyed accompanying his mother to the castle-like chateau to visit Mr. Martin. Mr. Martin was a strong man, though white-haired and elderly at the time. Young Peter particularly enjoyed Mr. Martin's hearty welcomes and the overstuffed sofas in his tiny servant's apartment in one wing of the mansion.

To this day Peter, now grown, cherishes warm memories of those days in his youth when he would ride his bicycle to Four Corners in the village of Pelham Manor to buy a newspaper for Mr. Martin and then pedal nearly to the end of Pelhamdale Avenue to deliver the paper to his friend in his apartment at the Priory. Jules Martin was always happy to see young Peter and to receive a Sunday paper. Young Peter enjoyed delivering a paper to Jules Martin not only because he was so fond of the old fellow, but also because he enjoyed visiting Bolton Priory. Once Mr. Martin gave young Peter a Swiss Army knife. More than fifty years later, Peter still has that knife, a special reminder of Jules Martin and the pleasant days Peter spent visiting the Priory.

During the spring of 1963, however, Jules Martin died of a heart attack. Young Peter was devastated by the loss of his mentor. His mother, likewise saddened by the loss of her friend, drove to the funeral service for Jules Martin held in the village of North Pelham. Not to be denied the opportunity to say his own goodbye, young Peter walked all the way to North Pelham and attended the funeral, an open-casket service.

At the service, Peter peered into the casket. As he said his goodbyes he thought, for a moment, that Jules Martin opened an eye and winked from the confines of the casket. Only a few days later, Peter's mother was sitting up late when she heard the distinctive voice of Jules Martin call her name.

Young Peter, of course, grew into an adult. His life took him to Denver, Colorado, where he settled. He never forgot Jules Martin, the Priory, or those pleasant days of his youth in Pelham when he rode his bicycle to visit Mr. Martin in his apartment at the Priory to bring him a Sunday newspaper. More ominously, he also never forgot the wink he knew he had seen, nor the story his mother told of Jules Martin calling her name after his death.

In late 1979, Peter traveled to New York City and to Pelham from his home in Denver. He was invited to a New Year's Eve party hosted by Columbia Records at Bolton Priory in Pelham. Peter had not been there since Jules Martin's death sixteen years before.

A host of the party led a handful of partygoers including Peter on a tour of the mansion. The host opened a door and led the group inside a room. Peter was surprised. He recognized the room as a familiar space. It was the old apartment in which the gardener and caretaker of the estate, Jules Martin, once had lived. Peter recognized the apartment immediately. The comfortable overstuffed sofa was gone, but waves of fond memories of Jules Martin instantly washed over Peter.

Late in the evening, as revelers celebrated the New Year in the Priory, Peter took a break from the celebrations. He wandered down a dimly lit hallway searching for one of the bathrooms he had seen on the earlier tour of the Priory. As he walked down the hall, he froze in his

Figure 28.2. Engraving of Bolton Priory by Richardson-Cox, SC, from a watercolor painting by William Rickarby Miller executed in 1855.

tracks. Shimmering near the end of the hallway in front of him was a luminous apparition of a man looking directly at him. The glimmering specter did not linger long, but there was no doubt in Peter's mind that a ghostly spirit was present. Indeed, Peter was so struck with a sense of awe and felt such a profound sense of comfort when he saw the apparition that he advanced toward the specter as it vanished in front of him. It was then that Peter realized that the entrance to the apartment in which Jules Martin once had lived was only a step or so beyond where the apparition vanished before his eyes.

One might wonder now, even if it causes a little chill to run up the spine: Did the shimmering apparition at the end of that long, dim hallway on that celebratory night seem to wink at Peter the moment it vanished?

Read More

Bell, Blake A. "The Ghostly Gardener of Bolton Priory: A Pelham Apparition." *Historic Pelham* (blog). October 27, 2015, https://historicpelham.blogspot.com/2015/10/the-ghostly-gardener-of-bolton-priory.html, accessed October 29, 2019.

Chapter 29

Ghostly Matron of the Manor Club

The members of the Manor Club in Pelham Manor were excited. The club's "Evening Section" hoped to arrange an entertaining program in celebration of Halloween 2015. It planned to hire an experienced Ghost Whisperer to explore ghostly aspects of the historic clubhouse listed on the National Register of Historic Places. Such Ghost Whisperers, made famous by a television supernatural drama of the same name that ran from 2005 until 2010, are said to be psychic mediums who are "receivers of paranormal communications."

The Manor Club promptly contacted a well-known Ghost Whisperer in the region. The medium made clear, however, that before he could agree to host an investigation of the clubhouse, he first would have to visit the building to assess it. With time running short, the club readily agreed.

At the appointed time, the medium appeared at the clubhouse and began his investigation. What happened next promptly became the stuff of legend, adding to the already rich history and lore of the storied Manor Club.

The Clubhouse

The Manor Club, located at 1023 Esplanade in the village of Pelham Manor, is a cultural, civic, and 501(c)(3) organization. The club had its beginnings in the 1870s. It was not, however, organized formally until January 10, 1882.

The clubhouse that stands today is not the original clubhouse. Today's clubhouse opened in 1922 on the site of the original clubhouse built 1887–1888. On May 12, 2014, the Manor Club clubhouse was listed on the National Register of Historic Places.

Beloved Mrs. Secor, Club President for Twenty-Six Years

For a quarter century, a Pelham Manor resident named Joan Elizabeth Klink Secor was the driving force behind, and leader of, the Manor Club. Joan Secor was a social and cultural force in the village of Pelham Manor. She lovingly devoted much of her adult life to the success of the club. She nurtured the club and its members tenderly and with great attention.

Mrs. Secor, as she was known to most, became president of the Tuesday Afternoon Club in 1900. When that club merged into the Manor Club (which became a women's club) in 1914, she served as president of the newly merged institution as well. She stabilized club finances. She presided over the fund-raising for, and the construction of, the new clubhouse. She grew the club and oversaw it as it became an important part of the social fabric of the town, a role that it continues to serve.

In May 1925, Mrs. Secor retired from service as club president after twenty-six years when she departed for California to live with family members. She died suddenly in her home in San Francisco on Saturday, July 23, 1932.

Mrs. Secor was a prim, proper, loving, and intelligent gentlewoman with a patrician air and a philanthropic focus. Beloved by all, she carried herself with dignity. She was responsible for implementation of the club rule that stood for many years banning alcohol. Out of her love for the club, she was a stickler for rules. Consequently, she managed the club during her tenure as president with love, care, and—when necessary—an iron fist.

A beautiful oil portrait of Mrs. Secor, painted by George Brehm, still hangs in the assembly room of the Manor Club. Via that portrait, Mrs. Secor's ever-watchful eyes take in all that occurs in the club she loved and oversaw for more than a quarter century.

The eyes of Mrs. Secor's portrait have followed many societal changes since 1925. Members now include women with breathtaking careers. Men, once again, are welcomed as members, something not permitted in her day. No longer do the club's women members don white gloves when they leave home. The days of beautiful, formal bonnets and hats are gone, replaced by commonsensical fashion and even, "gasp" (as Mrs. Secor would say), pants or knee-length skirts worn by some women. Men no longer wear jackets or ties. The eyes of Mrs. Secor's portrait even seem to cringe when club members walk in wearing their coats rather than carrying them or, heaven forbid, carrying umbrellas into the clubhouse rather than checking them at the entrance where they belong. Yes, things are different now. There even is loud and boisterous laughter among members, as well as occasional interruptions of smartphones (whatever those are, at least in the eyes of Mrs. Secor). These days the portrait of Mrs. Secor must suffer the indignities of presiding over members who excuse themselves to go to the bathroom rather than beg pardon to "powder the nose." Yes, things are very different now.

Back to the First Ghost Whisperer

The Ghost Whisperer walked the quiet hallways of the clubhouse. "Indeed," he said, "spirits are present." He continued, saying, "Some spirits are supportive of the club's efforts to become more modern. However, one spirit is upset because there have been so many changes in the club, in the lives of the club's members, and in the very village within which the clubhouse stands." White gloves are gone! Women are engaged in breathtaking careers outside the home! The standard rules of etiquette by which society forged its way in the 1920s have evolved into standards of etiquette the spirit no longer seems to understand. Clothes are different; cars are different; language is different; all is different.

The Ghost Whisperer said that the spirit is anxious about the changes, is not happy with the Ghost Whisperer walking through the clubhouse, and does not want a Ghost Whisperer there for fear it would bring members' attention to the spirit's presence and its "manipulation" of events. "Mrs. Secor's spirit," the Ghost Whisperer declared, "is so upset with the presence of a Ghost Whisperer and modernization of the club as well as the societal changes, that it is interfering with my psychic faculties!"

A few days after the visit, the Ghost Whisperer called the Manor Club's chair of the planned event to say he would not participate in the planned event. The committee members wondered if the Ghost Whisperer program scheduled for Halloween week would have to be canceled.

Finding Another Talented Ghost Whisperer

What is Halloween without such entertainment? Research revealed other Ghost Whisperers in the region. One seemed particularly intriguing and especially talented. A club member called her to discuss the event.

During the call, the second Ghost Whisperer said she was intrigued but needed more background information. As the conversation continued with a description of the planned event and its proposed date and time, the call disconnected abruptly. There seemed to be odd noise as the call ended. Was it static, or a hiss?

No problem, of course. Only a quick call back would be required. That call, however, failed. Several more failed. In fact, days of efforts to reach the Ghost Whisperer failed. It seemed as if any effort to arrange a Ghost Whisperer was, well, cursed.

Persistence, of course, pays off. Club members were nothing if not persistent. After diligent efforts, a member was able to connect with the Ghost Whisperer who was fascinated, intrigued and, most importantly, unintimidated by the spirit of Mrs. Secor, the Ghostly Matron of the Manor Club. The new Ghost Whisperer agreed to lead a ghostly tour of the clubhouse.

On the appointed evening, the Ghost Whisperer stepped into the hundred-year-old clubhouse and felt immediately the wrath of an angry spirit. Mrs. Secor was present. Indeed, her spirit would not have missed such an opportunity.

As the Ghost Whisperer walked members through the clubhouse, the unseen spirit of Mrs. Secor followed, bombarding the medium with sensations of anger and disappointment. The medium kept her focus to the point of exhaustion as she paced the same floors the living Mrs. Secor once had walked. The medium occasionally stopped as if to listen and related Mrs. Secor's disappointment with the way things had changed and the disrespect she felt having a Ghost Whisperer. To the shock of all, though no one had conveyed any of the actual words used by the first Ghost Whisperer who left the clubhouse never to return, the medium repeated word-for-word what Mrs. Secor had said to the first medium. The new medium said that the spirit is anxious about the changes, is not happy with the Ghost Whisperer walking through the clubhouse, and did not want a Ghost Whisperer there for fear it would bring members' attention to the spirit's presence and its manipulation of events. "Mrs. Secor's spirit," the Ghost Whisperer declared, "is so upset with the presence of a Ghost Whisperer and modernization of the club as well as the societal changes that affected the club's members, that it is interfering with my psychic faculties!"

Read More

Bell, Blake A. "The Ghostly Matron of the Manor Club: Even a Ghost Whisperer's Nightmare!" *Historic Pelham* (blog). https://historicpelham.blogspot.com/2015/10/the-ghostly-matron-of-manor-club-even.html, accessed October 29, 2019.

Chapter 30

More Ghosts of the Old Stone House

It seems the Elegant Lady of the Old Stone House that still stands at 463 First Avenue in Pelham is not the only spirit that roams the halls of that beautiful house. The watchful ghost of Widow Parrish in that handsome ancient stone home is not alone. At least two more specters wander the same hallways.

Dorothea and Frank Snyder bought the old stone house in 1923. Frank Snyder died in the home on Sunday, March 5, 1939. The home is built of undressed Tuckahoe marble with cutout barge boards. It has a solid "four-square" look. For much of its history it had thirteen rooms, eight fireplaces, and walls of astounding thickness. During early renovations of the home, owners discovered a secret staircase. Its existence was unknown to owners for many decades. For decades, Dorothea Snyder told a strange story about the elegant home.

Not long after she and her husband moved into the house in 1923, while her husband was at work in his New York City office, she busied herself about the home. On a beautiful morning as she worked diligently on the second floor, she sensed something. She glanced up and was stunned to see a woman and child standing before her. The pair stood in a doorway and remained perfectly silent.

The lovely woman was dressed beautifully in a style common during earlier days. She wore a richly brocaded velvet gown accented with a stunning poke bonnet that had a small crown and a wide, rounded front brim that extended beyond her face, framing it quaintly and beautifully. Dorothea could see frill at the bottom of the woman's pantalets, peeking from beneath the rich gown. The woman also held a massive sheaf of golden chrysanthemums that added both beauty and wonder to the vision.

Standing next to the beautiful woman was a stunning youngster. The girl bore a marked resemblance to the woman and was dressed in a similarly dated and quaint manner. The angelic little one remained just as silent as her companion. Both the woman and the youngster wore broad smiles.

Dorothea Snyder felt no fear. Indeed, the vision did not even startle her. Instead, her first reaction was that a neighbor was playing a joke on her. As Mrs. Snyder stared at the silent pair, she soon realized it was no joke. She stepped forward to approach the two visitors.

As she did, both the woman and the youngster bowed graciously in an old style, continued to smile broadly, and backed away from her. With each step Mrs. Snyder took toward the pair, they backed one step away from her while continuing to smile broadly. This continued as the pair began to back down the stairway to the first floor as Mrs. Snyder approached them.

On the first floor, the pair continued to back away until they reached a corner. Once they backed around that corner, they disappeared, leaving Mrs. Snyder to ponder their purposes and their identities for the rest of her life. She always took comfort, however, that the Elegant Lady of the Old Stone House would not be alone for eternity.

Read More

Pelham Sun (Pelham, NY). "Legend Gathers about Old Stone House Landmark for 85 Years in No. Pelham—Georgian House, Occupied by Mr. and Mrs. F. M. Snyder, Unique in Village, Attracts Many Visitors." August 23, 1935, vol. 26, no. 21, p. 3, cols. 1–2.

PART IX

QUIRKY APPARITIONS AND SHADOW GHOSTS OF PELHAM

Ghost stories have featured prominently in Pelham folklore for more than two centuries. As has been shown, some tales relate to Indigenous Americans. Others involve the Revolutionary War. A number involve stories of treasure or ghostly fire ships. Some Pelham ghost stories, however, defy easy categorization.

A number of Pelham specters can best be described as "quirky." One such ghost is the Luminous Lantern-Bearer of Baychester and Pelham Bridge. Others are the Wandering Ghost of the Mad Chemist, Little Specter of the Field, Floating White Phantom of City Island, and Fiery-Eyed Phantom of Pelham Heights. The stories of these ghosts are told in this section. Also told here is a pair of darker ghost stories. They involve so-called shadow ghosts.

Chapter 31

Luminous Lantern-Bearer of Baychester and Pelham Bridge

Heinrich Nieman made a single mistake. It may have seemed a tiny mistake. But even a tiny mistake in Nieman's business could be disastrous.

Heinrich Nieman, you see, worked in the acid house of the Dittmar Powder Works in Baychester, not far from Pelham Bridge. There, workers handled nitroglycerin and made gunpowder, dynamite, and other explosives.

As soon as Nieman made his tiny mistake, a chill enveloped him. His first instinct was to flee. Before he could turn toward the door, however, a light luminous wisp of smoke burst from the vat. There followed a tremendous flash and an earth-shaking explosion. The blast broke windows throughout Baychester and Pelham. It blew the acid house and much of the remainder of the facility into teeny-tiny pieces that soon rained from the sky.

Heinrich Nieman was no more. He was "blown to atoms," as one news report related.

Nieman was one of a long line of employees of local explosives manufacturers who were blown to smithereens. Indeed, by the time of Nieman's gruesome death, such manufacturing facilities were already known as "earthquake factories." One article, published shortly after the explosion that killed Nieman, stated:

> New buildings for the manufacture of gunpowder and other explosives are nearly finished at Baychester, in Westchester

County, and it is said that the operations of the powder company will be carried on more extensively than ever. The first enterprise of the kind was established near the junction of the Harlem and New Haven Railroad, and it was destroyed by an explosion attended by the loss of five or six lives. The company was prohibited by the town authorities from resuming business in the town. The next giant powder factory was established near the railroad station at Pelhamville, and was destroyed by fire. The operations of the company under a new name were then located at Baychester, a short distance north of the railroad station. The works were destroyed by an explosion and resulted in the loss of several lives and injuries to others. New workshops were erected and the manufacturing operations resumed. Another explosion took place and several persons were seriously injured. A resumption of operations at Baychester creates some alarm, for, although the neighborhood is sparsely populated, persons while waiting for the arrival or departure of trains from the railroad station, will be exposed to great danger.[1]

Of course, those at the Dittmar Powder Works who survived the blast that obliterated poor Heinrich Nieman grieved his death. All who worked at the facility knew him well. All loved him. Moreover, everyone thought much about the poor fellow's death because, to a man, each understood, "There, but for the grace of God, go I."

Within a short time, new buildings for the manufacture of gunpowder and other explosives were completed and operations resumed at the powder works. Almost immediately, workers on the night shifts began reporting a most unusual occurrence.

The first worker to experience the oddity could not believe his eyes. He stepped out of one of the manufacturing buildings late one winter night to take a brief break in the cold air. In the distance, he could make out the glow of a bobbing light. It clearly was a lantern being carried through a wooded area near the facility. As the bobbing light approached, the worker became increasingly alarmed. The open flame of any carelessly carried lantern was a terrible risk to the explosives manufacturing facility. It had no business anywhere near the powder works.

The worker stepped into the darkness and walked toward the lantern-bearer, hoping to stop him and keep him away from the powder works. In the distance, the lantern seemed to cast an odd, luminous glow that lit the hazy figure from head to toe without lighting the surrounding countryside.

As the worker approached the lantern-bearer he stared at the figure's illuminated visage. The hair on the back of the worker's neck stood up. He blinked and rubbed his eyes in disbelief. The figure carrying the lantern was poor Heinrich Nieman! More accurately, the figure carrying the lantern was a luminous figure that seemed to glide along the ground with a shimmering face that once belonged to Heinrich Nieman. That face seemed angry and singularly focused. Indeed, it seemed to stare right through the worker while focused on the powder works behind him.

The worker stumbled backward in terror until he fell. He scrambled to his feet to flee the apparition. The ghostly lantern-bearer continued to glide toward the worker even as he fled. Not knowing the spirit's intentions, the worker ran past the powder works screaming warnings and continued into the night, utterly terrified that the phantom was there to ignite the facility and kill all inside. The worker never returned to the facility.

This was merely the first sighting of the angry ghost of Heinrich Nieman. Most workers at the facility who worked in the evening or night hours soon reported seeing the apparition carrying its lantern. The sightings frightened so many that a number quit their jobs. A local newspaper reported that "the ghost of the man blown up has been seen perambulating about the premises at night, carrying a lantern, and the workmen, not caring to be in company with that kind of 'spirit' have all cleared out."[2] Another local paper reported, "Since Heinrich Nimen [sic] was blown to atoms by the explosion of dynamite at Ditmar's [sic] works at Baychester, there are some persons who affirm they have seen his ghost about the works at night. Some of the employees have left in consequence."[3]

For years, explosions at Dittmar Powder Works continued to rock the Baychester and Pelham Bridge region. For example, on September 30, 1886, a massive explosion killed four workers and scattered their body parts throughout the grounds. On April 5, 1890, another explosion tore through the running house of the facility, killing two men and rocking houses at Pelham Bridge, in Bartow-on-the-Sound, and on City Island. Some claimed that on each occasion the spirit of Heinrich Nieman carried its lantern into the facility, causing an explosion.

To this day the spirit of Heinrich Nieman wanders the Pelham Bridge and Baychester region. Though explosives manufacturers no longer dot the heavily populated region, the luminous phantom continues to search for powder works, apparently hoping to use its lantern to ignite a blast to blow all within to atoms—exactly the fate that befell poor Heinrich Nieman more than 135 years ago.

Read More

Bell, Blake A. "The Luminous Lantern-Bearer of Baychester and Pelham Bridge." *Historic Pelham* (blog). http://historicpelham.blogspot.com/2019/10/the-luminous-lantern-bearer-of.html, accessed October 29, 2019.
Chronicle (Mount Vernon, NY). "Westchester." March 19, 1886, vol. 17, no. 864, p. 1, col. 5.
Yonkers Statesman (Yonkers, NY). "The County—A Ghost Scare." March 20, 1886, vol. 3, no. 722, p. 1, col. 4.

Chapter 32

Wandering Ghost of the Mad Chemist

For much of his career, no one expected Andrew J. Parker to live a long life. Over the years he worked as the "chief manager" of a number of dynamite manufacturing facilities in the town of Pelham near the settlement of Bartow and also in the Baychester section near Pelham Bridge. Indeed, throughout Parker's career as a chemist, a number of workers were blown to smithereens during accidents while manufacturing blasting powder or working with the nitroglycerin that was made on premises (see chapter 31).

Parker grieved the death of every such worker. Actually, he obsessed over the death of every such worker. He toiled day in and day out in the dark buildings in which the chemical formulae he devised were used to craft the nitroglycerin and explosives that so frequently erupted and killed many within the facilities. He knew that he might be next. The fear gnawed at his mind. It consumed his brain. It overwhelmed his conscience.

Parker began his career in the 1870s. Though he lived in Bridgeport at the time, he worked near Pelham Bridge at the Neptune Powder Mill. That facility was blown to bits on October 10, 1878, while workers were making nitroglycerin for use in the powder manufacturing process.[1] Parker was not on site on that occasion, but two workers who were making the nitroglycerin observed it catch fire. As they fled, the resultant explosion leveled the facility. Thankfully, both escaped with their lives.

Parker was lucky not to have been there when the facility was blown into the sky that day. He could not comprehend why he had been so lucky. He knew that, once the facility was rebuilt, every time he stepped inside might be among the last moments of his life.

Yes, no one expected Andrew J. Parker to live a long life—including Andrew J. Parker.

Parker, however, defied the odds. By 1885, after multiple explosions at local powder works had killed numerous men,[2] Parker could stand it no longer. He no longer could think of anything but death. He trembled each time he worked. The faces of his colleagues and friends killed by explosions swirled in his brain and eventually deprived him of reason—some might say sanity. Parker summoned what little reason remained within and retired from the career of dynamite manufacturing. He settled in a home with his wife in the Baychester section near Pelham Bridge not far from the Dittmar Powder Works.

In a terrible twist of irony, only a short time later, on September 26, 1885, Andrew J. Parker simply dropped dead in his home.[3] Years of overwhelming fear of impending death had ravaged his mind and body. Perhaps all-consuming guilt that he somehow played some role in the deaths of so many who followed his chemical formulae robbed him of the will to live. Worse yet, perhaps he willed his own death as some macabre form of penance for the sin of surviving when so many others had died from his work.

Parker was buried in Green-Wood Cemetery in Brooklyn (Lot 5908, Section 9). His will, dated January 17, 1885, left all his real and personal property to his son, Andrew D. Parker, and was proved through testimony provided by his wife, Helen, and another of his sons, Charles F. Parker, on February 2, 1888.

A few weeks after Parker's death, only days after All Hallows' Eve, all of Baychester was abuzz. Indeed, local newspapers reported that all of Baychester was "alarmed"[4] and "much exercised"[5] over the appearance of the ghost of Andrew J. Parker.

Though reports differed over the nature of the spirit, virtually all who saw it were scared out of their wits. The luminous figure clearly resembled Andrew J. Parker as it glided through Baychester and around Pelham Bridge. Yet, it shifted its appearance and could take the form of a man, a woman with the face of Parker, and a figure holding a lantern. Most eyewitness accounts agreed, however, that the ghost seemed to wander the region aimlessly.

Even in death, the spirit seemed to have lost its mind. The wanderings of the ghost of the mad chemist were aimless. The phantom could not even settle on a single apparition to define its afterlife. Instead, it transformed from man to woman to lantern-bearer. All who encountered the phantom felt profound fear, both the phantom's fear and their own. Eyewitnesses also felt a sense of piteous empathy for a spirit that seemed doomed to such forlorn, guilt-ridden melancholy.

James Montgomery, an employee of the nearby Dittmar Powder Works, was the first to see the apparition. The New York Herald reported that Montgomery had "obtained a fair and unobstructed view" of the ghost standing in the doorway of the house where Parker had died only a few weeks before.[6]

James Montgomery frequented the bar of a little nearby hotel called the Baychester House kept by William Jacobs. William Jacobs seemed to have his own interest in the world of spirits and ghosts, perhaps because he had lost his own wife, Mary, who had died unexpectedly in her sleep in her bed in the Baychester House only a few months before.

James Montgomery was dumbfounded by the apparition he saw and told his story to his friends and acquaintances in the bar of the Baychester House. He quickly found himself the butt of their jokes and mockery. Indeed, any time he tried to describe what he had seen, everyone in the bar would whistle loudly to drown out his words and humiliate him.

Montgomery became so furious that he offered a $50 reward to anyone willing to stay in the Parker house all night on any night from 11:00 p.m. until 4:00 a.m. According to one account, Montgomery placed the promised $50 reward in escrow in the possession of William Jacobs of the Baychester House with instructions that Jacobs pay the money to the first person who successfully stayed in the Parker house overnight, subject to various conditions. Jacobs readily agreed to hold the bet in escrow.[7]

Within a short time, the people of Baychester were being frightened frequently by the spirit of Andrew J. Parker. The apparition was beginning to expand its range from the Parker home throughout the Baychester section all the way to Pelham Bridge and, as one report suggested, nearby City Island. The people of the region became alarmed and even "much exercised" according to one news account.

Different witnesses in the region observed different things when they saw the apparition of Andrew J. Parker during those weeks in late 1885. Some reportedly saw an apparition carrying what appeared to be a lantern while wandering at night "with no apparent purpose, and frightening those who see him out of their wits."[8]

As alarm spread, more and more people in the region saw the apparition. Soon local residents were reporting that sometimes they saw the ghost "in the shape of a man with a lantern" while others saw the apparition in the shape of a woman. Of course, care must be taken when considering such reports since the region is crowded with ghosts. Those who saw a ghost in the form of a man with a lantern may well have seen the spirit of Heinrich Nieman, who was blown to bits in an explosion at the Dittmar Powder Works a couple of years earlier (see chapter 31).

Some said that the ghost of Andrew J. Parker was "a production of Jacob's whiskey" at the Baychester House bar.[9] Others claimed the alarming spirit that wandered the region aimlessly was simply "flesh and blood, and so will be found when captured."[10]

Two things are certain, however. First, James Montgomery knew what he saw in the doorway of the Parker house: Andrew J. Parker weeks after he died. Second, not one person ever took Montgomery up on his offer to pay $50 to the first person willing to stay overnight in the haunted Parker house for only five terrifying hours.

As you drive along Gun Hill Road in The Bronx or from Pelham toward The Bronx along Shore Road and cross the Pelham Bridge at night, look carefully. If you can make out the luminous figure of a man or a woman wandering aimlessly, say a silent prayer for the soul of poor Andrew J. Parker—but whatever you do, don't stop. Keep going! Otherwise, you may encounter the wandering ghost of the mad chemist of Baychester and Pelham Bridge.

Read More

Bell, Blake A. "The Ghostly Lantern-Bearer of Baychester and Pelham Bridge." Historic Pelham (blog). http://historicpelham.blogspot.com/2018/10/the-ghostly-lantern-bearer-of.html, accessed July 5, 2021.

Chronicle Supplement. "Westchester." November 20, 1885, p. 1, cols. 2–3 (one-page supplement to the November 20, 1885, issue of the *Chronicle* [Mount Vernon, NY], vol. 17, no. 844).

New Rochelle Pioneer (New Rochelle, NY). "Local Intelligence." November 14, 1885, p. 3, cols. 1–2. See also Untitled, *Recorder* (Mount Kisco, NY), November 13, 1885, vol. 12, no. 32, p. 8, col. 2 (same text).

New York Herald. "Died." September 27, 1885, no. 17933, p. 15, cols. 1–2.

New York Herald. "The Ghost and the Dynamiter." November 18, 1885, no. 17985, p. 8, col. 6.

Supplement to Eastern State Journal (White Plains, NY). "County Items." June 5, 1885, p. 1, col. 3.

Yonkers Statesman (Yonkers, NY). "Baychester Alarmed." November 13, 1885, vol. 3, no. 617, p. 1, col. 4.

Yonkers Statesman (Yonkers, NY). "They Do Not Want to See It." November 18, 1885, vol. 3, no. 621, p. 1, col. 4.

Chapter 33

Little Specter of the Field

During the dark, cold months of deep winter in the 1880s, City Island in the town of Pelham was desolate at midnight. Some homes on the summer resort island were unoccupied during the dismally cold season when chilling winds swept the island from Long Island Sound. There were no streetlights to pierce the inky blackness. Travelers had to wait until their eyes adjusted to the darkness before trying to stumble over vacant lots, open fields, and deserted streets to get home.

During the cold nights of those days of yore, City Island could be a scary place, as many discovered during the winter of 1887–1888. For a few months that winter, City Island in the town of Pelham was virtually overrun by phantoms. One such phantom was the Little Specter of the Field.

Alvarette B. Sturges, known as "Allie," was the first to be accosted by the specter. Allie was a rosy-cheeked young woman who worked behind the counter of a bakery on City Island during the winter of 1887–1888. She was the twenty-four-year-old stepdaughter of Jacob Smith, a City Island cigar-maker, and his wife (Sarah Sturges Smith). Allie was a beautiful woman who looked younger than her twenty-four years. Indeed, some mistook her for barely eighteen.

In November, 1887, Allie was engaged to be married the following April to Rochelle N. Horton of City Island. Allie Sturges was floating on air. It turns out Allie was not the only thing floating on air around City Island that winter.

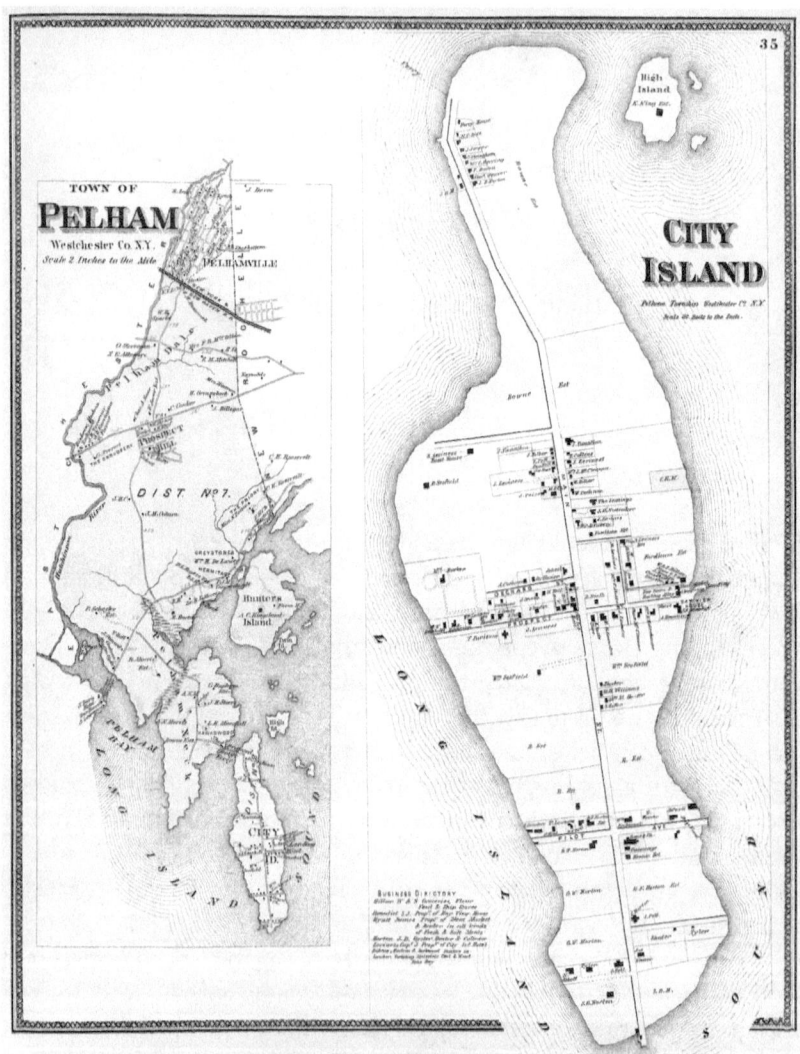

Figure 33.1. Nineteenth-century map of City Island and the town of Pelham.

Allie lived on the island with her mother, her stepfather, and a large extended family that included her older sister and eight additional stepbrothers and stepsisters who ranged in age from two months to fourteen years. Late one November evening, Allie left her work at Weber's Bakery for the long walk back to her home on City Island. Her clothes were lightly dusted with stray flour in a few places and retained the sweet yeasty scent of fresh rolls that she had served over the bakery counter throughout the day. Allie was tired, but happy, as she trudged home that evening.

As Allie neared her family home, the dirt road crept through fields and past vacant lots. Though her eyes were adjusted to the darkness, she kept her focus on the uneven, pothole-strewn road ahead to ensure sound footing. As she walked, head down, something caught the corner of her eye in the distance.

Allie looked up to see a terrifying "spectral apparition," as she later described it. At first, the specter seemed like a floating, luminous white mist. As she stared, however, the luminescence resolved into a spectral apparition that she later described as "a little one."

Allie was transfixed. The "little one" seemed to float above the ground. As she stared in wonder, the specter moved. Actually, it moved toward her.

Allie's eyes widened. At first, she saw the little specter float slowly toward her. As she stared, it seemed to speed more quickly in her direction.

Terror gripped Allie. As she watched, the apparition moved faster. Instinctively, she began to run toward her home. As she ran, she glanced at her pursuer only to see the specter continue its chase as it glided effortlessly across a rough field in her direction at an angle apparently intended to intercept her as she ran along the dark roadway.

Allie knew she could not reach her distant family home before the specter overtook her. She ran harder. She dropped a bag of rolls she carried for her family. She stumbled as she ran and cried in terror. All the while, the luminous little one sped faster and faster in her direction. As it approached, it no longer seemed so little.

Soon, the specter was upon Allie. She stopped in exhaustion and screamed as it raced by her. As it passed, Allie felt a terrible chill that shook her to her bones. It made her shiver, but the feeling was more than mere cold. It was a bone-rattling sense of icy terror and dark despondence that passed through her just as the apparition vanished.

Breathing heavily with tears streaming down her face, Allie began turning in every direction. She saw nothing but the blackness of the night. There was no specter, no luminous floating mist. She turned in an entire circle several times, terrified that the "little one" would appear from behind at any moment. She still felt the chill of icy terror and dark despondence.

The inky night suddenly seemed even more ominous. She feared it now hid some terrible spirit from her sight. Again, she ran.

This time, Allie ran nonstop to her family's home. As she reached the yard she began screaming as though the personification of evil had her in its clutch. She burst through the door of the house into the arms of her fourteen-year-old stepbrother, Jacob Jr., who had heard her screams and raced to the door.

Allie trembled violently. As family gathered about her, she related through tears her terrible story of the luminous spectral apparition and how it had chased her. She described how she had run for her life while it pursued her. She described how she had stumbled and dropped a bag of rolls she carried for the family.

Convinced Allie had been the victim of a prank, her stepfather, Jacob Smith, and her stepbrother, Jacob Jr., grabbed guns and retraced Allie's steps along the road. They found the bag with fresh rolls strewn along the roadway. In the distance, across the great field next to the road, they thought they saw a faint glow. With each step they took toward the glow in the distance, it seemed to retreat, ever faster, until it disappeared. As it disappeared, both men felt a chill of icy terror and dark despondence.

Read More

Bell, Blake A. "Pelham Was Overrun by Ghosts for a Few Months in the Winter of 1887–1888." *Historic Pelham* (blog). http://historicpelham.blogspot.com/2016/10/pelham-was-overrun-by-ghosts-for-few.html, accessed October 29, 2019.

Sun (New York, NY). "City Island's Big Ghost—It Moves Along without Touching the Ground—Sometimes White and Sometimes Black—It Looks Like a Woman, but Has No Face—If It Doesn't Look Out It Will Get Shot." February 12, 1888, p. 10, col. 7.

Chapter 34

Floating White Phantom of City Island

For three months in late 1887 and early 1888, all of City Island in the town of Pelham had been talking about the luminous Little Specter of the Field that had chased poor Allie Sturges and nearly scared her to death the previous November. Then, on Wednesday, February 1, 1888, there was an incident that became the new talk of the town.

Snow blanketed Pelham that brutally cold Wednesday. The waters of Long Island Sound between City Island and Hart Island were a frozen sheet of ice. Nevertheless, a festive and jolly crowd had gathered on the only hill on the island behind the local post office for a sledding party. One of the three Darling triplets, twenty-four-year-old William G. ("Will") Darling was there. Late in the evening, happy, exhausted, and cold, he left the waning festivities for home.

As Will made his way to his house, he approached Main Street (today's City Island Avenue). The street was deserted and dark. Will was cold. What he saw next worsened his chill. In fact, according to a later account, it "made his blood run cold." Floating above Main Street, almost as if it were "rolling along," was a tall, luminous, white apparition that glided along and never seemed to touch the ground. The terrifying specter seemed large and ominous.[1]

Will Darling had heard all the talk of the luminous Little Specter of the Field that had tormented Allie Sturges only weeks before. This, however, was no little specter. It was huge! Will never hesitated. He ran for his home, never looking back until he was safely inside.

Only a short time later that night, the apparition appeared to William Applebaugh, a telegraph operator in the Signal Service office on City Island. Applebaugh was walking along the roadway with drifts of snow piled on both sides when the tall, luminous apparition appeared and towered over him. Applebaugh turned to run. What happened next is unclear.

As he turned, Applebaugh felt what seemed like a shove. He fell into a deep snow drift along the side of the road. Whether he fell or was shoved made no difference. William Applebaugh scrambled out of the deep drift and took off down the roadway without looking back.

The Floating White Phantom of City Island was not finished that fateful night. Will Dayton, the son of a hardware merchant in town, was near Leviness's Hotel when he froze in his tracks. In the street opposite the hotel was a tall "grayish white something" that seemed to float along about three feet above the ground. Dayton could provide no more detailed description of the Floating White Phantom because he turned and "ran after the first glance."

For the next several nights, the Floating White Phantom frightened a number of other City Islanders who encountered it. On Thursday night, February 2, 1888, Stephen Collins was walking on Prospect Avenue on City Island opposite the Vail property. His house was nearby. He stopped cold when he saw the giant white apparition on Prospect Avenue. He later recounted that "it did not stand upon the ground. It seemed suspended several feet in the air." Collins could not describe the phantom with any additional particularity because, like so many others, he promptly turned, ran to his home, "quickly got indoors, and did not venture out until morning."

The following night, Friday, February 3rd, City Islander Eugene Hallet was returning home late on a "dismally dark night." Opposite Flynn's icehouse at the Forks, Hallet "saw the same white apparition." It was "white and tall." It seemed to glide over the ground without seeming to touch it. Though Hallet was a good half mile from his home, he turned and ran "at a hundred-yard pace." As he ran, the Floating White Phantom of City Island made "not the slightest sound" but followed him as he ran until he reached his home.

With so many sightings of the Floating White Phantom of City Island in such a short period of time, all on City Island were talking about the phantom. Local druggist George E. Reynolds had the most thoughtful explanation for the sightings. Given that most of those accosted by the phantom were young men, he noticed that "the girls don't go out alone nights any more [sic], and the boys have their hands full escorting them," just as the boys wanted.

Read More

Bell, Blake A. "Pelham Was Overrun by Ghosts for a Few Months in the Winter of 1887–1888." *Historic Pelham* (blog). http://historicpelham.blogspot.com/2016/10/pelham-was-overrun-by-ghosts-for-few.html, accessed October 29, 2019.

Sun (New York, NY). "City Island's Big Ghost—It Moves Along without Touching the Ground—Sometimes White and Sometimes Black—It Looks Like a Woman, but Has No Face—If It Doesn't Look Out It Will Get Shot." February 12, 1888, p. 10, col. 7.

Chapter 35

Faceless Shadow Ghost of City Island

Nineteen-year-old David Leviness, son of a City Island oysterman named Charles Valentine Leviness, was walking home late in the evening on Sunday, February 5, 1888. He was only a half mile from his home as he walked past Von Liehn's Bay View Hotel at the eastern foot of City Island Bridge. The moonless night seemed exceptionally dark, yet the skies were clear and stars twinkled. The hotel was dark—almost eerily quiet. There were no streetlamps along the roadway. Moreover, it was so late that no lamps were lit in the windows of any of the few homes and buildings he passed.

As Dave trudged along, he glanced toward the hotel bathing pavilions adjacent to the waters of the bay. He stopped dead in his tracks. A chill ran up his spine. On the shore near the pavilions was something that seemed to have a human form. It looked like a shadow barely darker than the darkness of the night that enveloped it. He estimated that it was at least six feet tall and quite large. Yet, it oddly struck him as though it had a woman's form. The shadow seemed three dimensional and moved slowly in the darkness.

At that moment Leviness realized that the six-foot-tall dark shadow was floating well above the ground. Indeed, he could make out the glint of dim starlight reflected off the waters of the bay underneath the floating specter. He froze in fear. As he later told a local reporter, he was "rooted to the spot in terror for a moment."[1]

Leviness squinted and stared at the creature, marveling that "it seemed suspended in the air." Though he could see where the dark shadow's face should be, there was no face. As he gawked at the faceless shadow, the apparition lurched toward him like a predator leaping for its prey.

Leviness stumbled backward, turned, and ran for his life. He ran along the dark dirt road toward his house. He ran as fast as he could. Indeed, as a reporter later wrote in a story about the incident, Leviness "ran as never he ran before." He was so terrified that, as he ran, he repeatedly glanced behind. With each glance he saw the faceless floating shadow specter following him closely at the same furious pace.

Finally, however, Leviness reached home and burst through the door. He was "completely exhausted."

Over the next few days, Dave Leviness became furious at the terrible fright he had suffered from the Faceless Shadow Ghost of City Island. When questioned a week later by a reporter from the *Sun* published in New York City, he threatened: "I'm going down that way to-night, and I'm going to carry a revolver. If she's layin' for me I'll give her a shot. I don't want to kill anybody, but that's a ghost. No live person could travel in the air." The same reporter interviewed the local justice of the peace, asking what he thought of the phantom sightings. The justice of the peace reportedly said, "Oh, there's some ground for it, of course; I suppose some one [sic] is masquerading around here, scaring folks. If it continues, I'm going to get detectives out and sift the thing to the bottom. It won't do to have women and children scared out of their wits. Everybody in town is talking about the thing, and a good many superstitious people believe it."

Epilogue

Readers may note that there is a common thread among this and the two previous chapters. "Little Specter of the Field," "Floating White Phantom of City Island," and "Faceless Shadow Ghost of City Island" all involved ghosts that terrorized Pelham during the winter of 1887–1888. Indeed, by late February of that Leap Year in 1888, nearly everyone in Pelham was talking about the phantoms that were stalking City Islanders. City Island, it seemed, was overrun by ghosts.

Though everyone in Pelham was talking about the phantoms, the conversations had taken a more ominous turn. City Islanders had observed a pattern to the appearance of the phantoms. The ghosts, it was said, appeared to be "most troublesome" to young men who lingered beyond the hour of midnight supposedly "in attendance at the bedsides of ill friends and family"—an excuse often used by local young men who, instead, visited their lovely young belles.

On Wednesday, February 29, 1888, young women of City Island hosted a Leap Year Concert filled with music and drama. The program was replete with beautiful costumes and charmingly framed tableaus. The "hit of the evening," however, was a two-part tableau presented by Josie Price and Susie Estes. In that "ingenious" two-part tableau, the pair "cleaned up the mystery of the City Island ghost," presumably by demonstrating to the audience how such a ghost could be fabricated.

While history does not record what Josie Price and Susie Estes presented to the crowd that evening, it is quite telling that the hit of the evening that night was something on the minds of every City Islander: the ghosts that overran City Island during that frightening winter of 1887–1888.

Read More

Bell, Blake A. "Pelham Was Overrun by Ghosts for a Few Months in the Winter of 1887–1888." *Historic Pelham* (blog). http://historicpelham.blogspot.com/2016/10/pelham-was-overrun-by-ghosts-for-few.html, accessed October 29, 2019.

New Rochelle Pioneer (New Rochelle, NY). "City Island." March 3, 1888, p. 3, col. 4.

Sun (New York, NY). "City Island's Big Ghost—It Moves Along without Touching the Ground—Sometimes White and Sometimes Black—It Looks Like a Woman, but Has No Face—If It Doesn't Look Out It Will Get Shot." February 12, 1888, p. 10, col. 7.

Chapter 36

Faceless Shadow Ghost of James Street

A silent, dark specter roams the streets of the village of Pelham Manor in the area of James Street near the Esplanade. It is a pitch-black specter—never luminous or shimmery. It takes the form of a human figure that is solid black from head to toe without exception. No eyes are visible. No clothing can be detected. It is simply the color of darkness from head to toe, entirely the same shade. It might be said to resemble a shadow in three dimensions. Indeed, on dark moonless nights, the shadowy specter is nigh impossible to see. It blends into the inky blackness of the nighttide.

One who has seen the Faceless Shadow Ghost of James Street is a jovial and intelligent fellow named Bardy who lived for years in Pelham Manor. Bardy will never forget the experience.

Bardy had a pair of dogs. One was a gentle giant named Sidney. She was part black Labrador Retriever and part Newfoundland. Those who knew Bardy and Sidney knew that neither had ever met a stranger. Bardy was friendly to all and happy to stop and chat with friends and strangers alike whenever and wherever an opportunity arose. For years, Bardy often could be seen walking Sidney on a leash in the Pelham Manor neighborhood that includes James Street near the Esplanade.

Sidney likewise loved people. When passing a friend or stranger during her walks with Bardy, Sidney strained at the leash to approach and say "hello" in her special way, with tail wagging, tongue panting, and a sparkle in her bright eyes.

While walking Sidney late one dark evening on James Street just south of the Esplanade, Bardy looked ahead into the darkness and noticed something odd. The overcast night was exceptionally dark. It was difficult to make out what he saw ahead. It seemed light-colored. Oddly, it seemed suspended in midair.

Bardy squinted and looked ahead into the ink-black shadows trying to make out what the odd item might be. Keeping his focus on the strange object floating in the darkness, he and Sidney moved a little closer until Bardy could make out what looked like an ordinary white plastic shopping bag. It was, however, far from ordinary. Momentarily, at least, it seemed to float motionless before Bardy's eyes.

As Bardy stared at the shopping bag, he realized that it actually hung from something. Then, a chill raced up his spine. In a flash, Bardy realized that only six feet away there stood in the darkness a shadowy black specter that, as Bardy described, "was solid black, same shade, head to toe; face, clothes everything." A shopping bag hung from an arm of the specter. The specter's featureless face seemed to have a cigarette dangling from where its mouth should have been, though there seemed to be no mouth. Though the cigarette glowed brightly, it oddly did not illuminate the featureless face.

The dark figure stood motionless and silently in the blackness directly beside Bardy. Its appearance was startling. Though Bardy stared at the specter, there was utterly no acknowledgment from the apparition of Bardy's presence nor that of Sidney. Even more oddly, though he and the ever-loyal Sidney were only a few feet from the shadowy figure, Sidney never acknowledged its presence; never tugged at her leash; never attempted to approach the specter with her tail wagging, her tongue panting, or her eyes sparkling as she typically greeted everyone, friend or stranger. Indeed, like the specter that stood motionless and took no notice of the pair passing it, Sidney took no notice whatsoever of the specter as she trotted by with Bardy in tow. The figure remained motionless and silent. It seemed content merely to wrap itself in the blackness of the night and to stand statuesque. Bardy felt a chill and quickened his steps to hurry away. As he hurried away, he glanced back. Nothing was there.

He will never forget the experience.

If you find yourself walking the streets of Pelham Manor after dark, particularly near James Street where it meets the Esplanade, pay close attention to the shadows. Even if you hear nothing, even if you notice nothing, and even if you sense nothing, you still may want to make certain that your eyes have adjusted completely to the dark. You may have to squint as you walk along, searching the shadows diligently. If you feel that you may have seen something in the corner of your eye, quicken your step. It is well-nigh impossible to see a dark, faceless shadow specter enveloped in the shadows on a dark night.

So far, at least, the Faceless Shadow Ghost of James Street remains silent and harmless. Be careful out there in the dark of the manor, however. One never knows.

Of course, the Faceless Shadow Ghost of James Street seen by Bardy while walking his dog, Sidney, in recent years seems eerily similar to the Faceless Shadow Ghost of City Island seen only a few miles away on February 5, 1888. The Faceless Shadow Ghost of City Island has been described as follows: "It is a pitch-black specter—never luminous or shimmery. It takes the form of a human figure that is solid black from head to toe without exception. No eyes are visible. No clothing can be detected. It is simply the color of darkness from head to toe, entirely the same shade. It might be said to resemble a shadow in three dimensions. Indeed, on dark moonless nights, the shadowy specter is nigh impossible to see. It blends into the blackness of the nighttide." Those who consider such things may well wonder if the Faceless Shadow Ghost of James Street is the same Faceless Shadow Ghost that haunted nearby City Island more than 125 years before. Those who believe in the paranormal have a name for such dark phantoms. They call them "Shadow People."

The Shadow People are out there haunting James Street in Pelham Manor and the streets of City Island. Watch out.

Read More

Bell, Blake A. "The Shadowy Specter of James Street: A Pelham Manor Ghost Story." *Historic Pelham* (blog). http://historicpelham.blogspot.com/2015/10/the-shadowy-specter-of-james-street.html, accessed October 29, 2019.

Chapter 37

Fiery-Eyed Phantom of Pelham Heights

Trolley conductor Joseph Martin bounced a little as he stood in the aisle of his Union Electric Railway trolley car. The little car clacked along the tracks of East Third Street in Mount Vernon as it neared the East Third Street Bridge over the Hutchinson River at the border with Pelham. He checked his pocket watch in the dim light of the car and smiled at his friend, the motorman operating the trolley. It was 7:59 p.m. as the trolley neared the bridge. It would arrive at its stop at the bridge exactly as scheduled at 8:00 p.m. on that evening of Thursday, November 29, 1894. The handful of passengers on board seemed drowsy with heads bowed or bobbing as they sat quietly in their cane seats.

Martin stood near the front of the little trolley car by the motorman. As the little car neared its terminus at the bridge, he and the motorman gasped. Ahead at the Pelhamville border they saw a luminous white cloud appear and take a human shape. It had "mammoth eyes like balls of fire."[1] As the pair stared, flames belched forth from the mouth of the phantom lighting the tracks and roadway ahead in a bright orange glow.

Startled by the gasps of the conductor and motorman, the passengers behind them leaned out of their seats and stared ahead into the darkness. They, too, saw the fiery-eyed phantom belching its frightening flames. Then, as quickly as the terrible specter appeared, it floated off the roadway and disappeared into the woods of Pelham Heights. The Fiery-Eyed Phantom of Pelham Heights was gone, leaving behind only the excited murmurs of the trembling operators and passengers of a dark trolley car at the East Third Street Bridge.

Pelham Heights in 1894

In 1894, the half-mile stretch along Boulevard from the Mount Vernon border was a quiet neighborhood of widely separated residential homes in a quiet, undeveloped area. It would be more than twenty years later when construction began on today's Pelham Memorial High School. A trolley line ran along tracks in the roadways from East Third Street in Mount Vernon onto a short stretch of Boulevard. The tracks on that short stretch of Boulevard ended when they joined those of the trolley line that ran up and down Wolfs Lane at that point.

For a time in late 1894, the Fiery-Eyed Phantom of Pelham Heights haunted the neighborhood where East Third Street in Mount Vernon becomes Boulevard at the border with Pelham Heights. The phantom wandered the neighborhood along Boulevard as far as a half mile from the Mount Vernon border. Some say that the frightful phantom wanders there still.

The phantom always emerged from the darkness of nearby woods in Pelham Heights near its border with Mount Vernon. The apparition danced in the roads, particularly on Boulevard. When approached, the frightening specter would "recede, wave its long arms and then disappear again, as if the ground opened to receive it."

The First Sighting by Those on Conductor Martin's Trolley Car

On December 6, 1894, daily and evening newspapers in New York City published sensational accounts of the initial sighting of the Fiery-Eyed Phantom. According to the news accounts, a week earlier trolley car conductor Martin was aboard his trolley at the Pelham / Mount Vernon border where East Third Street becomes Boulevard. There were passengers in the trolley car with him. Suddenly he saw a phantom ahead in the roadway. According to the account, he described the specter as follows: "It looked . . . like a white cloud shaped like a human being, with a large head and mammoth eyes like balls of fire, and from its mouth shot flames." The specter never spoke and, soon, disappeared. Significantly, Martin's trolley passengers also saw the ghost.

Martin was so frightened by what he saw that he reported the incident to the president of the trolley company. He reported he had never been so frightened in his life. Indeed, Martin and his motorman were so upset by the incident that later the same evening the motorman accidentally slammed his car into another trolley. The motorman was "almost killed" and Martin was "severely injured," though no passengers were hurt.

Martin convinced himself after the accident that the ghost actually had appeared to him and his passengers to warn them of the danger of the impending trolley car crash. Despite his conclusion regarding the ghost's beneficent motives, Martin remained so frightened that he refused to allow his trolley car to linger in the neighborhood and told others that he no longer wanted the company to run a car on the line.

Others See the Fiery-Eyed Phantom

Within days of the first sighting, "several citizens" reported seeing the same specter. Indeed, so many additional reports flowed in that Mount Vernon police officers began an investigation at the border with Pelham. Police Officer Emil J. Vollmer investigated but returned without apprehending the phantom.

Watch Officer Jacob Josephson, however, had an entirely different experience. He went to the area and saw the ghost. According to one account: "To him it looked large and formidable. It would come out of the woods and dance on the road, but when Josephson advanced the ghost would recede, wave its long arms and then disappear again, as if the ground opened to receive it."

A few days later, the Fiery-Eyed Phantom of Pelham Heights either changed shape or a second ghost began haunting the same neighborhood. The ghost appeared to Frank Peebles of New Rochelle as he walked through Pelham Heights toward New Rochelle on Boulevard about a half mile from Pelham's border with New Rochelle. According to a news report of the encounter:

> Frank Peebles, a resident of New Rochelle, reported to Chief of Police Foley, at Mount Vernon, last evening that he was intercepted a few nights ago by a ghost as he was walking through Pelham Heights, half a mile from where Martin says he saw it. His ghostship was standing in the middle of the road, and as Peebles would try to pass to one side, the ghost

would jump in front, all the time keeping well in advance. He had a good chance to see the spook. It was about seven feet in height, large head with horns, probably formed by a painted cap; hanging to its side it had large wings, which, when flapped, spread from one side of the road to the other. It seemed illuminated from within. Peebles says he does not know how he got past the ghost, but he shut his eyes hard and ran, and didn't stop until he fell exhausted at his house door in New Rochelle.

So many reports of the Fiery-Eyed Phantom of Pelham Heights surfaced in such a short time that the Mount Vernon police chief Jeremiah Foley decided to investigate the matter himself. Wisely, he chose to bring a group of fellows with him, apparently for comfort. Though research has not yet revealed an account of the investigation, the police chief surely knew that one of his own police officers had witnessed the Fiery-Eyed Phantom of Pelham Heights. A New York City newspaper reported:

> A ghost, white and cloudlike [sic], with wings and horns and with a mouth that breathes forth fire, is said to haunt the district between Mt. Vernon and Pelhamville. Car Conductor Martin, Police Officer Vollmer and Watch Officer Josephson say they have seen the ghostly visitor.[2]

Vigilantes Go on a Ghost Hunt

As the number of sightings rose, a young man named Hudson organized a group of armed vigilantes. Hudson announced that on the evening of December 6, 1894, he and his posse would arm themselves with guns and "patrol the haunted district." The announcement, of course, was laughable. Everyone knows you cannot shoot a true ghost with a gun . . . As one might expect, the announcement created a circus-like atmosphere.

Reporters for three New York City newspapers got wind of the ghost hunt. Each newspaper sent reporters to the border of Pelham Heights and Mount Vernon to cover the festivities. Nearly one hundred people flooded into the area on the appointed night expecting, as one newspaper reported, to witness "a contest between the ghostly being and its human hunters."[3]

Alas, the massive crowd of ghost hunters struck out. After roaming the region far and wide throughout the night, all they found was "a stuffed figure some fun-loving spirits propped up between the [trolley] car tracks, intended as a fright to the motorman."[4] The Fiery-Eyed Phantom of Pelham Heights, it turned out, was smarter than its pursuers that night.

Read More

Bell, Blake A. "The Fiery-Eyed Phantom of Pelham Heights." *Historic Pelham* (blog). http://historicpelham.blogspot.com/2016/10/the-fiery-eyed-phantom-of-pelham-heights.html, accessed October 29, 2019.

Chronicle (Mount Vernon, NY). "A Ghost Is with Us." December 6, 1894, vol. 25, no. 1666, p. 2, col. 2.

Chronicle (Mount Vernon, NY). "Sequel to Ghost Story." December 13, 1894, vol. 25, no. 1667, p. 8, col. 1.

Evening World (New York, NY). "To Lay Mt. Vernon's Ghost—It Has Wings and Fiery Eyes, and Police Chief Foley and Others Will Seek It To-Night—Citizens Have Been Frightened—Even a Trolley Car Conductor Dreads to Pass the Spot Where the Spook Has Made Its Home." December 6, 1894, p. 7, col. 1.

Evening World (New York, NY). "May Be a Christmas Ghost." December 6, 1894, p. 7, col. 1.

Notes

Preface

1. Diane E. Goldstein, Sylvia Ann Grider, and Jeannie Banks Thomas, *Haunting Experiences: Ghosts in Contemporary Folklore* (Logan: Utah State University Press, 2007), 26.

2. Goldstein, Grider, and Thomas, *Haunting Experiences*, 31.

Part I. Indigenous American Hauntings

1. See Robert Bolton Jr., *A History of the County of Westchester from Its First Settlement to the Present Time* (New York: Alexander S. Gould, 1848), 1: ix, 65, 517.

2. See, for example, Reginald Pelham Bolton, "Snakapins, a Siwanoy Site at Clasons Point," in *Contributions from the Museum of the American Indian Heye Foundation* (New York: Museum of the American Indian Heye Foundation, 1919), vol. 5, no. 4, part 2, 75–126; Alanson Skinner, "Exploration of Aboriginal Sites at Throgs Neck and Clasons Point," in *Contributions from the Museum of the American Indian Heye Foundation* (New York: 1919), vol. 5, no. 4, part 1, 46–74; John R. Swanton, "The Indian Tribes of North America," in *Bureau of American Ethnology Bulletin* (Washington, DC: US Government Printing Office, 1952), 145: 45–47; Reginald Pelham Bolton, "New York City in Indian Possession," in *Indian Notes and Monographs* (New York: Museum of the American Indian Heye Foundation, 1920), vol. 2, no. 7, 219, 254.

3. Notes of presentation by Dr. David Oestreicher delivered at Saint Paul's Church National Historic Site, 897 South Columbus Ave., Mount Vernon, NY 10550 on January 13, 2007 (copy in files of the author).

4. John Alexander Buckland, *The First Traders on Wall Street: The Wiechquaeskeck Indians of Southwestern Connecticut in the Seventeenth Century* (Westminster, MD: Heritage Books, 2009), xiii.

5. Paul Otto, *The Dutch-Munsee Encounter in America: The Struggle for Sovereignty in the Hudson Valley* (New York: Berghahn Books 2006), 4.

6. Otto, *Dutch-Munsee Encounter in America*, 3.

7. Otto, *Dutch-Munsee Encounter in America*, 4 (citing Robert Grumet, "'We Are Not So Great Fools': Changes in Upper Delawaran Socio-politico Life, 1630–1758," PhD dissertation, Rutgers, the State University of New Jersey, 1979, 23–28).

8. Otto, *Dutch-Munsee Encounter in* America, 4.

9. Otto, *Dutch-Munsee Encounter in America*, 4.

10. Otto, *Dutch-Munsee Encounter in America*, 4–5. Extensive research of period records has revealed to this author more than fifty spellings of the label for this Munsee group. This work will follow the custom of more recent scholarship including that of Dr. Paul Otto by referring to the group as "Wiechquaeskecks."

11. For a helpful map showing the approximate area inhabited by Munsee groups or bands including the Wiechquaeskecks in the early seventeenth century, see Otto, *Dutch-Munsee Encounter in America*, 5 ("Map 2: Munsee Bands in the Early Seventeenth Century").

Chapter 1. Headless Apparitions of the Haunted Cedar Knoll

1. Some accounts claim that the rival tribes were the Matinecocks of Sewanhacky and the Siwanoys of Laaphawachking. See, for example, Robert Bolton, *The History of the Several Towns, Manors, and Patents of the County of Westchester, from Its First Settlement to the Present Time Carefully Revised by Its Author* (New York: Chas. F. Roper, 1881), 2: 37.

2. "Legends of Pelham," *New-York Daily Tribune*, December 15, 1901, p. 2, cols. 1–4.

Chapter 2. Spirit of the Siwanoy Brave

1. All quotations in this chapter are from a fragment of an unidentified newspaper clipping in the collection of the Office of the Historian of the Town of Pelham (copy in possession of the author).

Part II. Revolutionary War Specters

1. James B. Saunders, ed., *The Pelham Manor Story* (Pelham Manor, NY: Privately printed, 1991), 32–44.

2. Alfred M. Franko, *Pelham Manor: The Forgotten Battle of the Revolution Near Mount Vernon, New York*, rev. ed (Pelham, NY: Bicentennial Committee of the Town of Pelham, New York, 1975), 3.

3. William Abbatt, *The Battle of Pell's Point (Or Pelham) October 18, 1776. Being the Story of a Stubborn Fight. With a Map, and Illustrations from Original Photographs and Family Portraits* (New York: Privately printed, 1901), preface (referencing "the official record of services of two regiments of the British Army—the Sixteenth and Seventeenth Lancers—it is stated that they were engaged in the battle of 'Pelham Moor' ").

4. George Athan Billias, *General Glover and His Marblehead Mariners* (New York: Henry Holt, 1960), 110–23.

5. Otto Hufeland, *Westchester County during the American Revolution 1775–1783* (White Plains, NY: Westchester County Historical Society, 1926), 467.

6. Abbatt, *Battle of Pell's Point.*

7. Susan Cochran, Swanson, "Colonel Glover's Stand at Pelham," *American History Illustrated* 15, no. 2 (May 1980): 14.

8. Billias, *General Glover.*

9. See, for example, Franko, *Pelham Manor*, 27.

10. Franko, *Pelham Manor*, 25.

11. Franko, *Pelham Manor*, 33.

12. Franko, *Pelham Manor*, 34.

13. Franko, *Pelham Manor*, 31 (quoting Glover's "Letter from Mile Square, Oct. 24, 1776" that was printed in the *Freeman Journal* and in the *New Hampshire Gazette* on November 26, 1776).

14. Thomas F. De Voe, *Genealogy of the De Veaux Family—Introducing the Numerous Forms of Spelling the Name by Various Branches and Generations in the Past Eleven Hundred Years* (New York: Privately printed, 1895), 110–11.

15. See *The American Heritage Dictionary of the English Language*, 4th ed. London: Houghton Mifflin, 2000).

16. See Franko, *Pelham Manor*, 39.

17. Franko, *Pelham Manor*, 32.

18. Franko, *Pelham Manor*, 32.

19. Franko, *Pelham Manor*, 32.

20. Franko, *Pelham Manor*, 32.

21. Franko, *Pelham Manor*, 32.

22. Franko, *Pelham Manor*, 32.

23. See Franko, *Pelham Manor*, 40.

24. Franko, *Pelham Manor*, 32–33.

25. Franko, *Pelham Manor*, 33.

26. Franko, *Pelham Manor*, 33.

27. De Voe, *Genealogy of the De Veaux Family*, 110–11.

28. David Osborn, "The Hessians," in *National Park Service History of St. Paul's Church*, https://www.nps.gov/sapa/learn/historyculture/upload/The%20Hessians.pdf.

Chapter 6. Ghostly Cow Rustlers of Pelham Road

1. Henry T. Cook and Nathan J. Kaplan, *The Borough of the Bronx 1639–1913: Its Marvelous Development and Historical Surroundings* (New York: Published by the authors, 1913), 130–31.

Chapter 7. Specter of the British Spy

1. Henry T. Cook and Nathan J. Kaplan, *The Borough of the Bronx 1639–1913: Its Marvelous Development and Historical Surroundings* (New York: Published by the authors, 1913), 130–31.

Chapter 9. Another Vanishing Soldier

1. See Pryer, *Reminiscences of an Old Westchester Homestead*, 104–09.
2. Pryer, *Reminiscences of an Old Westchester Homestead*, 108–09.

Part III. Ghostly Treasure Guards

1. See "Vicinity Notes," *Eastern State Journal* (White Plains, NY), August 29, 1884, vol. 40, no. 21, p. 2, col. 3.
2. See "Treasure in an Old Safe," *New York Times*, April 21, 1889, p. 20, col. 7.
3. See "Pewter Plates, Manufactured Before Revolution Unearthed in Pelham Manor," *Pelham Sun*, September 23, 1938, vol. 28, no. 25, p. 1, cols. 1–2.
4. Charles Pryer, "The Old Historic Buildings of Westchester County," in *The American Numismatic and Archaeological Society of New York City List of Meetings Held and Papers Read Before the Society under the Direction of the Committee on Papers and Publications, 1898–1899* (New York: American Numismatic and Archaeological Society of New York City, 1899), 38–39.
5. "William Kidd," Wikipedia, https://en.wikipedia.org/wiki/William_Kidd.
6. See, for example, "The Huguenots—The Settlement and History of New Rochelle . . . Captain Kidd," *Kansas Chief* (Troy, KS), January 18, 1877, vol. 20, no. 31, p. 1, cols. 4–5; Untitled, *Buffalo Commercial Advertiser* (Buffalo, NY), July 11, 1876, vol. 45, no. 15018, p. 1, col. 6.
7. "The Huguenots—The Settlement and History of New Rochelle . . . Captain Kidd."

Chapter 11. Elegant Lady of the Old Stone House

1. See "Almost Another Hull Case," *Rochester Daily Union and Advertiser*, July 18, 1879, vol. 54, no. 169, p. 1, col. 3 (reprinted from July 17, 1879 issue of *New York Herald*).
2. "Almost Another Hull Case."
3. See "Burglaries in Pelhamville," *Chronicle* (Mount Vernon, NY), July 18, 1879, vol. 10, no. 513, p. 2, col. 1.
4. Lockwood Anderson Barr, *A Brief, but Most Complete and True Account of the Settlement of the Ancient Town of Pelham Westchester County, State of New York Known One Time Well and Favourably as the Lordshipp and Manour of Pelham Also the Story of the Three Modern Villages Called the Pelhams* (Richmond, VA: Dietz Press, 1946), 135–36.
5. See "Legend Gathers about Old Stone House Landmark for 85 Years in No. Pelham—Georgian House, Occupied by Mr. and Mrs. F. M. Snyder, Unique in Village, Attracts Many Visitors," *Pelham Sun*, August 23, 1935, vol. 26, no. 21, p. 3, cols. 1–2.

Part IV. Phantom Ships Off Pelham Shores

1. Tom Nye, Subject Re: Rondel Painting: City Island, email from Tom Nye to Jorge Santiago, October 23, 2013, 9:48:37 a.m. Eastern Daylight Time (copy in files of the author).
2. Nye, Subject Re: Rondel Painting.
3. Nye, Subject Re: Rondel Painting.
4. Nye, Subject Re: Rondel Painting.
5. Nye, Subject Re: Rondel Painting.
6. See "Marine List," *Evening Post* (New York, NY), February 14, 1821, no. 5818, p. 3, col. 1.
7. Henry Wadsworth Longfellow, "The Phantom Ship," in *The Poetical Works of Henry Wadsworth Longfellow, with Bibliographical and Critical Notes in Six Volumes* (Boston: Houghton, Mifflin, Riverside Press, 1890), 3: 23–24.

Chapter 12. Fiery Phantom Ship of Long Island Sound

1. Augustus E. Silliman, *A Gallop among American Scenery: Or, Sketches of American Scenes and Military Adventure* (New York: D. Appleton, 1843), 265.
2. Robert Bolton Jr., *A History of the County of Westchester from Its First Settlement to the Present Time* (New York: Alexander S. Gould, 1848), 1: 434–35.

Chapter 13. Ghostly Gunship of Long Island Sound

1. Charles Pryer, *Reminiscences of an Old Westchester Homestead* (New York: G. P. Putnam's Sons, Knickerbocker Press, 1897), 72–73.

Chapter 14. Ghost Ship *Palatine* and Its Mad Specter

1. John Greenleaf Whittier, "The Palatine," in *Personal Poems—Occasional Poems: The Tent on the Beach by John Greenleaf Whittier with the Poems of Elizabeth H. Whittier and an Appendix Containing Early and Uncollected Verses* (Boston: Houghton, Mifflin, Riverside Press, 1888), 278.

Part V. Ghosts of the Murdered, Insane, and Suicidal

1. One of most terrible murder mysteries in Pelham history was the killing of wealthy Pelham Heights resident Julius Rosenheimer in 1906. He was beaten to death in the garden of his home known as "The Roses." Although police arrested several suspects over the years that followed, none was convicted of the murder, which remains unsolved despite a large reward offered by the family. See "Today's True Detective Story—The Murder in the Garden," *Brooklyn Daily Eagle*, August 19, 1930, 90th Year, no. 229, p. 14, col. 3.

2. On October 27, 1896, armed highway men sprang from behind a stone wall near the intersection of Jackson Avenue and Peace Street and robbed Josiah M. Bertine; his fifteen-year-old daughter, Mary; and their liveryman, John Royal, as they neared their home in the family's horse-drawn carriage. The liveryman fled. Josiah Bertine tried to wrestle a pistol from one of the men and shots were fired, striking the horse, which later died. The robbers later were identified, captured, and successfully prosecuted. See "Victim of a League to Kill," *New York Herald*, October 29, 1896, p. 5, col. 6 and p. 6, col. 1.

3. For example, in the late nineteenth century and the early years of the twentieth century burglars repeatedly used dynamite to blow up safes in the Pelham Manor post office located in the Pelham Manor Depot. See, for example, "Extra—Cracksmen at Pelham Manor Post Office—Baffled This Time by a New Safe—Their Fourth Visit of the Year," *Daily Argus* (Mount Vernon, NY), November 12, 1894, vol. 3, no. 798, p. 1, col. 6; "Burglars Use Dynamite," *New Rochelle Pioneer* (New Rochelle, NY), April 26, 1902, vol. 44, no. 6, p. 1, col. 1.

4. As noted in the chapter entitled "Elegant Lady of the Old Stone House," masked robbers reportedly broke into the home of the widow Mary Parrish in 1879, robbed her, and left her tied to her bed. See "Almost Another

Hull Case," *Rochester Daily Union and Advertiser*, July 18, 1879, vol. 54, no. 169, p. 1, col. 3 (reprinted from July 17, 1879, issue of *New York Herald*). Similarly, masked robbers invaded the home of the Emmett family (a home that still stands at 145 Shore Road) on December 23, 1873. They robbed and terrorized the family but were later identified, caught, tried, and convicted of the home invasion. See, for example, "The Masked Burglars—Trial of 'Patsy' Conway at White Plains, Westchester County—A Story of Nocturnal Violence Told by the Victims—The Prisoner Identified as 'Captain of the Gang,'" *New York Herald*, February 18, 1874, no. 13695, p. 4, col. 6.

 5. For some of hundreds of examples of news stories about the gruesome crime, see "The Eudora Tragedy," *Eastern State Journal* (White Plains, NY), May 16, 1856, vol. 12, no. 1, p. 1, col. 6; "The Eudora Tragedy—Capt. Palmer's Body Identified—Verdict of the Jury," *New-York Daily Tribune*, May 14, 1856, vol. 16, no. 4702, p. 7, col. 3.

 6. See "All about Oysters—Commissioner Blackford Enlightened by the Inhabitants of City Island—How the Beds Are Ruined—City Refuse Dumped on the Oysters—the State Investigation," *New York Herald*, November 24, 1884, no. 17627, p. 10, col. 3.

 7. Reginald Pelham Bolton, *A Woman Misunderstood: Anne, Wife of William Hutchinson* (New York: Printed for the author by Schoen, 1931), 123 ("It was a summer evening, probably the twentieth of August").

 8. Eve LaPlante, *American Jezebel: The Uncommon Life of Anne Hutchinson, the Woman Who Defied the Puritans* (San Francisco: Harper Collins, 2004), 237.

 9. See Katherine Kirkpatrick, *Trouble's Daughter: The Story of Susanna Hutchinson, Indian Captive* (New York: Delacorte Press, 1998), 228.

 10. LaPlante, *American Jezebel*, 237.

 11. Robert Bolton Jr., *A History of the County of Westchester from Its First Settlement to the Present Time* (New York: Alexander Gould, 1848), 1: 515.

 12. Robert Bolton Jr., *The History of the Several Towns, Manors and Patents of the County of Westchester, from Its First Settlement to the Present Time Carefully Revised by Its Author* (New York: Chas. F. Roper, 1881), 2: 29.

 13. Bolton, *History of the Several Towns*, 32 (emphasis added).

 14. Bolton, *History of the Several Towns*, 32 and n.b.

 15. See Otto Hufeland, "Anne Hutchinson's Refuge in the Wilderness—The Second Settler in Westchester County—Where She Settled in 1642 and Died in Anne Hutchinson—Did She Live in Pelham?," in *Publications of the Westchester County Historical Society* (White Plains, NY: Westchester County Historical Society, 1929), 7: 1–20.

 16. Hufeland, "Anne Hutchinson's Refuge in the Wilderness," 5–6.

 17. Bolton, *A Woman Misunderstood*, 110.

 18. Hufeland, "Anne Hutchinson's Refuge in the Wilderness," 10–11. See also Bolton, *A History of the County of Westchester*, 1: 122.

19. Bolton, *A History of the County of Westchester*, 1: 122.

20. Hufeland, "Anne Hutchinson's Refuge in the Wilderness," 11. See also Bolton, *A History of the County of Westchester*, 1: 125–26.

21. See Hufeland, "Anne Hutchinson's Refuge in the Wilderness," one of two maps between pages 18 and 19 ("Copy of map of land in Eastchester granted to William Peartree and Associates by Queen Anne in 1708. Original in Secretary of State's Office, Albany, N.Y.").

22. See Hufeland, "Anne Hutchinson's Refuge in the Wilderness" ("Copy of another map of land in Eastchester granted to William Peartree and Associates by Queen Anne in 1708. Original in Secretary of State's Office, Albany, N.Y.").

23. Hufeland, "Anne Hutchinson's Refuge in the Wilderness," 19–20. Even local historian Reginald Pelham Bolton, who had written a previous article that misplaced the location of Hutchinson's home, accepted Hufeland's conclusions. See Bolton, *A Woman Misunderstood*, 106–18.

Part VI. Wailing Ghosts of Pelham

1. For an interesting summary of such recent scholarship, including work by scientists at Laurentian University in Sudbury, Ontario, Canada; Goldsmiths, University of London College; Coventry University in England; and others, see Adam Marcus, "Mind: Ghost Lusters—If You Want to See a Specter Badly Enough, Will You?," *Scientific American*, October 27, 2008, https://www.scientificamerican.com/article/ghost-lusters-if-you-want/, accessed January 5, 2021.

2. Dale Kaczmarek, "A Typical Ghost?," Ghost Research Society, 2011, http://ghostresearch.org/articles/typical.html, accessed January 5, 2021.

3. Adam J. Powell and Peter Moseley, "When Spirits Speak: Absorption, Attribution, and Identity among Spiritualists Who Report 'Clairaudient' Voice Experiences," *Mental Health, Religion and Culture* 23, no. 10 (January 2021), https://doi.org/10.1080/13674676.2020.1793310, accessed January 20, 2021.

Chapter 19. Moaning Ghost of Hart Island

1. See, for example, *The War of the Rebellion: A Compilation of the Official Records of the Union and Confederate Armies*, Series 2 (Washington, DC: Government Printing Office, 1899), 8: 647–48, 660–61, 664–66, 684.

2. See "Spooks on Hart Island," *New York Evening Express*, September 25, 1865, p. 4, col. 6 (remaining quoted references in this chapter are from this source).

Chapter 20. Shrieking Ghost of Wolfs Lane

1. "Posse after a Ghost—Many Pelhamites Had Heard It and Some Said They Had Seen It," *New York Times*, August 21, 1905, vol. 54, no. 17376, p. 7, col. 2 (remaining quoted references in this chapter are from this source).

Part VIII. Haunted Houses and Ghosts of Pelham Mansions

1. Barbara G. Bartlett, Mary B. Buckley, Nancy M. Wheeler, and Gwendolyn B. Wolf, *A Glance at the Past* (Pelham, NY: Junior League of Pelham, 1975), 3.

Chapter 26. Ghost of the Haunted Hardenbrook House

1. See "All Sure They Saw a Ghost," *World* (New York, NY), October 8, 1893, vol. 34, no. 11737, p. 19, cols. 1–3 (remaining quoted references in this chapter are from this source).

Chapter 27. Spirits of Bartow-Pell Mansion

1. Margaret Highland, "Crowning Glory: Bartow-Pell's Lannuier Bedstead," *Mansion Musings* (WordPress blog), June 27, 2016, https://mansionmusings.wordpress.com/2016/06/27/crowning-glory-bartow-pells-lannuier-bedstead/, accessed January 5, 2021.
2. "Haunted by Houses," *Villager*, October 22, 2015, https://www.thevillager.com/2015/10/haunted-by-houses-3/, accessed January 5, 2021.

Chapter 28. Ghostly Gardener of Bolton Priory

1. See "Fire Rages through Upper Story of Historic Bolton Priory; Loss May Total $100,000; Will Be Rebuilt," *Pelham Sun*, July 22, 1932, vol. 23, no. 18, p. 1, cols. 3–5, and p. 8, cols. 6–7.
2. See "Negro Prowler at Bolton Priory Gets 15-Day Jail Term," *Pelham Sun*, May 3, 1935, vol. 26, no. 4, p. 1, col. 3.
3. See "Christ's Church Guild Holds Charming Tea at Bolton Priory," *Pelham Sun*, June 5, 1931, p. 5, cols. 5–7.

Chapter 31. Luminous Lantern-Bearer of Baychester and Pelham Bridge

1. "Story of Explosions—People Object to an Earthquake Factory in Their Midst," *Republic* (Columbus, IN), January 23, 1884, p. 1, col. 3.
2. "Westchester," *Chronicle* (Mount Vernon, NY), March 19, 1886, vol. 17, no. 864, p. 1, col. 5.
3. "The County—A Ghost Scare," *Yonkers Statesman*, March 20, 1886, vol. 3, no. 722, p. 1, col. 4.

Chapter 32. Wandering Ghost of the Mad Chemist

1. See, for example, "Blown High in the Air—A Nitro-glycerine Explosion That Shook the Town of Pelham—An Astonished Detective Seeing a Building Vanish from Sight—Two Men Making Haste for Their Lives—Suspicion Aroused," *Sun* (New York, NY), October 11, 1878, vol. 46, no. 41, p. 3, col. 5.
2. See, for example, "Blown High in the Air" (October, 1878, explosion that shook Pelham and destroyed the Neptune Powder Mill). See also "Powder Mill Explosion," *New York Herald*, October 11, 1878, p. 7, col. 4 (same); "Blown to Atoms—Explosion in the Neptune Powder Mill in Pelham," *Daily Graphic* (New York, NY), October 10, 1878, p. 700, col. 4 (same); "Casualties," *Syracuse Daily Journal*, October 11, 1878, vol. 34, no. 23, p. 4, col. 4 (same); "Explosion in a Powder Mill—Richard S. Howe Loses His Life—Narrow Escape of His Assistant," *New York Tribune*, August 30, 1879, vol. 39, no. 11990, p. 10, col. 5 (August 28, 1879, explosion kills one at rebuilt Neptune Powder Mill).
3. See "Died," *New York Herald*, September 27, 1885, no. 17933, p. 15, cols. 1–2.
4. See "Baychester Alarmed," *Yonkers Statesman* (Yonkers, NY), November 13, 1885, vol. 3, no. 617, p. 1, col. 4.
5. See "Local Intelligence," *New Rochelle Pioneer* (New Rochelle, NY), November 14, 1885, p. 3, cols. 1–2. See also Untitled, *Recorder* (Mount Kisco, NY), November 13, 1885, vol. 12, no. 32, p. 8, col. 2 (same text).
6. See "The Ghost and the Dynamiter," *New York Herald*, November 18, 1885, no. 17985, p. 8, col. 6.
7. See "They Do Not Want to See It," *Yonkers Statesman* (Yonkers, NY), November 18, 1885, vol. 3, no. 621, p. 1, col. 4.
8. See "Baychester Alarmed," *Yonkers Statesman* (Yonkers, NY), November 13, 1885, vol. 3, no. 617, p. 1, col. 4.

9. See "Westchester," *Chronicle Supplement*, November 20, 1885, p. 1, cols. 2–3 (one-page supplement to the November 20, 1885, issue of the *Chronicle* [Mount Vernon, NY], vol. 17, no. 844).

10. "Westchester."

Chapter 34. Floating White Phantom of City Island

1. "City Island's Big Ghost—It Moves Along without Touching the Ground—Sometimes White and Sometimes Black—It Looks Like a Woman, but Has No Face—If It Doesn't Look Out It Will Get Shot," *Sun* (New York, NY), February 12, 1888, p. 10, col. 7 (remaining quoted references in this chapter are from this source).

Chapter 35. Faceless Shadow Ghost of City Island

1. "City Island's Big Ghost—It Moves Along without Touching the Ground—Sometimes White and Sometimes Black—It Looks Like a Woman, but Has No Face—If It Doesn't Look Out It Will Get Shot," *Sun* (New York, NY), February 12, 1888, p. 10, col. 7 (remaining quoted references in this chapter are from this source).

Chapter 37. Fiery-Eyed Phantom of Pelham Heights

1. "To Lay Mt. Vernon's Ghost—It Has Wings and Fiery Eyes, and Police Chief Foley and Others Will Seek It To-Night—Citizens Have Been Frightened—Even a Trolley Car Conductor Dreads to Pass the Spot Where the Spook Has Made Its Home," *World* (New York, NY), December 6, 1894, p. 2, col. 6 (unless otherwise indicated by note, remaining quoted references in this chapter are from this source).

2. "May Be a Christmas Ghost," *Evening World* (New York, NY), December 6, 1894, p. 7, col. 1.

3. "Sequel to Ghost Story," *Chronicle* (Mount Vernon, NY), December 13, 1894, vol. 25, no. 1667, p. 8, col. 1.

4. "Sequel to Ghost Story."

About the Author

Blake A. Bell served as town historian of Pelham, New York, from 2005 through 2020. Before that he served as deputy town historian. He sharpened research skills as a New York City attorney with 980-lawyer Simpson Thacher & Bartlett LLP for more than thirty years before retiring in 2020. Before that he practiced with Cravath, Swaine & Moore LLP. He has served as a member of the boards of trustees of the Westchester County Historical Society (including service on the executive committee), the Society of the National Shrine of the Bill of Rights at Saint Paul's Church National Historic Site (including service as chairperson), and the Pelham Preservation & Garden Society. He also served as Pelham town clerk for three years and as a member of the Pelham Town Board for eight years.

Blake is the author of two previous books on the history of Pelham: *Thomas Pell and the Legend of the Pell Treaty Oak* and *Town of Pelham's 350th Anniversary Celebration: Historian Blake Bell's Articles Published in the Pelham Weekly plus Photos of Key Events*. In addition, he is author of more than eighty articles on Pelham history published in history journals, magazines, and newspapers. He served as the editor and publisher of the award-winning HistoricPelham.com website (now archived) as well as author and publisher of the *Historic Pelham* blog (HistoricPelham.Blogspot.com) on which he published more than 2,350 articles on Pelham history.

Blake has researched and collected Pelham ghost stories for more than two decades. As Pelham historian, he delved deeply into historic events associated with the ghost stories he uncovered. He has documented the lives of local citizens who witnessed Pelham phantoms and has woven appropriate details of those lives with eyewitness accounts of strange and unusual Pelham ghost sightings.

Index

5 Manger Circle, 104, 105
  Suicidal Specter of Manger Circle, 104–105
45 Iden Avenue, 17, 94, 136. See also Pelhamdale
  Ghost of Anne Hutchinson, 91–94
  Ghost of the Indian Maiden of Pelhamdale, 13–18
  Poltergeist of Pelhamdale, 36–138
175 City Island Avenue, 68
463 First Avenue, 63, 65, 164. See also Old Stone House
  Elegant Lady of the Old Stone House, 61–66
  More Ghosts of the Old Stone House, 164–165

Adventure Prize, 53
Albany, 89, 202
Algonquian, 2
All Hallow's Eve, 100, 159, 161, 173. See also Halloween
American Society of Engineers, 33
Angelic Presence, 154
Anglican, 133
Anhõõke, 3
Antinomian Controversy, 91
Applebaugh, William, 181, 182
Army Corps of Engineers, 21

Baldwin, Col. Loammi, 29, 30. See also Battle of Pelham
Bardy (of Pelham Manor), 187, 188, 189
  Faceless Shadow Ghost of James Street, 187–189
Barr, Lockwood, 17, 65, 66, 199
Bartow, 95, 96, 97, 98, 99, 100, 101, 102, 103, 133, 139, 146, 148, 149, 150, 151, 152, 153, 154, 170, 172, 203
Bartow, Clarina, 153
Bartow Family, 149, 153, 154. See also Bartow
Bartow, George Lorillard, 151, 152
Bartow, Maria Lorillard, 151, 153, 154
Bartow, Reverend John, 133
Bartow, Robert, 148, 151, 154
Bartow, Settlement of, 99, 100, 101, 102, 103, 146, 149, 170, 172
Bartow Station, 100, 102, 149
Bartow-Pell Conservancy, 150
Bartow-Pell Mansion, 95, 96, 97, 98, 139, 148, 149, 150, 151, 152, 153, 154
  Ghost of the Murdered Traveler at Bartow-Pell Mansion, 95–98
  Spirits of Bartow-Pell Mansion, 148–154

Bartow-Pell Mansion Museum, 78, 79, 115, 116, 117, 118
  Ghost of the Murdered Traveler at Bartow-Pell Mansion, 78–79
  Spirits of Bartow-Pell Mansion, 115–119
Battle of Pelham, 14, 15, 23–31 passim, 36, 49
Battle of Westchester Creek, 24, 25, 36
Baychester, 167, 168, 169, 170, 171, 172, 173, 174, 175
  Luminous Lantern-Bearer of Baychester and Pelham Bridge, 168–171
  Wandering Ghost of the Mad Chemist, 172–175
Baychester House, 174, 175
Bay View Hotel, 184. See also Von Liehn's Bay View Hotel
Bell, 52, 118, 123, 124, 125, 126, 127, 128, 129, 130, 131, 133. See also Church Bell
  Phantom Bell Ringer of Christ Church, 123–125
  Whispering Bell of Saint Paul's Church, 126–131
Bell (Sloop), 69
Bell, Blake A., 8, 18, 66, 74, 105, 116, 154, 158, 163, 171, 175, 180, 183, 186, 189, 194, 207
Bell, Liberty, 126. See also Liberty Bell
Big Tom, 56
Black Dog Brook, 87
Black Family Mansion (Pelhamdale Avenue), 140
The Blauzes, 56
Block Island, 73, 79, 80
Bolton, Cornelius Winter, 86
Bolton, Jr., Robert, 1, 2, 8, 59, 73, 74, 85, 86
  Bolton's History of Westchester County (1848 Edition), 1, 73

Bolton, Rev. Robert, 19, 155
Bolton Priory, 19, 140, 155, 156, 157, 158
  Ghostly Gardener of Bolton Priory, 155–158
Boston, 2, 10, 79, 84, 85, 91, 92
Boston Post Road, Old, 10, 14, 15, 16, 27, 31, 136. See also Colonial Avenue
Boston Turnpike (New Boston Post Road), 10, 87, 136
Boulder, 5, 6, 10, 14, 15, 20, 21, 27, 34, 56, 57, 58, 59, 85, 87. See also Glacial Boulder
  Glover's Rock, 14, 20, 27, 28
  Grey Mare, 20
  Kemble House Rocking Stone, 20
  Mishow, 20
  Priory Rocking Stone, 20
  Split Rock, 8, 10, 20, 21, 85, 87, 88, 89
Boulevard, 191, 192
Brehm, George, 160
Brooklyn, 53, 173
Bronx, The, 8, 36, 42, 47, 68, 78, 152, 175
Buckland, John Alexander, 2
  The First Traders on Wall Street: The Wiechquaeskeck Indians of Southwestern Connecticut in the Seventeenth Century, 2, 195

Captain Kidd, 53, 54, 55, 56, 57, 58, 59, 60. See also Kidd, William and Pirate
  Ghost of Captain Kidd, 56–60
Caribbean Sea, 53
Carll, David, 68, 69
Carll, Jesse, 68, 69
Carol Place, 136
Carriage House of Bartow-Pell Mansion, 148, 150

Cemetery (*see also* Pauper's Cemetery), 109, 126, 127, 130, 152, 173
Christ Church (Pelham Manor), 5, 118, 123, 124, 125, 126
  Phantom Bell Ringer of Christ Church, 123–125
Church Bell (*see also* Bell), 52, 118, 123, 124, 125, 129, 130, 131
  Phantom Bell Ringer of Christ Church, 123–125
  Whispering Bell of Saint Paul's Church, 126–131
Church of England, 133
City Island, 20, 21, 25, 28, 67, 68, 69, 71, 75, 77, 83, 84, 86, 109, 149, 167, 170, 174, 177, 178, 180, 181, 182, 183, 184, 185, 186, 189. *See also* Minneford Island
  Faceless Shadow Ghost of City Island, 184–186
  Floating White Phantom of City Island, 181–183
  Little Specter of the Field, 177–180
City Island Bridge, 184
City Island Avenue, 68, 181
City Island Road, 28
Civil War, 109, 110
Clairaudient Communications, 108
Clark, Marvin R., 141–147 *passim*
  Ghost of the Haunted Hardenbrook House, 141–147
Clark, Mrs. (Wife of Pelhamville Postmaster in 1879), 63
Cliff Avenue, 136
Clinton, Sir Henry, 31. *See also* Battle of Pelham
Collins, Stephen, 182
Collins, William, 85, 92
Colonial Avenue, 10, 14, 15, 16, 17, 27, 31, 136. *See also* Boston Post Road, Old

Columbia College, 152
Columbia Records, 157
Columbia University, 152
Condon, Martin J., 140
Confederacy (Civil War), 109
Connecticut, 2, 3, 19, 20, 77, 88
Connor, James D., 115
Continental Army, 16, 40. *See also* Battle of Pelham
Co-op City (The Bronx), 90
Cotton, Rev. John, 91
Cowboys and Skinners, 37, 38, 40, 49, 50, 51, 52, 75, 128, 129
Cuban Ledge, 56

Dana, Lieutenant (Quartermaster of Hart Island Union Military Post), 112
Davids Island, 54, 56
Darling Triplets, 181
Darling, William G., 181
Dayton, Will, 182
De Lancey, Col. James, 37
Delaware, 2
Denver, 157
De Veau, Jr., Abel, 28
Devil, 19, 20, 21. *See also* Habboamoko
  Dark Spirit of the Devil and His Stepping Stones, 19–22
Devil's Stepping Stones, 19, 20, 21, 68, 71. *See also* Stepping Stones
  Dark Spirit of the Devil and His Stepping Stones, 19–22
  Stepping Stones Light, 21
Diack, Alexander, 63
Diack Family, 66
Dittmar Powder Works, 168, 169, 170, 173, 174, 175
  Luminous Lantern-Bearer of Baychester and Pelham Bridge, 168–171
  Wandering Ghost of the Mad Chemist, 172–176

Doty, Girard Post "Pop," 36
Doty, Edward, 36
Doty, Warren, 36
Durham University, 108
Dutch, 3, 80, 81, 84, 85, 86, 92, 93, 104
Dutch Elm Disease, 104

Earthquake Factories, 168
East No Nations, 56
East Third Street, 190, 191
East Third Street Bridge, 190
Eastchester Bay, 48, 71, 93
Eastchester Covenant, 88
Eastchester Planting Ground, 86, 88, 89
Eastchester, 16, 52, 57, 86, 88, 89, 93, 126, 127, 129, 134
Eastchester Village Green, 52, 126, 132
East No Nations, 56
East River, 24
East Tree, 10
Electromagnetic Field, 107
Elliott, Bradford, 94
Elliott, Le Roi Layton, 94, 137, 138
Elliott, Mr. and Mrs. Le Roi Layton, 94, 137, 138
Elmira, 102
En Echelon, 28
England, 54, 84
English, 3, 24, 38, 40, 49, 53, 77, 92, 97, 155
English Parliament, 53
Episcopal Church, 63, 133, 152. See also Christ Church and Saint Paul's Church
Esplanade, 159, 187, 188
Estes, Susie, 186
Eudora Imogene, 83, 84
Eustis, James, 86, 88
Execution Rocks, 32
  Shrieking Ghosts of Execution Rocks, 33–35

Execution Rocks Light Station, 33, 34, 35
  Shrieking Ghosts of Execution Rocks, 33–35
Explosion, 168, 169, 170, 172, 173, 175
  Luminous Lantern-Bearer of Baychester and Pelham Bridge, 168–171
  Wandering Ghost of the Mad Chemist, 172–175

Farmhouse, 15, 16, 17, 118, 119, 120, 136, 137
  Melancholy Apparition of the Old Pelham Farmhouse, 119–122
Fire Ship, 69, 73, 167
  Fiery Phantom Ship of Long Island Sound, 71–74
  Ghost Ship Palatine and its Mad Specter, 79–81
Fish, James D., 139
Flat Rock, 101, 103
Flynn's Icehouse (City Island), 182
Foley, Jeremiah, 192–194
Forks, The (City Island), 182
Fort Amsterdam, 92
Fourteenth Regiment Regular Infantry, 110
Foxe, John (Author of *Book of Martyrs*), 143
Franko, Dr. Alfred M., 26
  Pelham Manor: The Forgotten Battle of the Revolution Near Mount Vernon, New York, 26
Friday The Thirteenth, 141
Funeral, 157

Gallows Limb, 38, 39, 40, 41, 49. See also Spy Oak, Haunted Oak, Haunted Spy Oak, and Skinners Oak
  Ghostly Cow Rustlers of Pelham Road, 36–38

Specter of the British Spy, 36–39
Gardener, 119, 120, 121, 94, 95, 96, 120, 121, 122
   Ghostly Gardener of Bolton Priory, 155–158
   Melancholy Apparition in the Old Pelham Farmhouse, 119–122
Gardiner's Island, 53, 69
George Fox University, 3
Ghost Town, 99, 103
Ghost Whisperer, 159, 161, 162, 163
Gilmartin, Officer (New York Police Department), 102
Glacial Boulder, 5, 6, 10, 14, 15, 20, 21, 27, 34, 56, 57, 58, 59, 85, 87. *See also* Boulder
   Glover's Rock, 14, 20, 27, 28
   Grey Mare, 20
   Kemble House Rocking Stone, 20
   Mishow, 20
   Priory Rocking Stone, 20
   Split Rock, 8, 10, 20, 21, 85, 87, 88, 89
Glover, Col. John, 16, 23, 26–31 *passim*. *See also* Battle of Pelham
Glover Field, 27
Glover's Rock, 14, 20, 27, 28
Goose Island, 56
Gordon, Mrs. (Servant of John A. Hardenbrook), 142, 143, 144, 146, 147
   Ghost of the Haunted Hardenbrook House, 141–147
Gothic Revival, 120
Greek Revival, 155
Green Flats, 56
Green-Wood Cemetery, 173
Guion, Elisha, 51
Gun, 13, 14, 15, 16, 23, 27, 75, 76, 77, 78, 180, 193
Gun Hill Road, 175

Habboamoko, 19, 20, 21. *See also* Devil
   Dark Spirit of the Devil and His Stepping Stones, 19–22
Hallet, Eugene, 182
Halloween, 100, 159, 161, 173. *See also* All Hallow's Eve
Hardenbrook House, 141, 142, 146
   Ghost of the Haunted Hardenbrook House, 141–147
Hardenbrook, John A., 142, 143, 144, 145, 146, 147
   Ghost of the Haunted Hardenbrook House, 141–147
Harlem Branch Line (Harlem and New Haven Railroad), 169
Harlem Heights, 16, 23, 25, 31
Hart Island, 68, 71, 83, 108, 109, 110, 111, 112, 113, 181
   Moaning Ghost of Hart Island, 109–113
Hart, Samuel, 68, 69
Haunted Cedar Knoll, 5, 6, 7, 8
   Headless Apparitions of the Haunted Cedar Knoll, 5–8
Haunted Oak, 36, 39. *See also* Gallows Limb, Haunted Spy Oak, Skinners Oak, and Spy Oak
   Ghostly Cow Rustlers of Pelham Road, 36–39
   Specter of the British Spy, 39–40
Haunted Spy Oak, 36, 37, 38, 40, 41, 44, 46, 49. *See also* Gallows Limb, Haunted Oak, Skinners Oak, and Spy Oak
   Ghostly Cow Rustlers of Pelham Road, 36–38
   Specter of the British Spy, 40–42
Hawkswood, 139. *See also* Marshall Mansion
Hay, James, 137
Headless Apparitions of the Haunted Cedar Knoll, 5–8

Heath, William, 26. *See also* Battle of Pelham
Hell Gate, 68, 69, 71, 73, 79
Hessians, 31, 126, 128
High Court of Admiralty, 56, 60
High Island, 48
Highland, Margaret, 150, 151, 154
Historic Civil Engineering Landmark, 33
Historic House Trust, 150
Holland, 80
Horse, 14, 37, 40, 41, 43, 44, 45, 46, 52, 71, 72, 73, 74, 115, 116, 123, 152
   Fiery Phantom Ship of Long Island Sound, 71–74
Horton, Edward Everett, 66
Horton, George Washington, 67, 68
Horton, Jr., George Washington, 68
Horton, Rochelle N., 177
Hospital, 31, 126, 133
Howe, Lord Richard, 24. *See also* Battle of Pelham
Howe, Sir William, 24, 25, 26, 28. *See also* Battle of Pelham
Huckleberry Island, 54, 56, 57, 58, 59, 60. *See also* Whortleberry Island
   Ghost of Captain Kidd, 56–60
Hudson River, 3, 24
Hudson Valley, 2, 3
Hufeland, Otto, 87, 88, 89
Hunter, John, 139
Hunter Mansion, 103, 139
Hunter's Island, 56, 84, 103, 139
Huntington, Long Island, 68
Hutchinson, Anne, 8, 84–94 *passim*
   Ghost of Anne Hutchinson, 91–94
Hutchinson, Anne (Daughter of Anne Hutchinson), 85, 92
Hutchinson, Francis, 85, 92
Hutchinson, Katherine, 85, 92

Hutchinson, Mary, 85, 92
Hutchinson River, 14, 15, 16, 25, 27, 86, 87, 88, 90, 136, 190
Hutchinson River Parkway, 85, 114, 136
Hutchinson's Brook, 87, 88, 89
Hutchinson's Meadows, 86, 88, 89
Hutchinson, Susanna, 85, 92
Hutchinson, William, 85, 92
Hutchinson, Zuriel, 85, 92

Iden Avenue, 17, 94, 136. *See also* 45 Iden Avenue and Pelhamdale
Indians, 2, 6, 7, 8, 10, 13, 60, 87. *See also* Indigenous Americans and Native Americans
   Dark Spirit of the Devil and His Stepping Stones, 19–22
   Ghost of Anne Hutchinson, 91–94
   Ghost of the Indian Maiden of Pelhamdale, 13–18
   Headless Apparitions of the Haunted Cedar Knoll, 5–8
   Spirit of the Siwanoy Brave, 9–12
Indigenous Americans, 1, 2, 3, 10, 16, 19, 20, 84, 87, 88, 90, 96, 97, 167. *See also* Indians and Native Americans
   Dark Spirit of the Devil and His Stepping Stones, 19–22
   Ghost of Anne Hutchinson, 91–94
   Ghost of the Indian Maiden of Pelhamdale, 13–18
   Headless Apparitions of the Haunted Cedar Knoll, 5–8
   Spirit of the Siwanoy Brave, 9–12
Infrasound, 107
International Garden Club, 149
Interstate 95, 10, 27, 85
Irving, Washington, 19, 22

Jacobs, William, 174

Jacobs, Mary, 174
James D. Fish Mansion, 139
James Street, 187, 188, 189
　Faceless Shadow Ghost of James Street, 187–189
Josephson, Jacob, 192, 193

Kansas Chief, 54, 60
Kenny, John, 114, 115, 116
Kenny, Peter, 151
Ketcham, James, 68
Kidd, William, 53, 54, 55, 56, 57, 58, 59, 60. *See also* Captain Kidd and Pirate
　Ghost of Captain Kidd, 56–60
Kidd's Point, 54
Kieft, Director-General Willem, 84
Kieft's War, 84. *See also* Wappinger War
King Philip's War, 16
King's Bridge, 24
Kingston Head, 80
Knickerbocker Cottage (Sixth Ave. and 28th Street, New York City), 141

Laaphawachkins, 7, 8
Lannuier Bed, 150, 151, 154
Lannuier, Charles Honoré, 150, 151
Leap Year, 185, 186
Lenape, 1, 2, 84, 85
Leroy, Herman and Hannah, 148
Leviness, Charles Valentine, 184
Leviness, David, 184, 185
Leviness's Hotel (City Island), 182
Liberty Bell, 126. *See also* Bell, Liberty
Little Mothers Aid Association, 101, 102, 103
Locust Point, 75, 76
London, 54, 126, 133
Longfellow, Henry Wadsworth, 69

Long Island, 2, 3, 10, 19, 20, 21, 32, 34, 53, 55, 68, 71, 73, 76
Long Island Sound, 13, 14, 15, 19, 20, 24, 32, 33, 34, 53, 54, 56, 69, 71, 72, 73, 75, 77, 78, 79, 80, 81, 91, 97, 100, 101, 103, 109, 110, 113, 142, 177, 181
　Fiery Phantom Ship of Long Island Sound, 71–74
　Ghostly Gunship of Long Island Sound, 75–78
　Ghost Ship Palatine and its Mad Specter, 79–82
Main Street (City Island), 181
Mamaroneck, 40, 41
Manger Circle, 104, 105
　Suicidal Specter of Manger Circle, 104–105
Manhattan, 2, 3, 17, 23, 24, 44, 46, 141
Manor of Anne Hoocks Neck, 86
Manor Circle, 123
Manor Club, The, 159, 160, 161, 162, 163
　Ghostly Matron of the Manor Club, 159–163
Manor of Pelham, 14, 17, 25, 37, 75, 77, 84, 88, 90, 92, 96, 97, 126, 136, 148
Mansion, 95, 96, 97, 98, 103, 139, 140, 148, 149, 150, 151, 152, 153, 154, 156, 157
Marblehead Mariners, 16, 26
Marine Railway, 68, 69
Marshall Mansion, 139. *See also* Hawkswood
Martin J. Condon Mansion, 140
Martin, Joseph, 190, 191, 192, 193
Martin, Jules, 155, 156, 157, 158
　Ghostly Gardener of Bolton Priory, 155–158

Index | 215

Massachusetts, 2, 84
Massachusetts Bay Colony, 84, 91, 92
Memorial Stadium (Mount Vernon, NY), 16, 26, 30
Middle Reef Island, 56
Militia, 14, 27, 28, 31, 128
Miller Reid's House in Eastchester, 89
Mill Lane, 89
Minneford Island, 67. See also City Island
Montauk Light, 80
Montgomery, James, 174, 175
Morrisania, 26
Mount Vernon, 16, 26, 64, 66, 114, 116, 171, 175, 190, 191, 192, 193, 194
Munsee, 1, 2, 3
Music, 107, 153, 154, 186

Narragansetts, 92
National Historic Lighthouse Preservation Act of 2000, 33
National Register of Historic Places, 21, 33, 94, 126, 136, 150, 155, 159, 160
Native Americans, 1, 13, 17, 19, 85, 97. See also Indians and Indigenous Americans
  Dark Spirit of the Devil and His Stepping Stones, 19–22
  Ghost of Anne Hutchinson, 91–94
  Ghost of the Indian Maiden of Pelhamdale, 13–18
  Headless Apparitions of the Haunted Cedar Knoll, 5–8
  Spirit of the Siwanoy Brave, 9–12
Neptune Powder Mill, 172
Neutral Ground, 23, 37, 52, 53, 75, 128, 148
New England, 24, 69, 73, 81
New Haven Branch Line, 10, 100, 102, 123, 149

New Jersey, 2
New Netherland, 69, 71
Newport, RI, 58, 60
New Rochelle, 22, 31, 57, 60, 68, 95, 97, 98, 175, 186, 192, 193
New Year's Eve, 157
New York City, 10, 39, 43, 53, 65, 67, 69, 76, 78, 86, 90, 94, 101, 102, 103, 109, 139, 141, 142, 147, 148, 149, 150, 164, 166, 180, 183, 185, 191, 193, 194
New York City Department of Parks & Recreation, 166
New York City Police Department Firing Range, 86
New York Harbor, 67, 71
New York Evening Express, 112, 113, 202
New-York Daily Tribune, 8
New York Herald, 66, 102, 103, 141, 174, 175
New York State, 2, 8, 16, 22, 26, 42, 47, 50, 53, 54, 55, 59, 65, 66, 68, 74, 78, 94, 102, 122, 150, 157
New York Times, 115, 116
Nicholls, Governor Richard, 88
Nieman, Heinrich, 168, 169, 170, 171
  Luminous Lantern-Bearer of Baychester and Pelham Bridge, 168–171
Nitroglycerin, 168, 172
North Oak Triangle, 10
North Pelham, Village of, 114, 157
Northport, Long Island, 68, 69
North Tree, 10
Nye, Tom, 68

Old Boston Post Road, 14, 15, 16, 27, 31, 136. See also Colonial Avenue

Old Stone House, 61, 62, 63, 64, 65, 66, 164, 165. *See also* 463 First Avenue
  Elegant Lady of the Old Stone House, 61–66
  More Ghosts of the Old Stone House, 164–165
Orchard Beach Road, 27
Oestreicher, David, 2
Otto, Paul, 3
  The Dutch-Munsee Encounter in America, 3
Owl, 115, 116
Oyster Bay, 53

Palatine, 79, 80, 81
  Ghost Ship *Palatine* and its Mad Specter, 79–81
Palmer, Benjamin, 76
Palmer, William, 84
Parker, Andrew D., 173
Parker, Andrew J., 172, 173, 174, 175
  Wandering Ghost of the Mad Chemist, 172–176
Parker, Charles F., 173
Parker, Helen, 173
Parris, Alexander, 33
Parrish, James, 63
Parrish, Mary, 61, 62, 63, 64, 65, 66, 164
  Elegant Lady of the Old Stone House, 61–66
Pauper's Cemetery, 109. *See also* Cemetery
Pearson, Mrs. George, 63
Peartree, William, 89. *See also* William Peartree and Associates
Peebles, Frank, 192, 193
Pelham Bay Golf Course, 10, 27
Pelham Bay Park, 1, 3, 19, 20, 23, 27, 47, 69, 79, 99, 102, 139, 148, 149

Pelham Bit Stables (Bronx Equestrian Center), 99
Pelham Bridge, 44, 47, 48, 49, 51, 71, 90, 93, 167, 168, 170, 171, 172, 173, 174, 175
  Luminous Lantern-Bearer of Baychester and Pelham Bridge, 168–171
  Wandering Ghost of the Mad Chemist, 172–176
Pelhamdale, 13, 15, 17, 18, 94, 118, 136, 137, 138, 139, 140. *See also* 45 Iden Avenue
  Ghost of Anne Hutchinson, 91–94
  Ghost of the Indian Maiden of Pelhamdale, 13–18
  Poltergeist of Pelhamdale, 136–138
Pelhamdale Avenue, 140, 156
Pelham Heights, 23, 167, 190, 191, 192, 193, 194
  Fiery-Eyed Phantom of Pelham Heights, 190–194
Pelham Manor, Village of, 5, 16, 18, 23, 26, 51, 79, 94, 104, 123, 125, 136, 155, 156, 159, 160, 187, 188, 189
Pelham Manor Depot, 123
Pelham Manor Fire Department, 156
Pelham Memorial High School, 31, 137, 191
Pelham Neck, 20, 28, 85, 86, 95, 97, 139. *See also* Pell's Point and Rodman's Neck
Pelham Reservoir, 114
Pelham Road, 13, 18, 29, 36, 37, 39, 40, 73, 78, 79, 80, 94, 95, 97, 110, 114, 115, 135. *See also* Shore Road
Pelham, Town of, 7, 10, 12, 32, 48, 65, 66, 67, 83, 86, 88, 90, 94, 99, 109, 138, 139, 148, 172, 177, 178, 181

Pelhamville, 61, 63, 66, 169, 190, 193
Pell, David Jones, 15, 17, 136, 137
Pell, John, 97, 148
Pell, Philip, 136
Pell II, Philip, 136
Pell III, Col. Philip, 136, 137
Pell's Point, 13, 15, 16, 23, 25, 26, 27. *See also* Pelham Neck and Rodman's Neck
Pell, Thomas, 1, 3, 86, 88, 90, 97, 136, 148
   Pell Deed (1654), 1, 97
Pell, Thomas (so-called Third Lord of the manor of Pelham), 136
Pell Treaty Oak, 95, 96, 97
   Ghost of the Murdered Traveler at Bartow-Pell Mansion, 95–98
Pennsylvania, 2
Percy, Dr. William, 102, 103
Phantom Ship, 67, 69, 70, 71, 73
   Fiery Phantom Ship of Long Island Sound, 71–74
   Ghostly Gunship of Long Island Sound, 75–78
   Ghost Ship *Palatine* and its Mad Specter, 79–81
Philadelphia, 22, 80
Phyfe, Duncan, 150
Picnic Grounds, 123
Pilot Avenue, 68, 69. *See also* Pilot Street
Pilot Street, 68. *See also* Pilot Avenue
Pinckney, Philip, 88
Pirate, 53–60 *passim*. *See also* Kidd, William and Captain Kidd
   Fiery Phantom Ship of Long Island Sound, 71–74
   Ghost of Captain Kidd, 56–60
Poltergeist, 117, 118, 125, 132, 136, 137, 138
   Melancholy Apparition in the Old Pelham Farmhouse, 119–122

Pelham Poltergeists, 117–118
Petulant Preacher Poltergeist, 132–135
Phantom Bell Ringer of Christ Church, 123–125
Poltergeist of Pelhamdale, 136–138
Whispering Bell of Saint Paul's Church, 126–131
Portsmouth, Rhode Island, 92
Posse, 115, 116, 193
Prevost, George A., 87
Price, Josie, 186
Prospect Avenue (City Island), 182
Prospect Hill, 10, 27, 28, 87
Prospect Hill Elementary School, 30
Prospect Hill Road, 10
Prospect Lane, 10
Pumping Station, Pelham Reservoir, 114, 115
Puritans, 92, 133

Quartermaster, 112
Queen Anne (Queen of Great Britain and Ireland), 89

Rat Island, 56
Rattlesnake Brook, 89
Read, Col. Joseph, 28, 29, 30. *See also* Battle of Pelham
Reed's Mill (Reid's Mill), 86, 87
Revolutionary War, 16, 17, 23, 34, 40, 45, 47, 51, 52, 67, 75, 97, 126, 127, 128, 134, 136, 167. *See also* Battle of Pelham
   Ghostly Cow Rustlers of Pelham Road, 36–39
   Ghostly Gunship of Long Island Sound, 75–78
   Ghost of the Indian Maiden of Pelhamdale, 13–18
   Revolutionary War Specters, 23–31

Shrieking Ghosts of Execution
   Rocks, 32–35
Specter of the British Spy, 40–42
Vanishing Soldier, 48–50
Whispering Bell of Saint Paul's
   Church, 126–131
Reynolds, George E., 182
Rhode Island, 69, 71, 84, 92
Rhode Island and Providence
   Plantations, Colony of, 84
River Thames, 54
Road to New Rochelle, 98. See also
   Shore Road and Pelham Road
Rodman's Neck, 25, 86. See also
   Pelham Neck and Pell's Point

Sackett, James, 69
Sacred Place, 9, 11, 12
   Spirit of the Siwanoy Brave, 9–12
Saint Paul's Church, 31, 52, 118,
   126, 127, 128, 130, 132, 133,
   134, 135
   Petulant Preacher Poltergeist,
      132–135
   Whispering Bell of Saint Paul's
      Church, 126–131
Saint Paul's Parish, 133
Sandford Boulevard, 26
Sands Point, Long Island, 32
Secor, Joan Elizabeth Klink, 160,
   161, 162
   Ghostly Matron of the Manor
      Club, 159–163
Secretary of State of the State of
   New York, 89
Sexton of Saint Paul's Church, 127,
   128, 130, 132, 133
Sewan, 2
Shadow Ghost (Shadow People),
   167, 184, 185, 187, 188, 189
   Faceless Shadow Ghost of City
      Island, 184–186

Faceless Shadow Ghost of James
   Street, 187–189
Shepard, Col. William, 29, 30. See
   also Battle of Pelham
Shipbuilding and Ship Repair, 67, 69
Shipyard, 68, 69
Shore Park, 79
Shore Road, 5, 7, 10, 27, 28, 87,
   95, 97, 98, 99, 119, 120, 123,
   141, 142, 146, 148, 175. See also
   Pelham Road
Signal Service Office (City Island), 181
Siwanoy, 1, 2, 3, 4, 7, 8, 9, 10, 11,
   12, 19
   Dark Spirit of the Devil and His
      Stepping Stones, 19–22
   Ghost of the Indian Maiden of
      Pelhamdale, 13–18
   Headless Apparitions of the
      Haunted Cedar Knoll, 5–8
   Indigenous American Hauntings,
      1–4
   Siwanoy Country Club, 1
   Siwanoy Elementary School, 1
   Siwanoy Place, 1
   Siwanoy Trail, 1
   Spirit of the Siwanoy Brave, 9–12
Skeleton, 102, 103
Skinners Oak, 36, 50. See also
   Gallows Limb, Haunted Oak,
   Haunted Spy Oak, and Spy Oak
   Ghostly Cow Rustlers of Pelham
      Road, 36–38
   Specter of the British Spy, 39–40
Smith, Jacob, 177, 180
Smith, Jr., Jacob, 180
Smith, Sarah Sturges, 177
Snyder, Dorothea Jewell, 164, 165
Snyder, Frank, 164
South No Nations, 56
Split Rock, 8, 10, 20, 21, 85, 87,
   88, 89

Split Rock Golf Course, 10, 27, 29
Split Rock Road, 10, 27, 28, 30, 43, 46
Spy Oak, 36, 39, 50. *See also* Gallows Limb, Haunted Oak, Haunted Spy Oak, and Skinners Oak
   Ghostly Cow Rustlers of Pelham Road, 36–38
   Specter of the British Spy, 39–40
Standard, Rev. Thomas, 126, 132, 133, 134, 135
   Petulant Preacher Poltergeist, 126–135
Staten Island, 18, 53
Stepping Stones, 19, 20, 21, 68, 71. *See also* Devil's Stepping Stones
   Dark Spirit of the Devil and His Stepping Stones, 19–22
Stepping Stones Light, 21
Steppingstone Park, 20
Storm, 19, 71, 72, 73, 78, 81, 100, 101, 103, 121, 134, 135
Sturges, Alvarette B. ("Allie"), 177, 178, 179, 180, 181
   Little Specter of the Field, 177–180
Sturges, Dan, 117
Sturges Paranormal, 151, 152
Stuyvesant, Grandmother Baxter, 36, 38, 39
Sun (New York City newspaper), 185

Tales of a Traveller (by Washington Irving), 19, 22
Ten Families, 88
Ten Farms, 86
Thirteen Club of New York City, 141, 142, 144, 147
Three Trees, Place of, 9, 10
Throggs Neck, 24, 25, 26, 40, 75, 76
Travers Island, 11

Treasure, 43, 51, 52, 53, 54, 55, 56, 58, 59, 60, 61, 128, 129, 130, 167
   Elegant Lady of the Old Stone House, 61–66
   Ghost of Captain Kidd, 56–60
   Ghostly Treasure Guards, 51–55
Trolley, 190, 191, 192, 194
Tuesday Afternoon Club, 160. *See also* Manor Club, The
Twin Islands, 56, 139

UK Sailmakers LLC, 68
Union (Civil War), 109
Union Electric Railway, 190
United States Coast Guard, 21, 33
United States Department of the Interior, 33

Valentine Hill, 26
Vestrymen, 124
Vollmer, Emil J., 192
Von Liehn's Bay View Hotel, 184. *See also* Bay View Hotel
Vreedlandt (Vredeland), 84, 85, 86, 91, 92, 93

Walker, Abigail, 151
Walker, Nathan, 151
Wampum, 2
Wappinger's Falls, 10
Wappinger War, 84. *See also* Kieft's War
Washington, George, 16, 23, 24, 25, 26, 36, 40, 67, 68
Weber's Bakery (City Island), 178
Westchester Avenue, 36, 47
Westchester County, 1, 8, 19, 20, 39, 47, 50, 59, 66, 73, 74, 78, 85, 86, 87, 94, 122, 131, 138, 139, 168, 171, 175
Westchester County Historical Society, 87

Westchester Creek, 24, 25, 36
Westchester Square, 152
Westchester, Town and Settlement of, 89
Westchester Turnpike, 98. *See also* Shore Road and Pelham Road
West Tree, 10, 11, 12
Whaleboat men, 75, 76, 77
White Plains, 8, 16, 25, 31, 74, 84, 135, 176
Whittier, John Greenleaf, 80, 81
Whortleberry Island, 54, 56, 57. *See also* Huckleberry Island
  Ghost of Captain Kidd, 56–60
Wiechquaeskeck, 2, 3
  The First Traders on Wall Street: The Wiechquaeskeck Indians of Southwestern Connecticut in the Seventeenth Century, 2, 3
William Peartree and Associates, 89. *See also* Peartree, William
Wilson Brothers, 128, 130
Wilson, George, 83
Wilson, Harry, 128, 129, 130, 131
Wilson, Henry, 128, 129, 130, 131
Wilson, Mary, 129
Winslow, Mrs. Garnett Mabel, 137, 138
Winthrop, Gov. John, 91
Wolfs Lane, 17, 27, 108, 114, 115, 116, 136, 191
  Shrieking Ghost of Wolfs Lane, 114–116
Wood Famine of 1777, 76
World (New York City newspaper), 110
Wreckers, 80, 81

www.ingramcontent.com/pod-product-compliance
Lightning Source LLC
Chambersburg PA
CBHW020329170426
43200CB00006B/319